Tourism and Innovation

This book is the first attempt to provide a comprehensive review of innovation in tourism, while also considering how tourism itself contributes to innovative local, regional and national development strategies.

This is a timely book placing tourism innovation in the context of current academic and policy concerns relating to knowledge, competition and the management of change. An introductory chapter describes how innovation in tourism is both distinctive from and similar to innovation in other sectors. This is followed by three chapters that explore how competition drives tourism innovation, how knowledge transfers and creation lead the process, and how institutions shape innovation. These provide a coherent theoretical framework for understanding the roles of different agencies in innovation, ranging from the state, to firms, and consumers. The next four chapters analyse innovation at different scales, reviewing the territorial dimensions of innovation through the fresh perspectives of national and regional innovation systems, as well as the determinants of innovation in the tourism firm, and the contested and complex role of entrepreneurship. The final chapter summarises the importance of understanding tourism innovation.

This ground-breaking volume provides an accessible introduction to a key but neglected topic. A clear conceptual framework is complemented by numerous illustrative international case studies. This book will be a useful guide for researchers and students of tourism studies, management and business, geography and regional studies.

C. Michael Hall is Professor of Marketing at the University of Canterbury, New Zealand and Docent in the Department of Geography, University of Oulu, Finland. Co-editor of *Current Issues in Tourism*, his main research interests are in the relationships between mobility and regional development, tourism, food, global environmental change and environmental history.

Allan M. Williams is Professor of European Integration and Globalization at the London Metropolitan University, UK. He is the author and editor of a number of books on tourism including *Critical Issues in Tourism* (2002) and *Tourism and Tourism Spaces* (2004), both with Gareth Shaw; and *A Companion to Tourism* (2004), with Alan Lew and Michael Hall.

Contemporary Geographies of Leisure, Tourism and Mobility

Series Editor: C. Michael Hall
Professor at the Department of Marketing, College of Business &
Economics, University of Canterbury, Private Bag 4800, Christchurch,
New Zealand

The aim of this series is to explore and communicate the intersections and
relationships between leisure, tourism and human mobility within the social
sciences.

It will incorporate both traditional and new perspectives on leisure and
tourism from contemporary geography, e.g. notions of identity, representation and culture, while also providing for perspectives from cognate areas
such as anthropology, cultural studies, gastronomy and food studies, marketing, policy studies and political economy, regional and urban planning, and
sociology, within the development of an integrated field of leisure and tourism studies.

Also, increasingly, tourism and leisure are regarded as steps in a continuum
of human mobility. Inclusion of mobility in the series offers the prospect
to examine the relationship between tourism and migration, the sojourner,
educational travel, and second home and retirement travel phenomena.

The series comprises two strands:

Contemporary Geographies of Leisure, Tourism and Mobility aims to address
the needs of students and academics, and the titles will be published in hard-
back and paperback. Titles include:

Tourism and Global Environmental Change
Ecological, social, economic and political interrelationships
Edited by Stefan Gössling and C. Michael Hall

Forthcoming:

Understanding and Managing Tourism Impacts
C. Michael Hall and Alan Lew

Tourism and Innovation

C. Michael Hall and Allan M. Williams

Routledge
Taylor & Francis Group

LONDON AND NEW YORK

First published 2008
by Routledge
2 Park Square, Milton Park, Abingdon, Oxon OX14 4RN

Simultaneously published in the USA and Canada
by Routledge
270 Madison Ave, New York, NY 10016

Reprinted 2008 (twice)

Routledge is an imprint of the Taylor & Francis Group, an informa business

© 2008 Michael Hall and Allan M. Williams

Typeset in Times New Roman by
RefineCatch Limited, Bungay, Suffolk
Printed and bound in Great Britain by
MPG Books Ltd, Bodmin

British Library Cataloguing in Publication Data
A catalogue record for this book is available from the British Library

Library of Congress Cataloging in Publication Data
Hall, Colin Michael, 1961–
Tourism and innovation / by C. Michael Hall and Allan M. Williams.
    p. cm.
    Includes bibliographical references and index.
    1. Tourism – Management. 2. Creative ability in business. I. Williams, Allan
M. II. Title.
    G155.A1H346 2008
    910.68′4—dc22

                                                                2007034038

ISBN10: 0–415–41404–0 (hbk)
ISBN10: 0–203–93843–7 (ebk)

ISBN13: 978–0–415–41404–3 (hbk)
ISBN13: 978–0–203–93843–0 (ebk)

Contents

Figures

Tables

Boxes

Preface

The initial stimulus to writing this volume was our concern that although the tourism literature made constant reference to growth and change, there was relatively little understanding of the innovation processes that are central to these. That led to our decision to write a book that provided at least the first steps in exploring a topic that is only now emerging onto the agendas of academic researchers and, equally surprisingly, many policy makers.

The central aim of the book is to provide a theoretical framework for understanding tourism innovation. Given both the nature of tourism, and of innovation, this inevitably calls for a multidisciplinary, and multi-level approach. We have tried to weave together the, often disparate, strands of research in tourism and other social science areas. In contrast to the neglect demonstrated by tourism, there is a vast literature on innovation in the other social sciences, including several specialist journals. Our approach is, therefore, selective, and we have drawn particularly on research in the areas of the service sector, knowledge, the role of institutions, the national and regional organization of innovation systems, innovation policy, the firm and entrepreneurship. In seeking to build inter- and intra-disciplinary bridges, we have hopefully opened up the prospects of a two-way traffic in ideas. While tourism has much to learn from, say, economics, politics, regional studies and geography, so too does tourism studies have much to offer those interested in the creativity of tourists, the dynamism of tourism firms, and the influential role of tourism in local and regional development.

Against this background we have used an array of short case studies (presented in boxes) to illustrate our central themes. These provide insights into the complexities inherent in the innovation process, while also emphasizing that innovation has to be understood as temporally and spatially contingent. In a way, they also tease out some of the tensions between structure and agency, with many of the case studies illustrating the influential roles of particular individuals, firms or territorial policy initiatives – although these always have to be understood in context of specific politico-economic and cultural structures and institutions.

Innovation is, of course, not a new process. It is as old as economic activity itself. But, in an increasingly competitive world, product cycles are shortening and the pressures – or perhaps, more accurately, the clamour – to 'innovate or die' are becoming incessant. Innovation is, however, an easily romanticized and misrepresented process, and the associated risks and costs can just as easily lead to 'innovate and die'. Research on innovation, just as much as the successful implementation of innovation, requires a multidisciplinary approach that engages with the blurred and shifting sets of relationships that stretch across different spheres of work and non-work activities, and across different scales. This presents an enormous challenge, and we hope that this book represents a helpful starting point for those wishing to engage with this challenge.

We also wish to acknowledge the help and support of a number of people without whom this book would not have been produced. Michael would like to thank Tori Amos, Nick Cave, Bruce Cockburn, Tim Coles, David Duval, Nicolette Le Cren, Dieter Müller, Jarkko Saarinen and Nicola van Tiel for stimulating thoughts and examples on tourism innovation and services at various times, and Jody Cowper for assistance with the Tamaki Brothers case study. Allan has benefited from his collaboration with Vladimir Baláž, Sergio Salis, Gareth Shaw and Adi Weidenfeld, and the general support provided throughout by Linda Williams. Finally, we would both like to thank Jennifer Page and Andrew Mould from Routledge for their continued support of the project.

Abbreviations

ABRS	Australian Biological Resources Study
AGMA	Association of Manchester Authorities
APEC	Asia Pacific Economic Cooperation
CMM	Communauté Métropolitaine de Montréal
CORDIS	Community Research and Development Information Service
CPDB	central patron database
CRC	Cooperative Research Centre
CRS	computer reservation system
CSTA	Council of Science and Technology Advisors to the Government of Canada
CVB	convention and visitor bureau
DCC	Dunedin City Council
DIUS	Department of Innovation, Universities and Skills
DTI	Department of Trade and Industry
EU	European Union
FDI	foreign direct investment
FP	Framework Programme (EU)
GATS	General Agreement on Trade in Services
GDP	gross domestic product
GDS	global distribution system
GIF	growth and innovation framework
IRAP	Industrial Research Assistance Program
IT	information technology
KISA	knowledge-intensive service activity
MCC	Manchester City Council
NIS	national innovation system
NRC	National Research Council
OECD	Organisation for Economic Co-operation and Development
OSVC	Our Stadium Visionaries Club
R&D	research and development
RIS	regional innovation system
SIS	spatial innovation system
SME	small and medium sized enterprise

SPC	service-profit chain
SSIP	sectoral system of innovation and production
STCRC	Sustainable Tourism Cooperative Research Centre
STDC	Sustainable Tourism Development Consortium
TFP	total factor productivity
THE-ICE	International Centre of Excellence in Tourism Hospitality Education
WdW	Witte de Withstraat
WGF	Westergasfabriek
WIPO	World Intellectual Property Organization
WTO	World Trade Organization

1 Introduction

Changing pleasures: the centrality of innovation in tourism

It has been commonplace in tourism publications to start articles or books with citations of the numbers of tourists, their estimated economic impacts and the fact that the tourism industry is one of the fastest growing sectors in the world economy. Having invited readers to gaze in wonder at the scale and the rate of change in the tourism sector, these publications move on to consider the real objective of their analyses, with no more than a sideways glance at the innovation processes that drive the changes behind such 'startling' data. This applies as much to the constant accumulation of incremental changes as to the small number of revolutionary changes that redefine the arena of tourism occupied by firms, tourists and other agents. The growth of clubbing in Ibiza provides one of the more spectacular examples of innovation (Box 1.1) and shows how a single innovation can, under favourable circumstances, lead to reshaping of an entire tourism landscape.

One of the most frequently repeated observations about tourism concerns the rate of growth of activities, tourist flows, employment and economic impacts over recent decades. That is undeniable, but it should not be understood to imply that tourism was previously a largely unchanging form of activity that is now being revolutionized by new technologies (for example, internet bookings), new markets (especially in Asia), and new organizational forms (such as budget airlines). Tourism has always been subject to changes, reflecting shifts in tastes and preferences, technologies and politico-economic conditions. And the history of tourism is littered by landmark innovations such as the emergence of new centres of pilgrimage, the introduction of rail travel, and the popularization of credit cards (Löfgren 1999). But globalization trends have modified the stage on which innovations are played out, and the rhythm of change has intensified in recent years. More than a decade ago, Poon (1993: 3) noted:

> The tourism industry is in a crisis – a crisis of change and uncertainty; a crisis brought on by the rapidly changing nature of the tourism industry itself. . . . The industry is in metamorphosis – it is undergoing rapid and

Box 1.1 Innovation and the clubbing tourism scene in Ibiza

The first night club on Ibiza opened in 1973, at which time the island was considered an upmarket millionaires' playground. Initially, a relatively small-scale innovation, it was to spark a series of discontinuous or radical innovations that transformed Ibiza's tourism. From the late 1970s onward, British music and dance entrepreneurs and fans, in effectively an informal innovation partnership between tourism firms and tourists, developed the island as a party destination. Spanish entrepreneurs also became involved in the development of club attractions, as well as in linked innovations in the hotel and other tourism subsectors.

By 2001 there were several mega clubs on Ibiza, including:

Club	Date of establishment	Capacity
Amnesia	1987	5,000
El Divino	1993	1,500
Eden	1980s	5,000
Es Paradis	1975	3,500
Pacha	1973	3,000
Privilege	1978 (rebranded 1995)	10,000
Space	1988	3,000

The club scene was highly internationalized but at the same time it was influenced by British youth culture and tastes, so the innovations were characteristically hybrids of UK and local ideas. The clubs were in a highly competitive environment, and constantly re-invested to remodel and relaunch themselves in a changing market. In effect, they were engaged in both continuous and discontinuous innovations, as they re-invented themselves in terms of product, process and market innovations. Each club innovated in an attempt to create a unique product that would give them first entrant advantage in the market, but the difficulties of patenting innovations meant they were locked into a continuous process of innovation to survive and expand.

Source: After Swarbrooke (2002: 354–5).

radical change. New technology, more experienced consumers, global economic restructuring and environmental limits to growth are only some of the challenges facing industry.

Tourism is increasingly characterized by changes in markets and consumer preferences, in drives for competitiveness, in technology, in the organization of factors of production (especially new sources of workers, and new forms of investment) (Cooper 2006; Coakes *et al.* 2002). As a result, the products and processes of tourism are constantly being modified, seemingly at an increasing rate. These changes are bound together in complex patterns of innovation that are evident throughout the tourism sector, whether in transport, entertainment or hospitality. They are also manifested at different scales – whether the individual, the firm, the tourist resort, the destination or the national tourism system.

It is important therefore to see innovation as systemic, or as integral to the tourism system as a whole. Of course, when asked to name the most significant innovations in tourism, particular brands come to mind, whether individual entrepreneurs such as Thomas Cook, or major corporations such as South West Airlines or American Express. Similarly, when asked 'to place' innovation, specific places immediately come to mind, whether Baltimore, Las Vegas, Legoland or Orlando, Florida. But tourism innovation is not the preserve of elite places and elite individuals. Rather innovation pervades all corners of the tourism system, whether it is the small hotel that creates its first web site, the restaurant that introduces new dishes to appeal to an emerging tourism market, or the individual tourist who creates new ways of holidaying for himself or herself.

Not only is innovation pervasive in tourism, but there is also a need to understand this in terms of how tourism is situated in relation to broader economic, social and political changes. First, and most obviously, there have been changes in the organization of work, leisure time and in absolute and relative income distributions (Gershuny 2000). Baumol (2002: 3) captures the essence of these:

> Even the most well-off consumers in pre-Industrial Revolution society had virtually no goods at their disposal that had not been available in ancient Rome. In fact, many consumption choices available at least to more-affluent Roman citizens had long since disappeared by the time of the Industrial Revolution. In contrast, in the past 150 years, per capita incomes in a typical free-market economy have risen by amounts ranging from several hundred to several thousand percent.

Increases in disposable income, non-work time and also in consumption preferences have had profound impacts on tourism, including the development of new forms of holidays, that would have been almost unimaginable a century earlier, let alone before the Industrial Revolution. Equally important has been the extension of market economies, or proto market economies, to a raft of ex-state socialist and emerging market economies, where new forms of tourism are being favoured by the growing middle, and more affluent, working classes – whether in Eastern Europe, China or India.

Second, the sources of tourism innovation often lie outside the sector itself.

This is especially true of technology for, in common with most service activities, this tends to be sourced from other firms or organizations rather than from in-house research and development (Hjalager 2002). For example, investment in military technology during the Second World War contributed to the innovation of air charter holidays in the 1950s, and hotels and restaurants have bought in generic office systems software. 'External' regulatory changes, such as air travel deregulation and relaxation of foreign exchange controls, have also stimulated tourism innovations. Some of the technological innovations, sourced from suppliers, have also led to development of new labour practices. For example, the introduction of electric dishwashers into restaurants in the 1960s led to job losses for many back-stage restaurant staff.

Third, tourism is not only the passive recipient of innovations originating elsewhere in the economy, but it is also a powerful driver of innovation, whether through firm behaviour (for example, the role of American Express in popularizing a more general adaptation of credit cards), or through deliberate government policy making and intervention. Most obviously, tourism features strongly in many urban regeneration strategies (Law 2002), as evidenced in places as diverse as Sydney, Boston and Cape Town.

Fourth, tourism also acts as a powerful conveyer and transmitter of new ideas and innovations. Tourism has driven innovation in retailing, particularly in the form of fostering demand for 'exotic' cuisines in previously homogeneous food cultures – for example, the growth of tapas bars in Northern European cities. This has occurred both as a result of labour mobility, chefs and cooks travelling and gathering new ideas, as well as consumer mobility, as people return to their home environment with a literal taste for the places to which they have travelled.

Given the pervasive and persistent nature of tourism in the modern world, let alone the intensification of innovation in the face of increased competition, there is surprisingly little research in this field. Just over a decade ago, Hjalager (1996: 201) could write, in an article on tourism, the environment and innovation, that this constituted

> an explorative and analytic approach which tourism research has never before touched on in any systematic way: the dynamic innovative effects identifiable within the tourist industry as a response to environmental disequilibrium, policy regulations and changes in consumer demand.

Similar comments could have been written about other areas of tourism, with some notable exceptions such as Poon (1993). Subsequently, there has been an emerging literature on tourism innovation, with a number of notable academic contributions such as OECD (2003), Cooper (2006) and Buhalis (2004), as well as growing policy interest (OECD 2003). However, tourism innovation is still seen as a rather specialist subject, often isolated from broader economic analyses of tourism, and from the broader and long-established tradition of social science research on innovation (Hjalager 2002: 465). The aim of this book is to explore tourism innovation in such a broader context. Of course, care must be taken not to reify tourism innovation because, as Nowotny *et al.* (2001: 36) observe, innovation has become 'a new religion rooted in a continuous drive to bring forth the New'. As we have already stressed, innovation is not only a feature of recent decades, and the study of innovation can provide no more than one component of how we understand tourism change and tourism-related changes. But it is equally true that it would be futile to try and understand the contemporary shifting landscape of global tourism without also understanding the nature of tourism innovation. That is the central tenet that informs the book, but before elaborating this further, we first need to consider some essential features of tourism innovation, beginning with the question: 'what is innovation?'

Defining innovation: illusions and elusiveness

There are many popular and academic illusions about what constitutes innovation, and the concept remains elusive. Schumpeter (1934) saw innovation as being 'at the core of competition and the dynamic efficiency of firms and industries' (Cainelli *et al.* 2005: 437) but contended that 'standard theories' of the firm were poor at explaining innovations (Phan 2004: 617). He stressed that innovation did not equate to invention. Rather, he considered that inventions were connected with basic scientific or technological research, while innovations were further developments of these, or just the application of bright ideas. As Metcalfe (2005: 11) argues, such applications and developments involve 'judgment, imagination and guesswork, and the optimistic conjecturing of future possible economic worlds'. These various notions are caught by Kanter's (1983: 20–1) broad definition of innovation:

> Innovation refers to the process of bringing any new, problem solving idea into use. Ideas for reorganizing, cutting costs, putting in new budgetary systems, improving communication or assembling products in teams are also innovations. Innovation is the generation, acceptance and implementation of new ideas, processes, products or services. . . . Acceptance and implementation are central to this definition; it involves the capacity to change and adapt.

This only provides a starting point for our definition, because innovations take many forms and can be classified in very different ways, but especially in terms of 'newness', 'focus' and 'attributes' (see Box 1.2). For Schumpeter (1934) the essence of innovation was newness, but he considered this could be either incremental or radical, depending on whether it occurred within, or departed from, existing technologies and practices. Subsequently, there have been several competing interpretations of the notion of 'newness'. For example, Chan *et al.* (1988) considered there were three types of innovation:

- Incremental. Does not require a major breakthrough in either markets or technology. For example, reducing waste in a hotel kitchen or speeding up baggage handling at an airport by introducing larger pick up trucks.
- Distinctive. Usually demands adaptation of consumer behaviour, and possibly of company organisation. For example, advance purchase of discount travel tickets, or provision of in-flight telephone communications.
- Breakthrough. Involves a new approach in consumer behaviour, system organisation or new technology. For example, automatic check-in facilities in hotels or electronic ticketing.

There are of course other problematic aspects of 'newness'. First, what is the focus of newness (see Box 1.2)? Schumpeter himself recognized that innovation could take many forms: creating new products, development of new methods of production, opening of new markets, capturing of new sources of supply and new organizational forms. In practice, innovations tend

---

Box 1.2 The classification of innovation: an application to hotels

Adams *et al.* (2006) identify three main ways to classify innovation:

- On the basis of *newness*. This was most famously captured by Schumpeter (1934) who distinguished between radical and incremental innovations.
  Example: Does a new hotel have significant new design features or does it largely replicate an existing formula?
- On the basis of the *focus* of an innovation, that is, on whether it centres on product, process, administrative or technological dimensions, amongst others.
  Example: Does a new hotel innovate in the products it offers (for example in-room information technology (IT) facilities), its processes (how it provides services) or in some other way?
- On the basis of the *attributes* of an innovation, or its descriptive properties, qualities or features. This is exemplified by Rogers' (2003) framework of five key attributes: compatibility, observability, relative advantage, trialability and complexity.
  Example: Is the new hotel and its innovative products and processes compatible with other components of the local tourism system? Are they easily observable to their competitors and, if so, what are the relative advantages to the hotel as the originator?

Source: The generic conceptualization draws on Adams *et al.* (2006), but is applied here to a specific tourism example.

to be linked and, for example, a tour company's attempt to attract higher spending tourists by offering a new product – say an expensive and fashionable holiday destination – may also require innovation in how these services are produced. Second, there are also difficulties concerning what we may term 'the impact range' of an innovation. Here we follow Sundbo's (1998: 22) argument that in order to be considered an innovation, something need not necessarily be new at world or national level, only in a particular market segment.

These two dimensions of focus and range are combined in what is probably the best-known classification of the newness of innovation, that is Abernathy and Clark's (1988) transilience model (Figure 1.1). Based on the degree of conservation versus disruption in terms of technology–production and market–consumer linkages, they identified four types of innovation:

- niche (opening new market opportunities via the use of existing technologies);
- regular (incremental);
- revolutionary (involving significant new technologies but whose impact is not industry wide); and
- architectural (which can change the entire industry).

Hjalager (2002) has commented on the potential utility of this model for understanding tourism innovation, although there has been little detailed research on its application.

There are, of course, some critiques of this model, not least because it

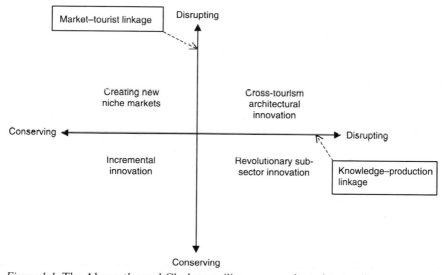

Figure 1.1 The Abernathy and Clark transilience map adapted to tourism.

Source: After Abernathy and Clark (1988).

under-estimates the extent to which innovation builds on existing technologies, rather than involves creative destruction (Andersen 1998: 36). Furthermore, it fails to allow for shifts in the nature of innovation over time: an innovation may begin serving specialized markets and a few lead users in the tourism industry (niche innovation), but it may 'take off' subsequently, and even become architectural innovation, with generalized impacts across sub-markets. This was the basis of the innovation 'S curve' (Utterback 1994). Nevertheless, the transilience model does provide an insight into the diversity of innovation, and the need to be specific about meanings when using this evasive term. In part, the specificity of tourism stems from being a service activity, which is considered in the next section.

The distinctiveness of service sector innovation

The literature on innovation has largely been dominated by manufacturing, reflecting the historical belief that this was the main driver of economic change, and also because of the high profile of technology as a driver of change in earlier research (Cainelli *et al.* 2005). More recently, however, the service sector has also been recognized as a site of innovation. Tether (2004) characterizes the different approaches to service sector innovation, in terms of their relative emphasis on assimilation and demarcation. The assimilation approach considers services to be fundamentally similar to manufacturing, but to have relatively restricted capacity for change. There is little endogenous sourcing of innovation, and technology in particular is externally sourced. Moreover, there is little creativity in the application of these technologies in the service sector. In contrast, the so-called 'demarcation approach' argues that the service sector is distinctive. Services are intangibles, involve considerable interaction with customers, and there are unique aspects of service delivery. This makes them distinctive from manufacturing although this argument should not be overstated. Drejer (2004: 560), for example, argues that many particularities of service innovation, such as organizational innovation, also apply to manufacturing.

In this book we favour the demarcation approach and consider services to be dynamic and fluid, constantly adjusting to customers' demands, and facing increasing competition as more and more services become (internationally) tradable, spurred on by the growth of internet trading, foreign investment, and efforts to liberalise international trade in services under the General Agreement on Trade in Services (GATS). Unfortunately, however, research on services innovation has tended to draw extensively on the research traditions of manufacturing, so that there has been undue focus on technological innovations rather than, say, organizational innovations (Van der Aa and Elfring 2002: 155–6).

Within these constraints, however, it is possible to outline those elements that make services innovation distinctive. In the following discussion, drawing particularly on Sirilli and Evangelista (1998), Tether (2004) and Van der

Aa and Elfring (2002), we identify four such distinctive features: the co-terminality of service production and consumption; information intensity; the importance of the human factor; and the critical role of organizational factors.

The co terminality of production and consumption. Services involve close interaction between the producers and consumers of services, evident for example in doctor–patient, or retailer–customer relationships. In essence, the customer becomes co-creator (Prahalad and Ramaswarmy 2003a, 2003b, 2004) or co-producer (Ramirez 1999; Bowen and Ford 2002) of the service experience, although this varies among types of services, among firms and among individuals, so that the border between the activities of producers and customers are necessarily flexible. Moreover, such flexibility provides opportunities for innovation (Vandermerwe 1993: 163).

There are two important implications of co-terminality. First, that customers can be see as 'partial' employees' (Schneider and Bowen 1995), so that motivating them is as crucial to effective service delivery as the motivation of employees. Examples include the cooperation and 'part-time work' of customers who take home self-assembly furniture, or work closely with an architect on the design of a new house. This means the customer has to be understood as a source of ideas that can be harvested by service providers as sources of innovation to the extent that it now becomes possible to talk of customer-made product developments. For example, research in product development and design has identified customer involvement as an important means to accelerate product development, improve product design, reduce development costs and enhance product value. This is grounded in customers' product knowledge as well as their market experiences. Therefore, customer involvement may provide access to innovative product ideas, new technologies, market information and development capabilities that firms lack in-house (Ritter and Walter 2003).

Second, the distinction between product and process innovations is particularly unsatisfactory when applied to services (Utterback 1994). Having a manicure involves purchasing a service product, but the service experience depends on the close interaction between producer and consumer. As a result, product becomes closely intertwined with process, and there is a similar blurring of product and process innovation.

Information intensity and the role of IT. Services are, by nature, potentially information intensive, because they are based on large numbers of individualized interactions with customers. There is therefore considerable scope for the application of IT to harvest, order and analyse such information. High street retailers, particularly those that have their own debit or credit cards, are especially effective in creating massive electronic data banks on their customers. These can be analysed to identify emergent trends that, in turn, can inform innovation.

IT systems enable point-of-sales data to be collected and filed virtually immediately. Hence, while technology in services has long been seen as lagging, 'many service sector firms play important roles innovation, not least in the creative use and diffusion of technologies' (Tether *et al.* 2002: i). Few of these technologies are developed in-house, so it is difficult for firms to capture monopoly rents from them by preventing imitation by competitors. Nevertheless, they remain a potent source of innovation and competitiveness, if information can be transformed into knowledge and applied to the operations of firms (Chapter 3).

Quality enhancement and human resources. Given the importance of consumer experiences in services, innovation is likely to focus as much on quality as on quantity. This is of course variable and there is a stark contrast between a major supermarket focused on driving down unit costs, and the boutique store selling a 'shopping experience'. There is also a contrast between front-stage employees, dealing directly with customers, and back-stage employees who provide essential administrative support for them (Drucker 1992). Writing about the so-called 'experience economy', Pine and Gilmore (1999: 12–13) argue that 'while the *work* of the experience stager perishes upon its performance . . . the *value* of the experience lingers in the memory of any individual who was engaged by the event'.

Therefore, in many arenas of service provision, there is considerable focus on quality management (e.g. Parasuraman *et al.* 1985; Grönroos 1994; Powell 1995), which cuts across the blurred boundary between product and process innovation. This means that human capital, understood as skills and competencies, is particularly important in the service sector that, in turn, places a premium on effective human resource management. Soft skills, such as inter-personal relationships, appropriate bodily behaviour and welcoming attitudes, often described under the rubric of 'emotional labour', are at a premium in the drive for quality-enhancing innovations – a stark contrast to much of the manufacturing sector (Guerrier and Adib 2003; Witz *et al.* 2003). 'Total quality management' is one strategy whereby managers seek to enhance the quality of service provision. This can lead to firms laying down specific guidelines on the bodily appearance and performance of front-stage workers, as McDowell (1997: 121) comments in relation to financial services: 'Workers with specific social attributes . . . produce an embodied performance that conforms to idealised notions of the appropriate "servicer" '. This is equally evident in the cruise industry (Weaver 2005) or in the hospitality sector, where – especially in some types of themed restaurants – customers expect particular types of performances from the waiters and waitresses, receptionists (and sometimes even the chefs) who make up the front-stage staff (Beardsworth and Bryman 1999; Pratten 2003; Skordoulis 2005). These are all key areas for tourism innovation.

The critical role of organizational factors. Organizational innovations are particularly important in services. Drawing on Van der Aa and Elfring (2002), this can be exemplified by multi-unit organizational forms, and new combinations of services.

First, as already noted, service provision mostly takes place close to the customer, so that firms that seek to expand their market share often have to open new establishments to serve localized markets in different places. This is particularly, but not only, evident in retailing. Applying the 'reproduction formula' (Normann 1984), firms seek to standardize service delivery in these additional branches in order both to drive down costs, and allow them to utilize their existing experience to enhance quality (Sundbo 1994). Benchmarking is often used by management so that different branches can learn from each other, although there are limits to standardization if there are significant cultural differences in consumption between sub-markets.

The production of new combinations of products is another important source of innovation in services, and this draws on Normann's concept of 'bundling'. If there are complementary demands for services, firms can increase their sales and reduce unit costs by providing bundles of these services. For example, financial services firms providing both pensions and insurance, or shops selling a range of 'lifestyle' goods that otherwise would be sold in separate retail outlets. As Van der Aa and Elfring (2002: 162) argue, in many new combinations: 'the components are not all that novel. Rather, the new concept derives its novelty from the way the components are combined.' Hence the key to innovation is finding novel ways of linking service components, thereby creating value for customers. This, of course, overlaps with the application of IT to harvest and analyse data on customer behaviour, as a prelude to innovation.

The four types of distinctive innovation identified above are not uniformly evident in all service industries, and over time they are combined in different ways. Innovation has to be seen not so much as a series of end products but as a persistent, linked but shifting set of endeavours over time. As Tether (2004: 6) argues, 'the firm can be perceived as holding an envelope of capabilities' and these will be drawn on and deployed in different ways to address the changing needs of customers. This is not to argue that service innovations constitute a chaotic or patternless landscape (see Box 1.3), but for avoidance of over-simplifications and over-idealised typologies. The next section considers the extent to which tourism innovation fits this broad picture for the service sector.

Tourism innovation: commonalities and distinctiveness

Tourism innovation has many features in common with innovation in the service sector as a whole, particularly those sub-sectors that deal mainly with final consumers, such as retailing, rather than intermediaries, such as business services or wholesaling. Hence, the four distinctive features of services considered earlier all apply, to some degree, to tourism (Figure 1.2):

- The co-terminality of service production and consumption. Tourism services are mostly intangible (with exceptions such as souvenirs), and simultaneously involve production and consumption. The tourist experience

---

Box 1.3 A cross-European study of service innovation

Expenditure on innovation in the service sector is relatively low, compared to manufacturing, but it is also highly polarized. A quarter of the European service firms surveyed spent less than 0.33 per cent of their turnover on innovation, while a quarter spent more than 7 per cent. They do, of course, devote resources to innovation within the firm but this only accounts for a quarter of the total. Instead, they spend relatively large amounts – compared to manufacturing firms – on purchasing equipment and machinery. There was evidence of firms collaborating externally with their customers or their suppliers. The authors conclude that key to innovation in services is therefore interactivity rather than internal research capacity, as in the manufacturing sector (Tether *et al.* 2002: 24).

Low spending totals do not, however, necessarily indicate low levels of innovation. Innovation – especially incremental innovation – may require relatively modest levels of investment in services. The most frequently cited type of innovation is the improvement of service quality, followed by extending the service range and developing new markets. This is relatively consistent across different service sectors. Most enterprises undertook both product and process innovations. Organizational innovations were more important than in manufacturing.

Source: After Tether *et al.* (2002).

---

is made up of, and defined by, multiple encounters with provides of tourism services over the span of a tourist's travel – whether in bars, in hotels or as tour leaders. But these are two-way encounters, and the tourist is an active collaborator, to varying degrees, in such encounters.

- Information intensity. The tourism industry is heavily reliant on information exchanges, whether in terms of information provided to tourists, or the information accumulated by tourism companies about tourists. Tourism has often been at the forefront of developing IT systems for information handling, and of e-commerce (see Chapter 3). But there are limits to the scope for innovation in this area. Keller (2006: 28) considers that tourism innovation has to be 'high tech and high touch' because investment in IT has to be balanced with greater emphasis on creating tourism experiences, so that the human factor remains critical.
- The importance of the human factor. Most tourism sub-sectors (with exceptions such as air transport) are labour-intensive. It is not just the labour-capital ratio that is important, but also the quality of labour input

Figure 1.2 Distinctive features of tourism and the shaping of tourism innovation.

that shapes the tourism experience. Hence, unit costs rather than nominal wages are critical (Hudson 2001: 109). There is, therefore, constant tension between managing labour costs and labour quality in tourism (Riley *et al.* 2002), and this is resolved differently across sub-sectors and places.

- Organizational factors. These are significant in tourism, being linked – often in the form of management changes – to process, product and market innovations (Hjalager 2002). For example, hotel chains can utilize multi-site management methods to reduce costs and maximize use of their expertise. New combinations of services are also important, as exemplified by the changing nature of tour packages: additional services may be added (car hire, excursions etc.) to generate greater revenue, or such services may be subtracted so as to reduce costs (as in the case of budget airlines). In addition, the multiple encounters with different service providers that constitute a significant part of the tourist experience may be coordinated via a web of economic, communicative and social networks of producers seeking to maximize their individual and collective customer returns. Therefore, the network concept has become a significant focal point for inter-firm tourism organizational innovation, particularly at the destination level (Michael 2006).

All the above dimensions are important foci of tourism innovation. And not only does tourism share these distinctive features of innovation with other service activities, but there are also similarities in the prevalent types of innovations, with process innovations being more common than product innovations. For example, Jacob *et al.* (2004) report that, in hotels in the Balearic Islands, process innovations were almost four times more frequent than product innovations (see also Chapter 7). In practice, of course, innovations tend to be linked and mutually dependent, as evidenced in the strategic innovations of the Scandic Hotel Group in the 1990s (see Box 1.4).

Box 1.4 Environmental sustainability: Scandic Hotels and innovation

In the early 1990s, Scandic Hotels faced bankruptcy. It's new chief executive, Roland Nilsson, proposed a strategy based on the Swedish concept of '*omtanke*', which emphasizes positive and caring attention. Nilsson was one of the first to recognize that sustainability offered a means to strengthen a tourism company's links with its customers. He sought to establish 'an emotional tie between company and customer' through joint commitment to an environmental improvement strategy.

The strategy also required organizational innovation. A more decentralized management approach was favoured, allowing employees greater scope for decision-making (and so become innovators in countless small ways) in the course of their daily interactions with customers. That, in turn, meant investing in human capital, and the company provided a new environmental training course that was delivered to some 5,000 employees in eight countries. Although the environmental training programme had a start-up cost of approximately $300,000, and annual operating costs of *c.*$100,000, these were offset by reduced costs and significant marketing advantages.

Scandic's other priority was upgrading its IT, and it invested $25 million to establish a customized reporting and benchmarking system. This allowed hotel managers to compare their performance against the best in the group on a weekly basis. Performance was measured across eight areas ranging from traditional financial indicators, through competitor status, to environmental measures relating to the use of energy and water, and waste disposal. They also entered partnerships with suppliers, to minimize the environmental impacts of their processes. For example, with Quadriga they developed temperature sensors, implanted in television sets, which monitored bedroom temperatures.

Source: After Goodman (2000).

There are, however, also some distinctive features of tourism (see Shaw and Williams 2002; Hall and Page 1999) to take into account. Although none of these is probably unique to tourism, in combination they make tourism innovation distinctive. In the remainder of this section, we consider five distinctive features: the clustering of related activities; temporality; spatiality; tourist–tourism industry encounters; and tourist–host community encounters.

Tourism as a complex of related activities. The tourism experience is delivered as a set of functionally linked tourism services by hotels, restaurants, transport companies, retailers, tourist attractions and others. This means that the tourists' assessment of the tourism experience depends on his/her cumulative quality perception (Weiermair 2006). Demand complementarities between these different sub-sectors arc also important (Papatheodorou 2006: 4). Indeed, Chapter 7 notes how tourism itself can be treated as a sectoral system of innovation and production.

There arc also innovation complementarities between the different activities that make up the bundle of encounters that constitute the total tourism experience. This has two consequences. Positively, it may mean that innovation in one sub-sector generates sufficient demand to stimulate innovation in another sub-sector. So marketing innovation by a large hotel that brings in more tourists may lead the next-door restaurant to innovate by extending its opening hours. But, negatively, it may mean that innovations in one sub-sector are held back by lack of changes in other sub-sectors. A tourist attraction may wish to extend its season, but finds this innovation is constrained because local hoteliers arc unable or unwilling to extend their season. It is not difficult to see that these individual relationships can become cumulative, with particular tourism arcas either being characterized by virtuous circles of innovation, or becoming locked into a circle of collective, despondent failure to innovate. To some extent this will depend on the stage of the resort life cycle (Butler 1980), but the process of innovation is more complex than this.

Temporality and the 'uno-actu-principle'. Most tourism transactions are characterized by the 'uno-actu-principle' that implies the availability of supply is highly time specific (Weiermair 2006). For example, a hotel bed or an aircraft seat is available for occupancy at a particular time. If it is not sold for that time period, the supply cannot be deferred until another occasion. Similarly, a major festival or sporting competition occurs in a fixed time period, and if any seats are not sold, the suppliers cannot resell these in another time period. Television rights and presentations of such events are, of course, time deferrable, but personal attendance is not. Not surprisingly, capacity utilization is one of the greatest challenges facing the tourism industry.

This temporal polarization is relational rather than absolute, and can be socially reconstructed (Shaw and Williams 2004: 22). Herein, lies the challenge for innovation. Organizers can reschedule events so as to increase the percentage of seats sold – shifting the dates or shortening the programme. Resort operators can overcome climatic constraints by installing indoor facilities or snow-making equipment. And individual hotels can introduce flexible pricing systems, or add new facilities or services, in order to increase low season occupancy levels.

Spatiality and innovation. Tourists consume tourism experiences at particular sites, hence tourism is considered to be characterized by spatial fixity. For example, Urry (1990) writes about spatial fixity as the outcome of how tourists consume particular tourism sites. However, as with temporality, this is not entirely fixed, and – at least in the long run – can be modified. It is difficult and sometimes virtually impossible to move a major tourism site, although transferring London Bridge from the UK to the US demonstrates that even the most challenging of constraints can be overcome. It is also impossible to recreate the full experience of visiting the Taj Mahal, but facsimiles can be created in theme parks that produce a simulated version of this experience. And it is certainly possible to create new individual sites for experiencing the generic tourism experiences of mountain skiing, tropical island holidaying or the Mediterranean beach experience. There is therefore important scope for innovation through site replication and this is exemplified by Club Mediterranean.

Despite some scope for longer term innovation, spatial fixity is a feature of tourism, and therefore an important focus, or determinant of innovation in the shorter term. Here we focus on four main features. First, spatiality is strongly associated with the clustering of tourism activities, and spatial polarization exaggerates the mutual innovation interdependencies of tourism as a set of related industries. Second, spatial polarization magnifies the difficulties of protecting intellectual property rights, because it makes innovations highly visible to competitors. Linked to this, the importance of public goods, such as a beautiful clean beach or harmonious urban building styles, demand collective action. An innovation by one hotel to improve the quality of the beach will be shared by all other hotels rent free, if access is unrestricted. Third, the tendency to spatial polarization creates potential for strong relationships between enterprises based on proximity. As will be seen below (and further elaborated in Chapter 6) this also creates considerable potential for trust-based collective learning and collaboration – although in practice this is problematic in many tourism areas.

Fourth, tourism facilities, and tourism resorts in particular, are characterized by significant sunk costs. As Papatheodorou (2006: 6) states,

> tourism is characterised by substantial fixed costs in transport, accommodation and in some cases technological infrastructure; airports, hotels and electronic reservation systems are good examples. These costs are largely sunk as they cannot be easily recovered due to their spatial fixity (e.g. a hotel cannot move) and asset specificity (e.g. the functionality of an airport is limited to air transport services).

This means that innovation is often constrained within the framework of sunk costs. Firms may focus on innovation *in situ*, because of the prohibitive sunk costs incurred in investing in greenfield sites, which offer different innovation possibilities. A further implication of the spatial fixity of tourism therefore is the potential for innovation being driven by inherent competition between fixed destinations, and the relative fixity of many of the firms that operate within them.

Tourist–tourism industry encounters. As previously argued, tourist experiences are strongly informed by a sequence of tourism encounters involving those who work in the tourism industry. These encounters, and the investments by firms in innovative facilities and services, are highly visible:

> By its very nature, the tourist sector makes it easy for enterprises to observe what others are doing, unless it takes place behind the scenes. Industrial espionage is inevitable, and ideas can seldom be fully protected by patent laws or other mechanisms.
>
> (Hjalager 2002: 469)

This has three important consequences.

First, because of the way the service encounter shapes the overall tourism experience, is a crucial focus of innovation. Second, given that it is difficult, if not impossible, to patent most front-stage innovations, there is constant pressure to innovate in order to stay ahead of imitators. Third, there is also an incentive to innovate in back-stage operations, such as the organization of the company, or its office systems, which is consistent with empirical evidence that organizational innovation is significant in tourism (Hjalager 2002).

Tourist–host community and environmental relationships. Some tourism sites, for example, high altitude ski resorts or Antarctic cruises, do occur in sites with zero or virtually no resident population. But most tourism sites are located in, or in near proximity to, existing centres of population. And all tourism activities, at whatever site, impact on the surrounding natural environment. These social and social-natural relationships inform, but also delimit, the tourism experience. Given rapid increases in tourism numbers, at increasing numbers of tourism sites, it is hardly surprising that sustainable tourism has become a feature of tourism discourses, particularly amongst academics and consumers, but also amongst some firms.

Not surprisingly, sustainability has become an important area of tourism innovation, at least in niche markets (Hall *et al.* 2004). It is probably no coincidence that two of the earliest papers on tourism innovation were concerned with tourism and the environment, and sustainable tourism (Hjalager 1996, 1997). This poses questions about organizational and institutional innovations, because all the major stakeholders understand effective sustainable tourism policies to require effective collaboration. But there is also scope for other types of innovation, whether in processes (for example, energy or water conservation methods) or products (environmentally friendly resorts or hotels can be marketed as distinctive products).

This brief review has highlighted some innovation features that tourism shares with other service activities (and indeed with some manufacturing), but also some features that, if not unique to tourism, are at least articulated in specific ways in this sector. We have not, however, sought to encapsulate these in any simple typology. Tourism is a diverse sector and there are sharp intra-sectoral differences in innovation. The transnational scheduled air carrier has very different innovation goals and methods to, say, the beach vendor or local restaurant. Moreover, there are also considerable differences across space and time, even within the same sub-sectors. This is because the drivers of innovation are time and place specific (reflecting institutional differences – see the final section of this chapter).

The drivers of tourism innovation

It is no longer sufficient – if it ever was – to view innovation as a matter of isolated individual inventors and entrepreneurs, or even of organized research in particular companies, universities or government research centres. Instead, innovation has to be understood in broader economic, cultural and political terms (Sundbo 1998: 160). These are not, however, mutually exclusive, as demonstrated in the following brief review of the drivers of tourism innovation.

Competition. Competition is one of the driving forces of innovation (see Chapter 2) generally as well as in tourism. There are several reasons for this, including the substitutability of different types of holiday activities and destinations. Reductions in travel barriers, including travel costs, have also intensified such competition as has growing inward investment, so that transnational companies increasingly compete directly against each other and against local capital in particular places (OECD 2003). In some sectors, such as air travel, competition is potentially ruinous, as evident in the string of major airlines that have become technically or effectively bankrupt, especially in Europe and the US. In such an environment, innovation is critical to survival, let alone expansion, in the face of intensified competition (Rubin and Joy 2005; Graham and Vowles 2006). This also makes it preferable for firms to seek innovations that are not easily copied by their rivals, that is process rather than product innovation.

Economic performance. Schumpeter provides insights into whether economic performance drives innovation, or vice versa (Cainelli *et al.* 2005). It is, of course, true that innovation is one of the drivers of performance, for example in terms of productivity – as evidenced by the impacts of automatic check-in facilities, freeze–cook food preparation, or the introduction of budget flights. But, strongly performing firms – as measured in terms of profits, growth rates and turnover – are also more likely to have the substantial financial resources required for major innovations. However, in tourism – in common with other service activities – there is relatively more scope for incremental, process innovations, and relatively less reliance on investments in technology, so that past performance may be less of a guide to innovation in many sub-sectors. Furthermore, relationships between innovation and economic performance tend to be cumulative: 'Asymmetries across firms in labour productivity and innovation performance not only tend to persist over time, but reinforce each other. Such a cumulative mechanism underlies the ability of firms to exploit the opportunities offered by ICTs' (Cainelli *et al.* 2005: 454).

Demand-led innovation. The general innovation literature has long recognized that innovation may be 'demand pulled' (Schmookler 1966). Empirically, this is based on evidence that cycles of output tend to lead cycles of patenting in the capital goods sectors. It can reasonably be argued that similar conditions apply in the service sector, although little researched (Cainelli *et al.* 2005: 438). This chimes with the observation that changes in working hours, the age structure of the population, and in incomes have shaped the growth of tourism demand (Shaw and Williams 2002). Large increases in tourist numbers, or increases in the distribution of demand, as countries such as South Korea and China become important generators of tourist flows, necessitate innovation. This may be in the form of replication, as more flights, hotels, package holidays etc. are created based on existing formulae. Or it may contribute to more revolutionary innovation, such as development of a new generation of larger aircraft. Beyond this, changes in the type of demands can also stimulate innovation: for example, preferences for greater flexibility within holidays contributed to development of fly–drive, and self-catering holidays. But it is also true that innovation may stimulate demand – as evidenced in the way that budget flights have increased air traffic between Australia and New Zealand.

Technology. Although tourism is more reliant on bought-in technology than technology developed in-house, it is still an important driver of innovation (see Chapter 3). Indeed, technology is usually considered to be one of the classic external drivers of innovation. For example, the internet has created opportunities for tourism businesses to provide information and sales electronically. This has also led to the need for innovation in terms of labour force skills, new services and new forms of organization, which together constitute what may be termed e-tourism (Weiermair 2006). Although e-commerce is probably the most spectacular, and commented on, form of technological innovation in tourism, there are many other examples ranging from changes in transport technologies, materials science (making possible new forms of sports equipment and clothing), and in-house integrated accounting systems in hotels, to minor innovations in kitchen equipment and bathroom design. See also Box 1.5 for role of jet technology and credit cards in the growth of international mass tourism.

Firm-level strategy and resources. Several aspects of the firm influence innovation. Most obviously, the strategic aims of the firm (see Keltner *et al.* 1999) – whether it is defensive or expansive, revenue maximizing or quality focused – will determine the degree of proactive innovation seeking, and the types of innovation. Resources, and the general absorptive capacity of the

---

Box 1.5 1958 as a turning point in mass tourism development

The year 1958 was a major landmark in the development of mass tourism in the developed world, and both the major innovations that sparked this originated outside of tourism:

- The introduction of the jet engine Boeing 707 and the Douglas DC–8 revolutionized travel. They had speeds of around 590 mph compared to only 350 mph in the previous generation of aircraft, and increased distances covered in a fixed unit of time by some 40 per cent. They also had double the carrying capacity of previous aircraft. By 1964, 72 per cent of air services were being provided by jet powered flights, ushering in economy fares while widening social access to medium-haul travel: both impacts were critical in the growth of modern mass tourism.

- In the same year, American Express introduced its credit card. It was not the first credit card. Bank America and Master Charge, the forerunners of Visa and Mastercard, had already been in existence for almost a decade, but their use was restricted to relatively few retailers. American Express was instrumental in the popularization of credit cards. Even so, their use and acceptance was relatively slow initially, and did not accelerate until the cards were accepted by American Airlines in 1964. Thereafter, they facilitated international travel both by extending credit and by easing purchases of a range of tourism services.

Source: After Poon (1993: 42–4).

---

firm, play a part in this, although they will not be drivers of innovation per se. The organizational features of the firm also play a significant role in the origination of innovation within the firm, and there is a classic division between the hierarchical and the dispersed organizational form. This is linked to the different requirements of incremental versus discontinuous or radical innovations (Tushman and O'Reilly 1996); there can be such a chasm between these innovation forms, that any organization that seeks to maximize both has to be 'ambidextrous'. Continuous incremental innovation in products and processes is usually more effectively managed in organizations that have strongly centralized procedures, allowing such innovations to be identified and redistributed between departments and establishments. In contrast, discontinuous or radical innovations are favoured by more entrepreneurial organizational cultures, which also tend to be more decentralised.

Individual entrepreneurship. Individual entrepreneurship is iconically associated with revolutionary innovations, but is important in all types of innovation. Even though research and development (R&D) (for example, in e-commerce software) tends to be concentrated in specialist suppliers, there is still considerable scope for entrepreneurs to innovate in terms of products, processes and as, for example, Ateljevic and Doorne (2000) report in relation to lifestyle entrepreneurs in outdoor activities in New Zealand. Entrepreneurs can be employees within companies, who innovate on behalf of their companies, often termed 'intrapreneurs', or leave that company to set up on their own in order to develop a new idea. But the classic individual innovator is portrayed as someone with a bright idea, who – in the face of considerable risk – sets up a new enterprise, which in due course revolutionizes an entire sector or sub-sector. The tour operator business is replete with examples of such innovators, dating back to at least Thomas Cook. A more recent example is provided by the Holiday Club of Upminster (Box 1.6).

Role of the state. The state may also play an important role in tourism innovation via its involvement in destination management and marketing. The state provides financial support for innovation, often through regional economic development programmes (for example in relation to attractions or even infrastructure); is involved in public–private partnerships with respect to redevelopment and infrastructure that would otherwise not be developed without public support (for example, new sports stadia); supports marketing innovations through national and destination branding; and also provides a policy and regulatory environment that can serve to encourage new innovations or protect existing ones, such as intellectual property laws.

Box 1.6 The Holiday Club of Upminster (UK): innovation in the package holiday business

The Holiday Club of Upminster illustrates the key role of individual entrepreneurs in innovation, particularly in the formative stages of company development. Shortly after leaving school in 1937, Harry Chandler persuaded his old school to let him organize a trip abroad for them. He secured group discounts for the trip to Portugal and also learnt how to organize such trips more effectively in future. The Second World War disrupted his enterprise, but he restarted the business after 1946, using the same model, thereby establishing the Holiday Club of Upminster.

Over time, the model was refined but future innovations were mostly incremental rather than discontinuous. More destinations were offered to club members, as well as more services including seat reservations, baggage transfers between trains and ferries, meals on trains, and the provision of information booklets to clients about their trips and destinations.

Although not the first to introduce air charter holidays, the Holiday Club was in the vanguard, and booked seats in advance on scheduled flights, at discounted prices. Then, in 1956, for the first time, Chandler gambled on renting an entire 44-seat charter aircraft from London to Basle, an innovation that had been pioneered by Vladimir Raitz, the founder of Horizon. This offered substantial savings over schedule-based group rate costs. It also meant that he made a hefty profit on the holidays in his current brochure, which had already been costed on the previous basis. There was, however, increased risk, as he now had 44 seats to fill, whereas the average party size hitherto had been about 10. In practice, he secured a high occupancy rate, the gamble paid off, and a new organizational model had been innovated.

Source: After Laws (1997).

The drivers of innovation vary over time and space, and between different types of tourism activities. Moreover, the roles that key individuals often play mean that there are also significant differences even within the same sub-sector in a specific place and time frame. The real landscape of tourism innovation and its drivers is, therefore, necessarily complex. This complexity is evident in Carayannis and Gonzalez's (2003: 595–7) generic review of the empirical evidence of the main drivers of innovation, which included:

- leadership, vision, strategic plan;
- innovation/creativity rewards system;
- protection of intellectual property rights;
- propitious organizational environment for converting tacit ideas and knowledge into explicit proposals for improvement: open and frequent dialogue;
- the right mix of people and *esprit de corps* manifested in teams that work together effectively;
- sense of urgency;
- response to need, or the classic notion that 'necessity is the mother of invention';
- willingness of governments to innovate;
- supportive management willing to take risk and encourage fresh thinking in the private sector;
- government support for R&D;
- availability of risk capital;
- effective compromise between political and economic power, and the existence of social control;
- innovation networks and clusters;
- social diversity and a free flow of ideas.

They also identified a number of inhibitors of innovation, including:

- resistance from elites as innovation may be viewed as disturbing the status quo;
- resistance to change   failures of courage and imagination;
- pervading sense of comfort and conservatism;
- lack of courage by government representatives faced by opposition from officials, or fear of electoral consequences;
- pressure on chief executives to take the short-term view;
- rigidity of hierarchical structures.

All these conditions, whether favourable or inhibiting to innovation, apply to some extent to tourism firms. The lengthy list of drivers reinforces the argument that there is no magic formula for devising sectoral, local, regional or national policies for promoting tourism (see Chapters 4–7). Our aim in this book, therefore, is to explore what we consider to be the main dimensions and determinants of tourism innovation, as a starting point for analyses that are sensitive to complexity, and the blurring of ideas, structures and processes.

The approach of this book

This book adopts a broad perspective on innovation that is based on three main premises. First, that there is an emerging research literature in tourism that deals with themes that are closely related to innovation, such as cultural districts, adaptation and change in resorts, product life cycles, re-imaging places, and entrepreneurship, as well as a small but important literature on tourism innovation. However, we concur with Hjalager (2002: 465) that there has mostly been a failure to recognize that 'innovation is actually a core issue in a research tradition that has gained its own respect in social science'. More precisely, we believe that research can be advanced by mutually interrogating the broader literatures relating to tourism innovation, and the extensive theorizing on this subject in other social sciences.

Second, we aim to provide a conceptual and theoretical framework for understanding tourism innovation, but at the same time seek to illustrate and explore these ideas through drawing on largely fragmented empirical research. Reflecting the realities of the published literature, most of the empirical material – much of which is explored through a series of boxed case studies or illustrations – is about the more developed world, but where possible we have also drawn from other regions. Innovation is not the preserve of particular places or companies, but a pervasive activity.

Third, and following Schumpeter's (1934) early lead, we emphasize that not only does invention not equate to innovation, but the latter has to be understood as more than an individual act, or series of individual actions. Instead, innovation is a relational activity – whether those relationships are between individuals, individuals and technology, firms and individuals, firms and other firms, research agencies or government bodies. At the same time, these relationships have to be understood as being situated in particular institutional contexts. Fischer (2001: 200) provides useful guidance on this, and we broadly follow his notion of 'systems of innovation':

> A system of innovation may be thought of as a set of actors, such as firms, other organizations and institutions that interact in the generation, diffusion and use of new – and economically useful – knowledge in the production process. Institutions may be viewed as sets of common habits, routines, established practices, rules or laws that regulate the relations and interactions between individuals within as well as between and outside the organization.

The structure of the volume flows from these three main premises. In Chapter 2, we address the relationship between *competition* and innovation. Baumol (2002) provides a compelling argument that increased competition has been the main driver of innovation. There is, of course, innovation in all types of economies, whether pre-capitalist or state socialist, but a distinguishing feature of late capitalist economies is that globalization has contributed to intensification of competition (although this is very uneven across sectors), leading to high and probably accelerating rates of innovation. Of course, firms (or places) can seek to protect their innovations, but this is generally difficult in the service sector as a whole, and tourism in particular. Some tourism products and processes can be patented, for example particular software, but satisfying experiences – whether in terms of ambience, beauty or harmony – are as difficult to protect from would-be imitators, as they are to create.

There is a popular maxim that firms must 'innovate or die', a theme that we return to in Chapter 9. Although this is necessarily an oversimplification, innovation is crucial to the establishment, growth and survival of firms, at least in the long term, even if they can sometimes shelter in protected market niches in the short term. Firms can use innovation in different ways in the face of competition. For example, product innovation can make them first movers in the market, although they have to balance higher initial returns against the lower risks incurred by imitative innovation. Process or organizational innovations may also reduce costs or generate originality, making them more competitive. This links to a persistent debate in economics, that is the role of innovation in productivity, which has particular resonance for tourism, where many sub-sectors are characterized by relatively low labour productivity. But innovation is not a magic wand with which to cure all economic ills. Innovations can be financially disastrous for firms. So the strategic goal of firms (or places) is, or should be, to identify and implement innovations that add value to their operations.

Innovation has several requirements, including the availability of capital and resources, and entrepreneurship. Chapter 3 considers another essential component: *knowledge*. There are many different types of knowledge but we follow Polanyi's (1966) classic distinction between tacit and explicit (or codified) knowledge. Explicit knowledge is represented by technology, databases and manuals, and the first two of these are particularly important in tourism, as noted earlier. Tour firms and large hotel groups have become adept at collating and managing databases on their customers, while tourism has also been at the forefront of e-commerce, with airlines playing a pioneering role in IT-based information, reservations and sales systems. The problem with explicit knowledge is that, at least in tourism where patenting is rare, it is difficult for firms to protect their innovations from imitation by competitors. That is one reason why tacit knowledge – the different types of embodied and embedded knowledge (see Blackler 2002) possessed by individuals, and difficult or impossible to express – is potentially such a valuable source of innovation. While such knowledge is most obviously possessed by individuals, organizations can be understood to possess collective knowledge. Indeed, one of the main challenges faced by organizations is how to capture, systematize and redistribute individual tacit knowledge.

Knowledge creation and transfers are best understood in terms of intra- versus inter-firm flows. There is a considerable debate as to what constitutes the most effective organizational forms, and management strategies for maximizing knowledge transactions (Sundbo 1998). In general, decentralized management is considered to favour discontinuous or radical innovations within companies, but there is an argument that centralized management, with well-defined routines may be more effective for transferring incremental innovations across companies. In any case, there is general agreement that the empowerment of individual, or groups of, workers is important in knowledge creation. That, in turn, raises important issues for tourism, given relatively low levels of human capital, skills and investment in training (Riley *et al.* 2002), as well as organizational citizenship. Inter-company knowledge transfer is probably even more complex. Ownership is considered to be particularly important, with transnational companies having significant knowledge advantages. But companies can also enhance knowledge transfers through formal and informal collaboration, with firms up or down the value chain, or with government bodies and agencies, many of which have been set up specifically to promote innovation. As well as planned knowledge transactions, there are also knowledge spillovers between firms, effected through 'industrial gossip', labour market turnover, migration and other channels. Firms may view this positively, as in knowledge communities where all firms mutually benefit from such exchanges, or negatively, as indicating loss of competitive advantage. Finally, customers, in this case tourists, are also a source of knowledge and the more progressive firms seek to harvest this as a source of innovation. Tourists can also be seen as innovators in their own right, in the way that they contribute to and create new forms of tourism experiences.

Innovations are shaped by the framework of governance and regulation, as well as by institutional factors. In Chapter 4 we address *the role of state and quasi-state institutions* in tourism innovation development and diffusion. The chapter focuses on issues of innovation policy within the context of the role of the state in innovation and tourism; the significance of institutions as an element of innovation systems; and the concept of governance. The chapter emphasizes that innovation policy needs to be understood as emerging out of a political process but that there have been significant changes in policy focus and the nature of state innovation agencies in recent years. The chapter provides a framework for understanding the multi-layered architecture of the innovation systems in which firms are embedded and which serves to contextualize the national, regional and firm analysis of tourism innovation in the following chapters.

The significance of scale and the embeddedness of different sets of scales was noted by Bunnell and Coe (2001: 570) who argued that

> if scale is viewed as relative and socially constructed, then events do not occur exclusively at one particular scale but instead across various scales simultaneously, making it difficult to assign causal priority to one scale over the others . . . influences can run in both directions, or, to use the language of Smith, it is possible to 'jump scales' in both directions.

As with Bunnell and Coe, our view is that scale is a fluid and multidimensional concept, delineating the complex interactions between physical space, institutional and regulatory jurisdictions, and the shifting levels at which the actors in innovation systems organize themselves.

The consideration of institutions, regulation and governance in the previous chapter leads us to consider the territorial dimension of innovation. While we consider the national and the regional/local in different chapters, these have to be understood as inter-related and fluid scales (Bunnell and Coe 2001: 570). Archibugi and Michie (1997: 2) express this clearly:

> To understand technological change, it is crucial to identify the economic, social, political and geographical context in which innovation is generated and disseminated. This space may be local, national or global. Or, more likely, it will involve a complex and evolving integration, at different levels, of local, national and global factors.

Chapter 5 considers innovation at the *national level* via the concept of *national innovation systems*. This is perhaps the scale at which institutional differences are most clearly articulated, whether in terms of values and norms, or the organizational framework for innovation. This is not to say that these are closed national systems. Rather, 'each [national] system is constantly changing and is open to influence from other systems' (Hollingsworth 2000: 623–4). However, national institutions do remain distinctive in the face of globalization, and are key sites for understanding innovation. These differences are encapsulated, although not entirely contained, in the notion of the national innovation system, a term that was first employed by Freeman (1987: 1) to indicate 'the network of institutions in the public and private sectors whose activities and interactions imitate, import, modify and diffuse new technologies'. The concept has been further elaborated, notably by Lundvall *et al.* (2002). The national innovation system is most obviously constituted of the framework for R&D, education and training, and the climate for enterprise. However, it also includes a range of indirect innovation policies – such as migration polices (whether they facilitate skilled labour migration) or the tax system – as well as investment in infrastructures that support innovation.

Innovation is 'an intrinsically territorial, localized phenomenon, which is highly dependent on resources which are location specific, linked to specific places and impossible to reproduce elsewhere' (Longhi and Keeble 2000: 27), so that the *regional and local levels* are also important sites for innovation. Chapter 6 considers some of the main theories of localized learning and knowledge creation, which emphasize concepts such as Marshallian external economies, learning regions, and clusters. These mostly emphasize five main features that facilitate innovation. First, how trust, knowledge sharing and collective learning are facilitated by proximity. Second, the role of localized social networks in providing various forms of support amongst firms. Third, the existence of territorially-based cultural systems that favour innovation. Fourth, the existence of local and regional agencies that support innovation. And fifth, the existence of pools of skilled and knowledgeable, mobile workers who contribute to the creation of knowledge communities and to positive knowledge spillovers. The net effect is to reduce the transaction costs of innovation, including associated levels of risk. (Sternberg and Arndt 2001). So-called 'soft location factors', such as housing quality, amenities and the natural environment, can also be conducive to attracting innovative workers and entrepreneurs (Marinova and Phillimore 2003: 51). Moreover, Florida (2002) argues that social diversity and tolerance are critical features of creative regions.

The above observations are, in effect, comments on what may be termed the local of *regional innovation systems* (Chang and Chen 2004: 22), which, in common with national innovation systems, are defined by territorially distinctive institutions. Interesting questions are posed as to the extent to which local and regional innovation systems map onto the territorial configurations analysed by tourism researchers. Can, for example, local institutional features be integrated into the tourism resort life cycle model – indeed, might this not be a source for, at least partially, explaining which of the alternative pathways a resort follows in the 'rejuvenation stage'? And how do these theories of regional innovation systems relate to features such as the cultural district, the museum district or the clustering of hotels in particular zones, such as city centres?

Although the regional is a key level for analysing innovation, as stressed earlier neither the regional nor the national innovation system is closed. There are overlaps between regions and localities, with blurred boundaries, while the institutional context in any particular territory is also shaped by the national and the global. This is evident in firm behaviour, as Simmie (2004: 1103) argues:

> [I]nnovative firms are part of an internationally distributed system of innovation. They use localities as places primarily to operate from, rather than within. Firms and clusters that do not have this outward orientation are liable to suffer from too much intellectual inbreeding and lock-in. From this perspective, local clustering is just as likely to deliver economic decline, low productivity and a lack of innovation as the reverse.

In other words, national and international linkages are essential to the innovation performance of firms. This leads to consideration of the *firm level* and the place of the firm within *sectoral innovation systems* in Chapter 7. Sternberg and Arndt (2001: 380) remind us that the emphasis on the territorial organization of innovation systems should not imply neglect of the fact that 'a region represents an ensemble of individual innovation players (mostly firms)'. Although they use the regional environment, as well as helping to create it, their primary focus is the economic welfare of the firm itself. This is probably the level at which theorization of innovation is most sophisticated, and certainly most extensive. Some of the key issues will already have been covered in the earlier chapters on competition and knowledge, but this chapter explores the importance of organizational features. It examines R&D in different types of firms, especially transnational companies versus small and medium sized enterprises (SMEs). It also looks at the different theories of the innovation process. Linear theories, assuming a direct flow from invention through to market, are increasingly seen as oversimplified and are being challenged by theories that see more complex backwards and forwards linkages, and simultaneous developments of different stages in the innovation process – for example, of the basic research, some of the detailed design work, and market testing.

Tourism firms are, of course, heterogeneous in terms of ownership, scale and positions in the production chain. But there are some prevalent features that, although not unique to this sector, do inform innovation. First, there are very high rates of firm births and deaths in some sub-sectors, such as restaurants and cafés. This means there are high rates of inflow of knowledge, but it also signals that innovators operate in a high-risk environment. Second, there is strong polarization between those firms that compete on cost – an important feature of mass tourism – and those that compete on the basis of quality: these offer contrasting returns for different innovations. Third, temporality is a major issue. There are distinctive rhythms of demand with daily, weekly and seasonal peaks, which means that capacity utilizations are variable, posing particular challenges for the effective organization of labour. This is a stimulus to, and a constraint on, innovation. Fourth, the absorption capacity of tourism firms in some areas and sub-sectors can be constrained by lack of capital and entrepreneurship, and this is especially true of traditional tourism resorts, dominated by SMEs.

Following on from the above, *entrepreneurship* is the focus of Chapter 8. Baumol (2002: 58) argued that '[t]he entrepreneur is at once one of the most intriguing and one of the most elusive in the cast of characters that constitutes the subject of economic analysis'. Even Schumpeter was undecided as to whether to conceptualize the entrepreneur as the originator of innovation, or the vehicle for effecting this. The answer probably lies in understanding entrepreneurs as having a number of blurred and variable roles. At one level, heroic entrepreneurial figures are major landmarks in the evolution of tourism. But most entrepreneurs are involved in imitative innovation. That is not to say that they do not take risks or that they are not essential to innovation, but they do not bring about the discontinuous innovations that radically change the face of tourism.

One key issue in this chapter is the importance of scale – in particular, are entrepreneurs in smaller firms more likely to be innovative than those in larger ones? This is especially germane in discussing the tourism industry, given the size distribution of firms. There are also issues concerning family ownership, where entrepreneurship and innovation have to be understood in context of tangled social relationships. In some instances, firm strategy and operations including innovation can be highly contested within families. It is particularly important, in this context, to be sensitive to the highly selective nature of much of the available evidence on entrepreneurship, which tends to draw on relatively small numbers of case studies in particular economic environments in a few countries.

Finally, in the conclusions in Chapter 9 we review some of the emergent themes of the book, focusing first on the issues around innovation policies at the territorial level, especially relating to why the landscape of tourism policies is so patchy and uneven. In general, tourism is poorly represented in national innovation policies, while national tourism policies tend to neglect innovation. However, a number of conditions have coalesced, leading to tourism featuring more prominently at the regional level. Second, we revisit the theme of 'innovate or die' for the local firm, while posing the alternative of 'innovate and die' in recognition of the risks and costs inherent in innovation. Finally, and this is perhaps the central theme of this book, we emphasize that despite the many gaps in our understanding of tourism innovation, this is a theme that researchers and policy makers need to engage with, as much as firms. Innovation does not guarantee higher welfare levels in particular territories, or the survival of firms in the medium to long term, but these are also inconceivable without innovation.

2 Competition and innovation

Competition and the 'innovation arms race'

The 'innovation arms race' is a colourful phrase coined by Baumol (2002: 55) when describing innovation as 'a primary competitive weapon'. Although an emotive phrase, it catches the urgency and centrality of the relationship between competition and innovation. This is particularly strong within and between market economies.

Of course, there is also innovation in non-market economies, such as in the state socialist economic systems of Central and Eastern Europe before 1989 (Williams and Baláž 2000: chapter 2) or China before marketization reforms. However, the relationship between innovation and competition was muted within these very different institutional frameworks. Centrally directed R&D programmes, and systems of allocated outputs and inputs militated against innovation, especially discontinuous or disruptive innovations. The lack of incentive systems also dampened the potential for incremental innovations.

In contrast, the increasing rate of innovation in modern capitalist economies is considered to be driven by, above all, competition (Baumol 2002). For Metcalfe (2005: 23; emphasis added), there is a particular symbiosis between innovation, competition and entrepreneurship in capitalist economies.

> Modern capitalism is a particular kind of knowledge-based economic system, one in which *innovation, enterprise and competition* are connected through systems of complementary market and non-market instituted frameworks. These three processes are mutually defining and together they form the connection between the growth of knowledge and the expansion of material welfare that defines a modern economy.

Entrepreneurship is essential to the dynamic rivalry that faces any firm, which never quite knows where the threats to its existence will come from. Markets provide the incentives and market signals that guide entrepreneurial behaviour. The relationship between innovation and enterprise is examined in Chapter 8, and here we focus on the relationship between innovation and competition.

While competition is a defining characteristic of capitalist markets, this is not to say that markets are invariable across time and space. Rather they have diverse and changing forms. In Europe, some of this diversity is caught by Esping-Anderson's (1990) typology of national politico-economic models, ranging from the strongly social welfare Scandinavian model, to the corporatist German model, to the more neo-liberal UK model (see Shaw and Williams 2004: chapter 2). In essence, the idealized markets of free competition are modified in significantly different ways by regulations, institutions and state interventions in these countries. Other such politico-economic differences are evident between these European economies, and other advanced economies, such as Japan and the US, as well as the many different variants of emerging market economies. These and other differences related to institutions, and national innovation systems, are considered further in Chapters 4 and 5, respectively.

Markets are also imperfect due to varying degrees of regulation, concentration of ownership, imperfect information and market dominance by a small number of operators. In other words, markets are characterized by varying degrees of contestability (Baumol *et al.* 1982). In some markets, there may be a monopoly or oligopoly, and consequently very limited competition, such as on a flight route served only by a single airline. Contestability is, however, scale-dependent. A hotel may be the only such establishment in a particular area, and so may be considered to exercise a local monopoly. But it will also be in competition with hotels in other areas for some market segments, as well as with alternative forms of local accommodation (self-catering, small guesthouses or home stays, for example). What really matters, therefore, in respect of contestable markets 'is not whether an industry is actually a monopoly or not, but whether there is a real threat of competition' (Lei 2006: 21).

Although there are limits to market contestability, in particular sectors or at particular times, there is generally a strong and mostly positive relationship between innovation and competition, driven by the need to survive, or strategies to increase market share or profits. However, the relationship is not always so benign: innovation can also inhibit competition (Baumol 2002: 55). This is especially so where innovation raises the entry cost threshold for new entrants to a sector or sub-sector. A notable example of this is the early innovations in computer reservation systems (CRSs) by the major airlines (Box 2.1): substantial development costs became a strong deterrent to later new entrants. Other examples include the development of mega theme parks: in the UK, for example, few theme parks can compete with the year-on-year investments in new attractions at the largest theme park of all, Alston Park.

Despite the above qualifications, innovation and competition are mostly considered to be locked into a positive and mutually reinforcing relationship. Competition stimulates innovation, and the resulting increase in competition leads to further innovation by competing firms. More precisely, competition drives innovation in a number of ways:

Box 2.1 Innovation as an inhibitor of competition: airline CRSs

It is estimated to have cost $581 million to develop the five main competing CRSs by 1986. These development costs represented a very significant barrier to other firms seeking to compete in the market for providing such systems. In addition, there were several other related barriers to competition.

1   The CRS software was constructed around the airlines' own reservations systems. This meant that any non-airlines seeking to enter this market faced substantial additional adaptation costs.
2   There are major economies of scale and strong marginal rates of return. It is estimated that 80 per cent of the additional income generated via these systems was captured as profits by the operators. While advantageous for existing companies, it also meant there were very high initial costs compared to revenues, for new entrants.
3   The contractual relationships signed between CRS suppliers and travel agencies posed strong barriers for new entrants from the latter sector. They would have had to buy out their existing contracts, incurring major costs before even investing in project development.

Source: After Baumol (2002).

- First, constant competition from existing, and new entrant, firms generates compelling pressures to minimize costs, that is to pursue various forms of process and organizational innovations, both incremental and discontinuous, that will make the firm more competitive. For example, hotels are finding a succession of new means of reducing reception labour costs by automating the provision of services such as reservations, checking out or payment.
- Second, competition is dynamic and rests on innovation that seeks out strategic differences (Porter 2000a: 19). Entrepreneurs seek 'to position a company strategically in the market-place in such a way as to produce products that are both different from and superior to those of rivals' (Simmie 2004: 1109–10). Differentiation between sub-sectors, and of companies from their main competitors (Crevoisier 2004: 369), is the central logic here. Such strategies include all types of innovation, including product innovation and, especially in the service sector, process innovation. This is exemplified by the way in which 'adventure tourism' companies seek out ever-remoter and more challenging environments for

the holiday packages that they market. It also demonstrates the close relationships between production and consumption in tourism: competition between individual tourists, in terms of social emulation (Williams and Shaw 1992), both responds to and informs differentiation of the products and processes provided by tourism firms and, therefore, the innovations that keep reinventing strategic differences (Ateljevic and Doorne 2003: 123).

- Innovation provides 'first mover advantage'. The first entrant into a submarket, for example where a firm introduces a new product or process, whether in a specific local or national market, or globally, encounters particular conditions. On the one hand, it is easier to capture market share and to charge higher prices in the absence of competition. The first movers can also establish a comparative knowledge advantage and brand loyalty advantage before any competitors enter the market. To some extent, the early success of Disney reflects such first mover advantages, although this is also a story of effective marketing. However, first movers also encounter disadvantages for two reasons. First, because of the generally higher costs of the first wave of new technology, compared to subsequent imitations and modifications. Second, because of the higher risks in largely untested markets for new products. For example, the introduction of an American airline CRS at French Railways in the 1990s – the first such innovation in rail transport – ran into considerable difficulties because of differences between US air and European rail market structures (Mitev 1999). In part, the balance between such advantages and disadvantages is highly place and time contingent. The key question, therefore, is how long can first movers secure above average returns on their innovations, in particular places, before being challenged by new entrants? That, of course, raises questions about the contestability of markets or, more specifically, the extent to which their innovations can be protected from imitation, or from being outflanked by further innovations, a theme we return to later in this chapter.

Figure 2.1 suggests an idealized set of pathways that an individual firm may take, as defined by costs and returns. As first entrants (FE) firms have high costs and high returns, but then in the face of competition pressures (CP), their returns decline. At this stage they can follow one of three pathways. Innovation to differentiate themselves from their competitors (DI) may increase returns, but assuming this is an incremental innovation, the competitive pressures on costs remain high. Or they may pursue competition via innovations to reduce costs further (CR). Or they may simply fail to innovate, and end up in an untenable market position, with high costs and low returns, signalling bankruptcy and market exit (B).

Innovation has always been a feature of economic activity but globalization and neo-liberal deregulation tendencies have also increased competition, thereby intensifying the drive to innovate. For David and Foray (2002: 11),

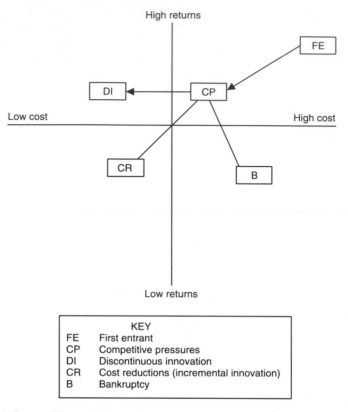

Figure 2.1 Competition and innovation: costs versus returns.

'the need to innovate is growing stronger as innovation comes closer to being the sole means to survive and prosper in highly competitive and globalised economies'. For individual firms, however, it is not a simple case of 'innovate or die' (see Chapter 9): for example, some innovations may raise quality, but there may be no market for this – an example of 'innovate and die'. Rather, firms have to innovate in a highly focused way: they have to prioritize those innovations that create value.

Value innovation and competing perspectives

If competition drives innovation in capitalist economies, then innovation has to fulfil competition-related goals for individual firms. We have already noted that there are different types of innovation – product, process, market, organizational and institutional, among others (see Chapter 1). Successful innovation by firms, within or across these types, will be shaped by the dictates of competition. In essence, innovation has to increase returns (of which profit is a key measure) to a tourism firm if it is to survive in a competitive market.

That, in turn, means the innovation must enhance the value of the product or tourism experience in relation to costs. In other words the innovation must create value for the firm. Kim and Mauborgne (1999: 6) summarize what they understand by the concept of 'value innovation', in terms of negating competition, at least temporarily.

> [M]ost sustained success comes from value innovation, which makes competition irrelevant by offering fundamentally new and superior buyer value in existing markets and by enabling a quantum leap in buyer value to create new markets.

It also requires creating value in terms of a consumption perspective, that is the customers' perceived quality of a tourism service or product, relative to the price (cost). Successful innovation (in terms of enhancing profits or ensuring the survival of a firm) has to increase value by improving quality or by lowering price for the tourist, or both of these. Of course, this does not apply to every single innovation – the owner of a hotel may decide to invest in replanting its gardens, because of a personal passion, even though the anticipated returns may be less than the costs incurred. In other words, there is scope for a range of entrepreneurial motives (see Chapter 8). But the market is a brutal place for most firms, and competition invariably demands value innovations. The French hotel chain Accor is often cited as an example of successful value innovation (see Box 2.2). Interestingly, Kim and Mauborgne (2004) argue that value innovation via the creation of new products or services in unoccupied product territories, for which there are no direct competitors, requires a different competitive mindset from other competitive strategies.

This discussion may appear to be emphasizing a rather obvious point about the constraints that markets and competition place on innovation. However, this is also a device for highlighting the existence of other understandings of innovation. From a production perspective, a successful innovation maximizes economic output, but from a welfare perspective, innovation increases social and environmental returns. The latter may sometimes coincide with value innovation. For example, an innovation such as improved glazing and insulation in a hotel may make it more comfortable to guests, improve the image of the hotel, reduce costs for the hotel owners, and be environmentally friendly by reducing energy consumption. However, it is rare for perspectives to coincide in this way, which is why state or voluntary intervention may be required to realise some innovations in tourism (see Chapters 5 and 6). But value innovation by firms is the cornerstone of innovation and adaptation, in the face of intense competition, in market economies. Arguably, neo-liberal tendencies have tended to reinforce this.

Box 2.2 Value innovation and Accor Formule 1

Accor discarded conventional notions of what a budget hotel should be and offered what most value-conscious customers really wanted: a good night's sleep for a low price. They did this by asking key questions:

- Which of the factors that the hotel industry takes for granted should be eliminated?
- Which factors should be reduced well below the budget hotel sector's standard?
- Which factors should be raised above the budget hotel sector's standard?
- Which factors should be created that the budget hotel sector has never offered?

In response to these questions, Accor developed a new hotel concept that led to the launch of the Formule 1 brand. Formule hotels provide less value compared to the average one-star and two-star hotel with respect to eating facilities, architectural aesthetics, lounges, room size, receptionist availability, and furniture and amenities in rooms. However, they provide greater value than the competition with respect to bed quality, hygiene and room quietness for a price marginally above that usually associated with one-star hotels. At the end of 2006 there were 317 Formule 1 hotels in 14 countries in Europe, South Africa, Australia, Brazil and Japan. This represented approximately 8 per cent of the Accor hotel portfolio at the time.

Source: Derived from Kim and Mauborgne (2004) and Accor http://www.accor.com/gb/.

Tourism: innovation in contestable markets?

Tourism is a complex mix of activities, involving several distinctive sectors, so it is hardly surprising that levels of competition are highly uneven both between sub-sectors and places. Sinclair and Stabler (1997: chapter 4) have reviewed the extent to which tourism sub-markets are contestable and conclude that in the hotel, accommodation and travel intermediaries sectors 'there are elements of contestability . . . alongside the dominant market forms of monopolistic competition and oligopoly' (Sinclair and Stabler 1997: 93). Paptheodorou (2006: 7) concurs that 'concentration and market structure dualism prevail nowadays in the transport for tourism, accommodation and travel distribution sectors'. Moreover, competition is articulated in different ways within each sector or sub-sector. For example, Box 2.3 summarizes some of the main and highly diversified forms of innovation in the airline sector, where competition and innovation are mutually informing.

In reality, competition is even more complex than this, and has to be understood as spatially specific. A large tourism attraction may dominate visitor flows in a particular area, suggesting a weakly contested market. But not only can tourists choose to visit other types of attractions within the same area, they can also choose to visit competing and similar mega attractions in different areas. The same applies to major hotels: they may dominate particular localized markets, but tourists can choose to stay in adjoining areas, trading off proximity for price or quality. Travel intermediaries, such as

---

Box 2.3 The many faces of competition: models of airline innovation and competition in the early 2000s

There has been strong innovation in the air travel sector, driven by increased competition. This is due in part to deregulation that has lowered some significant barriers to air transport. The main forms of innovation include:

- New full-service airlines, such as Etihad based in the United Arab Emirates, established in 2003.
- Low cost airlines such as Air Asia in Malaysia and Air Arabia in Sharjah.
- Traditional airlines being rebranded as low cost operators, such as Aer Lingus and American West.
- Low cost carriers being created within full-service carriers, such as Ted (UAL), and Atlas Blue (Royal Air Maroc).
- New regional airlines such as Lagun Air in Spain and Styrian Sprite in Austria.
- The conversion of traditional full-service, regional airlines into low cost carriers, such as Independence Air in the USA, and Norwegian Airlines.
- The creation of independent charter airlines such as Air Finland, and Zoom in Canada.
- The introduction of niche carriers such as Air Bourbon, linking Paris to the Island of Reunion.

These innovations have been driven by competition, but have also intensified the competition faced by individual operators.

Source: After O'Connell (2006: 58).

travel agents and tour operators, are also subject to intense competition, due to relatively low entry barriers (in terms of costs) and this has been further intensified by the rise of web-based marketing and reservations, empowering individual tourists. Moreover, there is also competition *between* sectors and sub-sectors as they bid to capture discretionary consumer spending. Tourists allocate their spending between types and categories or qualities of transport, accommodation and tourism attractions. Innovations in one of these may change the balance between price and quality, making it more attractive to tourists who may, therefore, redistribute their total holiday budget. For example, they may decide to travel economy rather than business class, in order to spend more on a new type of hotel that offers innovative services, but at a relatively higher price.

In common with most other economic sectors, globalization is increasing the extent to which markets are contestable in tourism. For example, within the American market the seaside resorts of New Jersey are no longer just in competition with, say, Florida, but also with Thailand and the Caribbean. But despite the globalization of competition, this remains territorially bounded to a significant extent: for example, domestic tourism is still several times greater than international tourism. A striking example of this is the US, where outbound international tourism is relatively modest compared to domestic tourism. Yet there is a very high level of tourism innovation in the US, compared to, say, most national tourism systems in Europe. This is because, as Keller (2006: 22) emphasizes, the US constitutes a large and relatively liberalized tourism market, where internal competition drives the tourism innovation system. Examples include: hub and spoke air transport systems, low cost airlines, hotel chains, standardized gastronomy, car rental, leisure parks and credit cards. In Europe, the most intense competition is probably to be found in the Mediterranean seaside holiday sector (Koutoulas 2006: 119), which has been associated with significant innovations in package holidays (Bray and Raitz 2001).

One of the distinguishing features of tourism innovation is the centrality of tourist–tourism industry interactions, which are necessarily highly visible (Chapter 1). This poses problems for tourism firms in concealing innovations from their competitors because – other than some back-office operations – these are easily viewed and imitated by other firms. The difficulties of patenting in the service sector underline the severity of this challenge. Restaurants may introduce new tariff arrangements, new types of meals or higher levels of service at meal times, but they cannot patent these.

Another distinctive feature of competition in tourism is the prevalence of public goods. Public goods are those for which no direct user fees can be charged. They are considered to be both 'non-excludable', which means that their use cannot be limited to those who pay, and also 'non-exclusive', which means that their use by one individual does not exclude them being used by others. Examples include paving the promenade along the sea front, subsidizing transport for tourists, and destination marketing campaigns. Even if one private company did invest in such innovations, it would be unable to exclude 'free riding' by other companies and individuals. As a result, individual firms will be unwilling or unable to invest in some types of innovations. State intervention may therefore be needed to collectivize the costs of certain types of tourism innovation (Hall 2005). At the heart of this lies the tension between competition and collaboration.

Because, as we argued in Chapter 1, the tourism experience is produced by a complex of tourism and non-tourism providers, firms have to walk a very fine line between competition and collaboration (Michael 2006). Thus hotels in a mountain ski resort may, at one level, be competing directly against each other, and the extent of such competition will drive innovation. For example, individual hotels may introduce new types of evening entertainment in their bars or restaurants, or may upgrade rooms by adding spa baths or other facilities. However, the hotels also know that they need to collaborate in order to realize some forms of innovation. They may need to come together to share the costs of a new resort-level information or marketing web site. And hotels that seek to innovate by extending their season know they cannot do so unless the owners of skiing facilities also agree to innovate in a similar way. Despite these limitations, tourism innovation is driven by competition and, as discussed below, is central to understanding both productivity and competitiveness in the industry.

Closing the gap: tourism innovation, productivity and competitiveness

Value innovation is central to the long-term survival of individual firms in contestable markets. Innovation potentially strengthens the competitiveness of the firm and, as argued later in this section, this implicitly also addresses productivity issues. Of course, what matters for firms, or territorial economies, in relation to competition is not so much the absolute level of productivity, but the relativities with their main rivals. In other words, how does innovation affect productivity (and marketing and sales) compared to competitors, and how does this, in turn, influence competitiveness (see Figure 2.2)?

The classic work on competitiveness is Porter (1990), which reviewed a wide range of evidence from both relatively advanced and emerging industrialized economies. Porter argued that economic success is determined by how an economy scores in terms of the drivers of competitiveness: the conditions relating to factors of production, demand conditions, relationships with related industries, and firm strategies and rivalry in the industry (including the intensity of competition). These four determinants are captured in his famous diamond model. One of the key conclusions (developed further in Porter 2000a: 18–20) is that firms can significantly enhance their competitiveness by addressing microeconomic conditions. In particular, demand conditions are determined by whether firms focus on imitative, low quality products,

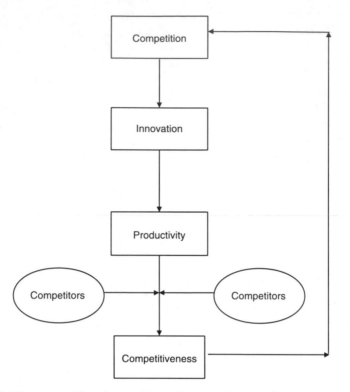

Figure 2.2 The competition, innovation and competitiveness chain.

or on competing via differentiation; that is whether their strategies are based on incremental as opposed to discontinuous or disruptive innovation.

Asheim and Coenen (2006: 163) similarly emphasize the centrality of innovation to competitiveness:

> [T]he theory of competitive advantage is dynamic, and thus, can be influenced by innovation policies and supporting regulatory and institutional frameworks. In this way innovation plays a central role in attaining and sustaining competitive advantage.

This view is echoed by Chell (2001: 44) who argues that innovation is the principal means by which firms can secure a competitive advantage over rivals. There are several ways in which this can be achieved: technological change, responding to or generating new or shifting buyer needs, the emergence of an entirely new industry segment, or modifying the costs or availability of inputs. The entry of Airtours of the UK into the cruise ship holiday market illustrates one such innovation (Laws 1997). Airtours entered what was, at that time, a new market segment for the company, by purchasing the Norwegian Cruise Line's ship, *Southward*, in 1994. Airtours was determined to take an innovative approach to make the cruise ship's operations more profitable. Its strategic aims were based on changes in volume and services. Whereas the ship had previously taken *c*.750 passengers, Airtours increased its capacity to 1,000, reducing unit costs and increasing discretionary spending on board. It also redesigned the ship's facilities, taking out the cinema and adding new bars, a casino, gym, teenage disco and children's play areas. The aim was to create a new, more affordable cruise package that would attract a new market segment to this type of holiday. It worked, in that 60 per cent of passengers in the first season were new to cruising. Airtours had managed to combine product, process and market changes in a high-yielding value innovation.

Porter's framework provides perspectives on the competitiveness not only of firms but also of territorial economies, whether national or local, and he explicitly wrote about this (Porter 1990; 2000a). The approach has obvious application to understanding the competitiveness of tourism destinations, as demonstrated by Crouch and Ritchie (1999: 146). They proposed a model of tourism destination competitiveness based on four main determinants: core resources and attractors, supporting factors and resources, destination management, and so-called qualifying determinants. We consider local-level innovation further in Chapter 5, and it is sufficient here to note that the transformation of competitiveness, via innovation, is as critical to particular areas – for example, waterfronts, seaside or mountain resorts, and rural areas – as it is to individual firms.

Competitiveness has many different determinants, as Porter noted. One of these is the conditions relating to the factors of production and, in essence, this is about productivity. Productivity is an expression of the relationship between inputs and outputs, and it is possible to refer to either firm-level productivity, or productivity levels in territorial economies, whether local, regional or national. Productivity is usually measured in terms of either labour productivity or total factor productivity (TFP).

The most widely used concept of productivity is labour productivity, not least because it is relatively simple to operationalize and measure. Labour productivity can be computed as a simple ratio of output per input of labour (e.g. number of workers, working days, hours worked). This is a particularly attractive concept for studying tourism given commonly held beliefs that the industry is characterized by low levels of labour productivity (Blake *et al.* 2006). However, the marginal productivity of labour (the amount produced by each extra hour worked, or worker employed) changes with the amount of other substitute/complementary inputs that are used in the production process, such as capital or knowledge. Therefore, although an useful concept, labour productivity only provides partial information about how inputs are transformed into outputs.

The second approach to measuring productivity nominally takes into account the inputs of all the factors of production. In practice, these tend to be reduced to labour, capital and a 'constant' that captures the level of technology, technical efficiency, managerial capacity or any other unobserved components in the firm (Barro and Sala-I-Martin 2003). The 'constant' is also known as TFP, which is usually calculated as the change in production that is not explained by a change in the other two inputs – in other words, it is a 'black box' concept. The residual includes innovation – whether in terms of technology or management – but it is notoriously difficult to deconstruct TFP so as to provide measurements of its constituent parts, including innovation.

Despite these operational difficulties, innovation is a critical determinant of productivity levels. For example, innovation accounts for some 80 per cent of productivity growth in the European economy, while productivity growth, in turn, accounts for some 80 per cent of gross domestic product (GDP) (Sternberg and Arndt 2001: 365). These bald numbers underline the role of innovation in competitiveness and growth at the territorial level. But it is, of course, equally crucial to the performance of individual firms, and there is considerable evidence that innovative firms consistently out-perform non-innovative firms in terms of both productivity and growth (Cainelli *et al.* 2005: 454).

Most research on productivity – as on innovation – has focused on manufacturing, but there is increasing analysis of innovation as a driver of productivity in the services. As might be anticipated, this has been highly problematic, not least because of the difficulties of defining and measuring real output and inputs in the service sector. Most services, including tourism, are characterized by non-material outputs and inputs, which are difficult to capture statistically, and this is one reason why services are generally seen as 'low-tech, low productivity industries with little impact on a country's economic performance' (Preissl 2000: 125). This problem is compounded because services are often produced and consumed simultaneously (see Chapter 1), so that real time quality control is of the utmost importance to services productivity. This is in sharp contrast to manufacturing, where quality control can be exercised after production. Although it is possible to measure the number of hours worked, or the formal skills of the workers, it is very difficult to quantify 'quality control', based on inter-personal skills and other elusive competences, which are vital in services.

Tourism, as noted in Chapter 1, shares many of the generalized characteristics of the services; in other words, productivity issues assume a distinctive but not a unique form in tourism. Tourism is commonly asserted to have low levels of productivity, and especially low labour productivity (Keller 2006: 20), although this does not apply to all the diverse sub-sectors that make up this complex industry, such as air travel. A notable feature of low productivity industries is that they tend to encounter difficulties in factor procurement, particularly labour, which therefore necessarily becomes a focus of innovation (Scheidegger 2006: 13). More specifically, given the importance of the tourist–tourism employee encounter in the production of tourism experiences, real time quality control is important and often central to tourism innovation – whether as its object, or as a constraint on the replacement of workers by technology.

In practice, there has been surprisingly little research on productivity in the tourism industry as a whole, although there have been studies of particular branches, notably airlines and hotels. Blake *et al.* (2006: 1100) have reviewed the available literature and conclude that the key drivers of productivity are: 'physical capital, human capital involving skills and training, innovation and the competitive environment'. Human capital has already been emphasized, as has the competitive environment (the contestability of markets). But technological innovations are also important in tourism productivity – and this is formally recognized as a component of TFP. Technology is discussed further in Chapter 3, but here we consider one element of this: IT, one of the principal dimensions of tourism innovation.

It is no exaggeration to state that IT has taken by storm some branches of the tourism industry, particularly via internet and web-based innovations. Porter (2001), commenting on the use of the web, states that the main impact has been seen in the reorganization of existing industries that previously were characterized by high costs of communication, gathering information and accomplishing transactions. This is a very apt description of the impact of IT on tourism. Tourism firms and tourism economies face a number of competition challenges, and web technology can be harnessed in response to these (see Box 2.4), whether at the level of firms, destinations, or sectorally (for example, from new media forms).

While IT innovations are commonly held to be drivers of productivity in tourism, in response to different forms of competition, there is a counter argument based on the notion of the 'IT productivity paradox'. Brynjolfsson (1993) first coined the term the 'IT productivity paradox', arguing that the benefits of spending on IT are not always reflected in aggregate output increases and, therefore, not necessarily in increased productivity and competitiveness. The evidence on this point is rather mixed. Sigala (2002) reviewed the hotel sector and, initially, concluded that the IT productivity paradox was present. And David *et al.* (1996) report that hotel managers believe that while some IT applications (for example, reservation management systems, rooms management systems) have improved productivity, others (for example, vending and entertainment) have led to decreases. Finally, Baker and Li (1996) used financial performance data from 29 Taiwanese hotels to analyse past investment and corporate performance, but failed to isolate IT as having a distinctive impact, separate from other factors. However, Sigala *et al.* (2004: 189) urge caution in their conclusions, arguing that the 'productivity paradox' may be due to measurement difficulties, or what they termed 'a methodological artefact'. The difficulties of measuring productivity are well established in the service sector (for example, Reardon and Vida 1998) but this is compounded where ITs have transformed the content and provision of service activities. According to Petit (1995) the quality improvement of those services may well have been significantly under-assessed in national accounts.

Box 2.4 Competition intensity, tourism challenges and IT solutions

Level of competition	*Technology solution*
Competition from similar service providers	Extranets facilitate collaboration amongst producers and destinations
Competition from similar or undifferentiated destinations	Internet representation helps tourism destinations to reinforce their image nationally and internationally and to promote their uniqueness
Competition from differentiated destinations	Internet can reinforce uniqueness and extranet can bring together all partners to develop themed experiences
Competition within destination channels	Technology enables disintermediation, giving suppliers the opportunity to reach their customers directly and strengthen their position. When intermediation is inevitable, inter-operability tools can reduce distribution costs allowing a higher margin to be shared by all partners
Competition with alternative leisure activities	IT produces activities, e.g. computer games, that allow people to stay at home for leisure. In reality many of these activities are also provided at destinations, so that internet representations can be used to promote a variety of alternative leisure and recreational activities at the destination

Source: Based on Buhalis (2006: 146–7).

The full impact of investment in IT on productivity therefore only becomes apparent when the exploitation of the network/integration, informational and transformational capabilities of IT are considered, and this usually requires qualitative research.

In summary, then, innovation lies at the heart of competitiveness, although it is not sufficient in itself to guarantee this, whether for individual firms or for tourism destinations. Tourism firms need to address productivity levels – traditionally considered to be relatively low in much of the industry – via innovation. Those innovations may focus directly on the costs and quality of labour or on capital, management and technology, especially IT. Moreover, firms or places not only have to focus on their own innovations, but also have to be constantly vigilant of the innovations being undertaken by competitors. Defensively, this means they have to seek to close the competitiveness and productivity gap with their leading rivals, or offensively it means they seek to open a gap over their rivals. The former is more likely to involve imitative innovations, and the inherent risks that this may involve (see Chapter 7), and the latter is more likely to be based on innovations that provide differentiation from competitors.

Once tourism firms or destinations have secured a competitive advantage through innovation, they have to protect this in one of two ways. One approach is constant review of their own performance, and that of their competitors, as a basis for continuous innovation. This can be formalized through benchmarking (Box 2.5). Benchmarking involves systematic comparisons to the performance of competitors, with a view to identifying significant gaps, the

---

Box 2.5 Benchmarking and destination competitiveness

Reasons to benchmark:

- Helps organizations understand they have strengths and weaknesses.
- Helps to meet more effectively customers' needs for quality, cost, product and service by establishing new standards and goals.
- Motivates employees to reach new standards and to be keen on new developments.
- Allows organizations to realize what levels of performance are really possible by looking at other organizations, and how such improvement can be achieved.
- Documents reasons why these differences exist.
- Helps organizations to improve their competitive advantage by stimulating continuous improvement in order to maintain world class performance and increase competitive standards.
- Promotes changes and delivers improvements in quality, productivity and efficiency, which in turn brings innovation and competitive advantage.
- Provides a cost efficient and time efficient way of establishing a pool of innovative ideas from which the most applicable practical examples can be utilized.

Benchmarking can focus on:

1 Internal benchmarking – which aims to improve the internal performance of a destination, by bringing the standards of all firms up to those of the most competitive.

2   External benchmarking – which uses tourist motivation, satisfaction and expenditure surveys to investigate how one destination
performs compared to another.
3   Generic benchmarking – which uses the adoption of 'absolute'
quality and eco-label standards.

Source: After Kozak (2004: 2).

means to close these, or the harvesting of knowledge about alternatives. In
essence, it involves learning and innovation. Alternatively, firms may seek to
protect their innovations from imitation, through creating barriers to entry
whether legal (for example, patenting), in terms of start-up costs, or simply
concealing the true nature of such innovations. However, as will be seen
in the following section, it is particularly difficult to realize protection of
innovations in tourism.

To the (fragile) barricades: reducing competition and protecting innovations

Innovations can require major investments of resources, whether measured in
terms of time, capital, creativity or management. But irrespective of costs,
their initiators have an inherent interest in seeking to protect these from
imitation or – even worse – enhancement by competitors. This is in effect a
rallying cry to reinforce the barricades against competitors. Moreover, the
intensification of competition has increased the return on protecting innovations, that is on constructing barriers to their adoption by potential rivals.
This is a challenging task in most sectors, let alone tourism, where the barriers
are often fragile if non-existent.

Baumol (2002) provides convincing evidence of the difficulties faced by all
firms in protecting their innovations over more than a relatively short time
period. His study of 46 major product innovations (across all areas of the
economy) reveals that the time span over which innovations offer a competitive edge – measured as the gap before competitors enter the market – has
fallen from 33 to just 3 years between the late nineteenth and the early
twenty-first centuries. Three years represents a remarkably short time period
in which to try and recoup a major investment in a particular innovation.
This time lag is even shorter in some sub-sectors, say for a hotel that introduces a new facility: the likely time span for enjoying a competitive edge,
before this is copied by its neighbours, may well be no more than a single
season.

This is not to say that firms necessarily seek absolute protection of their
innovation from imitation. Rather, as Baumol (2003: 435; emphasis added)
argues,

possessors of intellectual property characteristically have much to gain, not only by sharing them passively yet voluntarily even with direct competitors, but by actively devoting effort and resources to getting others to use them, *on suitable terms*, of course. This can demonstrably be profitable, and not only in theory. It is widely done in practice via licensing, trading and other means, and the activity, that began no later than the early 19th century, is evidently expanding.

Baumol (2003: 437) further contends that, because firms differ in their capacities and in the activities at which they are relatively efficient, some firms will be better at innovation while others will be more effective in the use of inventions as inputs to final products. For example, one firm may have expertise in inventing a new type of biotechnology process, while other firms have the expertise and resources to apply this to the mass production of new commercialized pharmaceutical products. In other words, it may be economically logical for 'inventor firms' to specialize in innovations that they subsequently profit from largely by licensing or selling their innovations to other firms, rather than by directly exploiting these on a large scale themselves. And if there are massive development costs associated with such innovations, the only way to recoup these may be to plan future licensing revenues into the original business plan. Hence, there may be a logical division of labour in the different stages of evolving and adapting innovations.

However, the key words in Baumol's quote are '*on suitable terms*', which in practice implies various forms of licensing and patenting. Herein lies a problem for tourism firms: in general, it is much easier to patent technologies or products than services or processes. But it can be very difficult to limit the use of innovations by your rivals, even in manufacturing and for technology. Görg and Greenaway (2004) have reviewed the difficulties inherent in controlling technology transfers. Essentially, knowledge is a partially excludable good because the proprietary firm encounters major difficulties in seeking to prevent its use by other firms. There are a number of channels of knowledge spillover (see Chapter 3) ranging from the mobility of key workers, leaving to set up businesses on their own or to work for a rival, to unlicensed applications in countries where intellectual rights and patenting are not recognized or are not effectively policed.

The difficulties faced by most service firms, and tourism firms in particular, when seeking to protect innovations are even more challenging. Only very rarely can they patent and license their innovations, as exemplified by the cruise ship sub-sector, where there are strong convergence tendencies in both products and processes (see Box 2.6). Some of these limitations are outlined here.

Public goods. It is not possible to patent public goods, such as views of the Taj Mahal and Sydney Harbour Bridge, or the excitement of anchoring in a Caribbean port while on a cruise. By their nature, these are open to other tour operators, and to a multitude of accommodation providers who can locate within daily travelling distance, even if not necessarily within sight of these attractions. It may be possible to protect geographical designations in some circumstances, for example, Champagne, but the intellectual property of place is grounded in branding rather than actual goods or experiences (Hall and Mitchell 2008).

Tourism products are characteristically impossible to patent or protect. For example, if a tour operator offers a holiday to a new location, then it cannot protect this against imitation – as evident in the example of cruise tourism (Box 2.6). Other tour operators could imitate this product in their holiday brochures in the following season, unless there was only a single hotel at the destination that was tied into an exclusive contract with the first tour company. Even then, this would be a relatively short-term barrier, as other hotel operators would enter the market if returns were sufficiently high – provided that there were no other restrictions on building, such as an absolute ban on new construction in a national park. The same difficulties in protecting innovations can also be seen at the micro scale. For example, Hitchcock (2000) describes how many women entrepreneurs in Bali, with limited capital, set up catering outlets. They innovated menus, based on trial and error, without incurring too much risk to their capital. However, their successful formulas were easily visible to competitors, who quickly copied these, providing very short time spans for reaping the returns from being first entrants with a particular product.

Technology. As noted in Chapter 1, internal R&D expenditure on technology is characteristically very low in the tourism industry, with a few exceptions such as the specialist area of travel book systems. Instead, there is a tendency to buy in technologies, either off-the-shelf, or adapted to their needs through collaboration with suppliers. Consequently, little of their technology is proprietary (Pfeffer 2002), and so is easily copied by competitors. Indeed, the suppliers may promote further sales of the technology to their rivals on the basis of having sold or successfully adapted it for their first tourism client. For example, most of the back-office IT software used in hotels is based on relatively minor modifications to basic systems provided by specialist suppliers.

Tourism processes. Tourism is generally a labour-intensive sector, where both the cost and the quality of labour are critical. Not surprisingly, firms pay particular attention to either one or both of these criteria. While some of the underlying labour processes may be concealed in the back office, the critical tourism encounter and much of the labour input is front stage and highly visible. It is therefore difficult to conceal innovations, such as the quality of service in a restaurant, the excitement provided by a new form of entertainment in the hotel bar, or the employment of bilingual guides to accompany holiday tour groups. It only requires a visit to the restaurant or hotel bar, or a report from someone on one of these tours, to effect the simplest of learning by observation. However, it may be difficult to reproduce these experiences in another firm, because of the intangible nature of service delivery. But you cannot conceal at least the outward signs of these innovations, which rivals can then seek to imitate or further enhance.

Box 2.6 Imitative innovation in the holiday cruise sector

Cruising has become an increasingly popular form of tourism, with the cruise ship itself being as much the destination as the places it visits. Many tourists remain on board the cruise ship throughout, preferring its security and controlled environment to the perceived uncertainty of visiting the ports of call. The larger ships have effectively become floating resorts, representing an extreme form of enclave tourism.

As a lucrative sector, even though one with relatively high entry costs especially for those operators who wish to own rather than lease ships, there has been intense competition to capture a share of the growing market for cruising. There are two main foci of innovation: the services and facilities provided on the ships, and the places visited. In respect of the latter, a notable innovation was introduced by the Norwegian Cruise Line: the private island concept. In 1977, they initiated the practice of landing passengers, by tender, on Great Stirrup Cay, a supposedly 'deserted island' in the Bahamas, for a day's relaxation. This product innovation was so popular that the cruise line purchased it in 1986, as a means to protect its innovation. Once it was no longer a public good (that is, open to use by other cruise ships), the company considered it worthwhile to invest $1 million to upgrade its facilities.

Although they could exclude other cruise ships from using Great Stirrup Clay, the Norwegian Cruise Line could not patent this innovation. It was easily observable, and was soon imitated. By the mid-1990s most of the cruise lines operating in the Caribbean had purchased their own private islands, or called by arrangement at particular 'out islands', which offered a similar blend of tranquillity and security. In most cases, the notion of 'the private, pristine and deserted island' is a myth. Instead, the destinations are usually located on coves on peninsulas that are not easily accessible except by small boats, and they are located on inhabited islands to ensure there is a ready supply of local labour to service them. And the local environment has usually been significantly improved, and is not a natural habitat in any meaningful sense.

The private island concept was an innovation that initially provided a competitive advantage to one company. However, in common with most innovations in the cruise ship sector, it could not be protected from imitation, and had been widely copied by competitors in less than two decades.

Source: After Laws (1997: 78–9).

Given the difficulties of constructing barriers, or barricades, to the imitation of innovation, it is hardly surprising that there tends to be widespread passive acceptance of the difficulties, or impossibility, of protecting most tourism innovations. For example, a survey of accommodation establishments and tourism attractions in the UK found that 83 per cent of respondents believed they were under strong competitive pressures from potential new entrants (Blake *et al.* 2006: 1108). Significantly, 58 per cent of accommodation and 63 per cent of attractions managers concluded that if they invested in innovations, their competitors would copy these. This inability to protect investments in innovations can evolve into a vicious circle of innovation passivity.

Of course, some forms of tourism experiences or tourism services can be protected from imitation, through the exercise of particular types of rights, or the creation of economic barriers. To some extent, this is a matter of scale. For example, reflecting further on the example of the Taj Mahal, mentioned earlier, it is possible to come to two distinct conclusions: first, that the Taj Mahal is unique and, because of its particular combination of architecture, site and image, cannot be replicated in another place. It may be possible to copy the building, but not its site, or its historical and cultural associations. Second, hotels offering services to tourists visiting the Taj Mahal do compete against each other. If one hotel innovates in the services it offers, other establishments can imitate this. With this important caveat in mind, we consider five ways in which tourism innovations can be protected from imitation or emulation by competitors (Figure 2.3).

First, the provision of tourism services, or the construction of tourism facilities, may be regulated and limited. Such regulation is usually effected through the national or the local state (see Chapter 4). Most obviously, only a single company, or a small group of operators, may be licensed to provide tourism services in a particular area, such as a national park, or some other environmentally sensitive area via concession agreements. For example, the driving of coaches onto Farwell Spit, or the provision of overnight accommodation on Doubtful Sound, both in South Island, New Zealand. Innovations by one company can be imitated by other licensed operators in other locations, but not by new entrants within that particular regulatory space. Such regulations are double-edged in terms of innovation. On the one hand, and positively, they may provide companies with greater scope to secure a return on their innovations, because of lack of imitators, and a greater willingness to take risks. But, on the other hand, and negatively, limiting competition may dull the incentive for firms to innovate: it is no longer a case of innovate or die for them (Chouinard 2005).

Second, firms may obtain exclusive proprietary locational rights over particular tourism sites. They may literally be able to purchase a particular tourism site, and exclude their competitors from that space. If the tourism attraction has non-reproducible characteristics, then they can establish a monopoly over the direct commodification of the tourism attraction. One

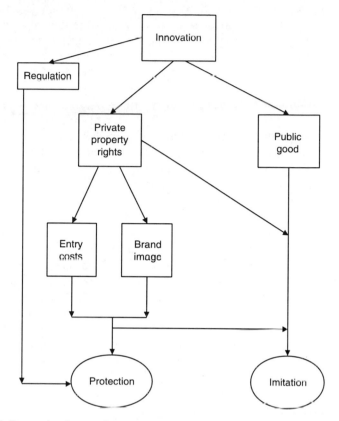

Figure 2.3 Protecting innovations.

example would be the purchase of a castle or house with historic or other associations. Alternatively, they can purchase a larger area – such as Land's End in the UK – charge entry to the site, provide additional services for tourists and exclude other operators.

Third, some innovations may be so expensive to develop that this creates cost barriers that deter new entrants. One well-known example is the development of airline CRSs, discussed earlier. There are however limits to the effectiveness of such barriers. There may be potential new entrants with sufficient resources to overcome such barriers. Furthermore, the advantage enjoyed by the innovators may be relatively short lived: for example, over time autonomous technological developments – in computing hardware and software in this case – may reduce the costs to competitors. Finally, with venture capital having evolved into a global industry, resource constraints within particular regional or national economies have also become less effective, although still non-negligible, barriers to innovation.

Fourth, it is easier to protect innovation in tourism processes than products, although these tend to be intertwined. To some extent, this is about the greater scope to conceal innovations when they are back stage rather than front stage in the production of tourism services. But it is also about the difficulties of imitating management practices. For example, the remarkable success of Southwest Airlines in the USA, the pioneering low cost scheduled airline, is well-known. It reorganized working practices, so that it had fewer employees per flight, and flew more passengers per employee than its rivals. It also turned around 80 per cent of its flights in 45 minutes or less, creating a productivity gap over its rivals that yielded significant competitive advantage. The broad strategy behind their innovative approach was observable by their rivals, but 'the culture and practice of the company are less obvious than its technology' (O'Connell 2006: 66). It may be relatively easy to emulate particular innovations, but far more difficult to imitate the complex set of innovations, and the way in which these are managed as a whole. Consequently, none of its significant rivals has hitherto been able to imitate their innovative approach in its entirety, and to close the productivity gap.

Fifth, it may be possible to establish a reputation for quality and 'exclusiveness' as part of branding strategies that are difficult for competitors to challenge, thereby allowing extraction of above average returns. In tourism, this applies to some of the world's most famous hotels, such as Reid's on Madeira, or Raffles in Singapore. However, such protection is precarious as can be seen for instance in relation to tourism-based urban regeneration strategies. Places such as Baltimore and Boston enjoyed the associated advantages of being first entrants in this field. However, their approaches could not be patented or protected from imitation, and over time there was 'serial reproduction' of such regeneration schemes (Harvey 1989: 10). The outcome was a congested sub-market, and waterfront regeneration schemes have been locked into a continual struggle to innovate and differentiate themselves from their competitors (Jessop 1998). The outcome, however, has tended to be predictability and standardization, with strong convergence in the approaches adopted. However, although precarious, establishing a strong brand identity does offer some protection for innovation. A notable example is provided by the Guggenheim branded museums (Box 2.7). After establishing two major museums, the Guggenheim has since, effectively, franchised its name in three further major museums. These were developed by local funders, in collaboration with the Guggenheim, which provided expertise, access to its collections and exhibitions, and – most importantly – a strong brand name, partly associated with innovative architectural forms.

Conclusions

Competition is probably the main driving force of innovation in tourism, at least in capitalist economies. The collapse or the partial marketization of state socialist economies in the late twentieth century has extended the reach of competition, at the same time as globalization has intensified it. Innovation offers a number of competitive advantages to firms and places, as first

Box 2.7 Urban branding: Guggenhcim Bilbao – the first global museum?

The Guggenheim Museum in Bilbao was an overnight sensation when it was opened, not so much for its contents, as for the building itself, designed by architect Frank Gehry, and costing over £70 million. In some ways it reproduced the impact of the striking New York Guggenheim muscum, designed by Frank Lloyd Wright, three decades earlier. But, at the same time, it created the idea of franchising a museum brand name that destinations became willing to bid for – usually, by offering to fund the construction of a striking new building.

The Guggenheim Bilbao helped transform the city, previously perceived as a stagnating centre of heavy industry, into a major visitor attraction. It attracted 1.3 million visitors in its first year alone, and justifiably was labelled 'one of the most transformative symbols of place making in the last decade' (Evans 2003: 432).

Transformation of the city's image was a catalyst for major urban improvements, and almost overnight recognition of the Guggenheim as a global museum of the first rank. Not surprisingly, it was soon imitated, but in the novel form of a museum brand. Branded Guggenheims were opened in Berlin and Las Vegas, adding to the earlier museums in New York and Venice, with discussions proceeding to open further 'branded cultural exhibition spaces' in other places.

Museum	*Opening of museum building*
Venice	1949
New York	1959
Bilbao	1997
Berlin	1997
Las Vegas	2001

The Guggcnheim Bilbao was a disruptive innovation and providcd the city with a competitive edge in national and global tourism markets. Although the actually brand name was protected, the innovative idea of a striking architectural museum building was not, and has since been imitated. At the same time, the Guggenheim itself has been subject to 'the reproduction formula' (Normann 1984) with new Guggenheims being franchised in other cities. However, the latter brings problems for Bilbao, if not for the Guggenheim brand name: 'over-reliance on a single brand . . . also risks image decay as the brand dilutes' (Evans 2003: 432).

Source: After Evans (2003).

entrants, or via differentiation or cost reductions. Such innovations are associated with the struggle of firms to enhance their productivity, and open up a productivity gap over their rivals.

Competition is particularly strong in the tourism industry, because it is difficult for places or firms to patent their innovation, or to put up effective barriers to imitation by their rivals. This stems from the importance of public goods, reliance on external suppliers of technology, and – above all – the intangible and highly visible nature of tourism services. Of course, firms and places do find ways to protect innovations from imitation, at least in the short term, whether by concealment in the back office, creating powerful brand images, establishing absolute proprietary rights or erecting cost barriers. None of these are fixed, however, because the story of innovation in tourism is a tale of shifting relationships between the principal agents.

Although competition is the main driver of innovation, this does not explain how or why this is articulated in particular ways. In the remainder of the volume, we examine innovation processes and outcomes in more detail, commencing with a review of the role of knowledge in the next chapter.

3 Knowledge, creativity and innovation

Knowledge at the heart of innovation

Knowledge of course lies at the heart of innovation; indeed, innovation is the process of applying new forms of knowledge. This poses the question of what we understand by knowledge. One response is that knowledge is what is gained through experience or study that enables a person to perform a specific task (Awad and Ghaziri 2004). It is more than information, which is essentially about meaningful data, because it involves elements of interpretation (Wiig 1993). As Chang and Chen (2004: 24) explain:

> Knowledge is different from information. Information relates to data, while knowledge involves a wider process that involves cognitive structures that assimilate information and put it into a broader context, thereby allowing actions to be undertaken on that basis. Information exists independently of the receiver and transmitter. Knowledge is information that has been translated so that humans understand it. Knowledge cannot be said to 'flow' but can be said to be 'shared' or 'transferred'.

Almost by definition, knowledge has always been critical to innovation, productivity and competitiveness. But the availability of information and knowledge have increased exponentially in recent years (Chang and Chen 2004: 33), driven by both IT changes and globalization. It is increasingly seen not as *a* factor, but the *key* factor in economic performance, as is epitomized by the fashionable notion of the 'knowledge-based economy'. Although the latter is overstated, in its implied ahistoricism, and failure to recognize the critical role of knowledge throughout the economy, this concept does highlight the need to understand knowledge – how it is created, transferred and applied.

Moreover, knowledge is not the preserve of elites, or of central management, or of cutting-edge companies or major transnational corporations. Rather as Metcalfe (2005: 12) reminds us, 'perhaps the most obvious characteristic of modern economies is the distributed nature of knowledge generation and the consequent distributedness of the resultant innovation processes across multiple organizations, multiple minds and multiple kinds of knowledge'. Most obviously this implies distributedness within companies, and the need to recognize that knowledge resides in individual workers, or groups of workers. Effective companies – notably the so-called 'learning organizations' (Garvin 1993; Bayraktaroglu and Kutanis 2003) – seek to capture and share this information within the company, a theme that we refer to later. But distributedness also refers to the existence of critical sources of knowledge in all areas of the tourism economy, including some of the more obscure corners of the informal economy. For example, Hitchcock (2000: 219; emphasis added) has described how many Balinese work in kiosks and hotels, or as guides, in occupations where there are very few other Indonesians: 'In these contexts, local *knowledge* of customs and festivals may provide the Balinese with a competitive edge.'

While knowledge transfers are central to innovation, as evidenced for example by the revolutionary changes in work practices that followed the introduction of chill–cook technologies or electric dishwashers into restaurants, this is not always viewed as a positive process by individual companies or by employees. There can be both intended and unintended, foreseen and unforeseen, knowledge transfer. The originators of knowledge may suffer from knowledge spillovers (Arrow 1962) when other firms are able to acquire their knowledge without hindrance or payment. This is particularly prevalent in tourism where, as noted in Chapter 2, it is difficult for firms and places to protect service innovations from imitation. In formal economic terms, this is because knowledge and innovation are partially excludable and non-rivalrous (can be reused many times) goods (see Chapter 2). In simple terms, it means that tourism firms and destinations cannot easily prevent their rivals from copying their latest attractions, or more recent improvements to their facilities – without having had to bear the risks or the start up costs of these innovations.

Types of knowledge

Not only is there a need to differentiate between information and knowledge, but also between different types of knowledge. The classic work in this field is Polanyi's (1958, 1966) famous distinction between tacit and codified knowledge. Codified knowledge is that which can be made explicit, and therefore can be transmitted in formal and systematic ways, whether in a manual, a data set or a software programme. In contrast, tacit knowledge is person and context specific and, paraphrasing Polanyi, this is epitomized by the notion that 'an individual knows more than can be expressed in words'. Later writers, such as Nonaka and Takeuchi (1995), have argued that effective knowledge creation and transfer requires a combination of these types of knowledge. As Asheim and Coenen (2006: 164) argue, even if knowledge can be transferred with very little friction across space, 'it relies on tacit knowledge embedded in people and organizations to be understood and applied'. For example, a hotel could buy a training manual about improving the quality of service provided by its front-line staff (codified knowledge), but it would be much more effective if they also brought in a trainer from another firm to train up the staff who were applying this manual; in other words supplementing codified with tacit knowledge. Let us consider these two types of knowledge in more detail.

Codified knowledge: the limitations of manuals and data sets

Codified knowledge assumes many forms, including written and figurative documents, computer data systems, and databases generally. Of particular note in recent years has been the growing importance of databases, particularly – but not only – on customers. These have been given added importance by IT developments that have allowed the assembly, analysis, management and rapid transfer of increasingly large databases. This allows firms to either purchase data sets – for example, from specialist consultants – or to create their own data sets. Moreover they can link different databases – for example, across all branches of a hotel chain, or a restaurant with the accommodation section within a resort hotel – and so can build up relatively comprehensive pictures of the spending behaviour and preferences of their clientele. Such databases can be invaluable sources of knowledge for innovation, whether in marketing or in terms of products and processes. Harrison (2003: 143), for example, notes how IT developments have revolutionized the uses made by the Ritz-Carlton group of its guest database:

> Current technology has made it much less expensive to implement a wide range of service procedures. Rather than use file cards (as occurred in an earlier day), hotels can maintain customer profiles on computer. Ritz-Carlton, for instance, tracks the tastes and preferences of its regular visitors. Ritz-Carlton properties use their guest database to good advantage by arranging for express check-in for regular guests, who need only to call and say when they plan to arrive. All is in readiness when they drive up to the curb. The technology to track this sort of information was not affordable even a few years ago – and the size of the market made manual operations infeasible. Hotel companies can also use technology for data mining, the intensive search for and compilation of information found in databases.

Hotels are not alone in making innovative use of IT and codified data. Tour operators, transport firms and credit card companies similarly centralize, marshal and transfer vast data sets on their customers, and this information – transformed into knowledge through its interpretation and application – has become an important driver and means of realizing innovations. It is no exaggeration to argue that IT developments have had a liberating effect on knowledge-based innovation in tourism, as indeed in many other economic sectors. Information systems in tourism have been among the pioneers of leading-edge technology applications: (discussed in Chapter 2) CRSs or global distribution systems (GDSs) have been among the first international inter-organizational systems. Yield management systems are among the most advanced data mining applications. Tourism marketing systems typically represent the forefront of multimedia and virtual-reality applications. The World Wide Web is also profoundly changing the production, distribution and consumption of tourist products. Werthner and Klein (1999) go so far as to argue that IT is probably the strongest driving force for changes within the tourism industry, while tourism is also of great importance for the IT and e-commerce sector. As Buhalis contends (2004: 814) in relation to airlines,

> in the last few years, ICTs emerged from a pure infrastructure department to a critical enabler of the entire range of the airline business processes. ICTs effectively determine the competitiveness of airlines, as they are embedded in every simple element of the airline value chain.

It is hardly surprising, therefore, that IT has become a key area of innovation.

The early developments in IT, however, gave few indications of how pervasive these would become in many areas of innovation, only a generation later. The earliest IT applications were stand-alone computers, within hotels for example, and these were essentially used to speed up back-room operations. Then, in the late 1970s, the introduction of CRS by the major airlines started to demonstrate the innovative potential of inter-firm links, and of linking databases. This subsequently spread to tour operators and travel agents, pioneered by Thomson in the UK. Later, individuals were given direct access to these databases – initially via teletext but subsequently, and critically, via the web – both for information and reservations purposes. The rate of such innovations, based on codified databases, characteristically displays a sharply rising curve over time (Poon 1993: 158). The use of IT depends on other firms also taking up a particular technology. Thus, very few travel agents in the US initially used CRSs because they simply lacked the appropriate technologies, but within ten years, 96 per cent were able to access these. With time, the increasing compatibility of IT equipment, centred on increasingly powerful and flexible PCs, has meant that many innovations have required no more than purchasing and installing new software onto existing and increasingly widely available equipment (O'Connor *et al.* 2001: 341).

The combination of codified data and IT offers a number of innovative advantages to firms, and for early movers these can provide competitive advantages (Buhalis 2004, 2006; Poon 1993; Werthner and Klein 1999):

- Cost reductions and productivity improvements. IT innovations allow firms to reduce their costs in a number of ways including the substitution of capital for labour, reducing communication costs, and achieving more flexible production and marketing strategies. Poon (1993: 183) considers that the introduction of CRSs reduced the cost per reservation to airlines from $7.50 to a mere $0.50, and that it also increased the productivity of travel agents by over 40 per cent.
- There have also been significant cost-reducing innovations in the hotel sector (O'Connor *et al.* 2001: 342):

> The advantages of setting up their own site are clear – lower distribution costs, increased sales as a result of specific promotions and increased customer loyalty . . . gives them a risk-free supplemental source of confirmed reservations, allowing them to take advantage of endless marketing opportunities. . . . Thus they can avoid GDS fees and, in certain cases, travel agent commission, and more importantly they can reach the customer directly. . . . Furthermore little or no capital investment is required. . . .

- More efficient management of yields and capacity in the face of changing conditions. It becomes easier for firms to adjust to changing conditions – whether amongst their markets, suppliers or competitors. Sophisticated yield management systems allow faster and more informed pricing changes (a form of innovation) in response to demand fluctuations, and inventories can also be closely monitored in line with these (Buhalis 2004; Gratzer *et al.* 2004; Klein and Loebbecke 2003).
- Electronic communication diminishes the barriers posed by spatial distance, even if it cannot completely eliminate these – as discussed later in relation to the selectivity of knowledge transfer mechanisms. This provides the basis for innovative forms of management and ownership across multi-branch, multinational companies, groups and partnerships, to some extent regardless of the nature of national politico-economic systems (Werthner and Klein 1999; Ma *et al.* 2003).
- The relationships between consumers and the providers of tourism services can be revolutionized through the use of IT (Gratzer *et al.* 2004). Firms can make their databases available online, so that customers can book cars, flights, hotels, tickets etc. directly. Some of the most disruptive forms of tourism innovation in recent years have been in this realm of disintermediation. For example, whereas in April 2002 British Airways sold 54 per cent of its tickets through the travel trade and only 20 per cent via the web, by late 2004 the relative shares have been inverted to 38 per cent and 53 per cent respectively (Buhalis and Ujma 2006). In fact, the innovations can be characterized more as a process of reintermediation rather than of disintermediation. Whereas initially air lines, for example, bypassed travel agents to sell directly to tourists, specialised web companies, such as Expedia, now sell the products of a number of airlines, and not only do they sell flights but they also act as agents for hotels, car rentals and insurance companies. More generally, as Buhalis and Ujma (2006: 178) state, 'as a result of speed and connectivity, the boundaries between various channel players are getting blurred. Companies are refocusing and taking on a variety of responsibilities that earlier belonged to interdependent channel players.'

These are substantial advantages stemming from IT-related innovation. However, as with all innovations, the introduction of IT, allied to more effective data set management, does not constitute a magic wand bringing about sweeping changes. Rather it makes demands on the organization – for major ITs may require a very different organizational structure and orientation (see Sigala 2003). This is evident in the convention and visitor bureau (CVB) sector, where the introduction of IT does not of course level the competition playing field, but rather differentiates firms in new ways (Box 3.1). It is those firms that have the most effective organizational capacity – especially in terms of leadership and learning capacity – that benefit most from such innovations, and potentially can construct competitive advantage around this.

Box 3.1 IT and innovation: US CVBs

IT is an important source of innovation in tourism, and most hardware and software is purchased 'off the shelf', rather than being specifically designed, whether externally or via in-house R&D. However, as a study of IT in the CVB sector demonstrates, this is never simply transferred into organizations. Rather, both the organization and the technology are transformed in the process of transfer and adoption.

IT, by providing new ways to access information, potentially increases the capabilities of firms, which in turn assists organizations to modify and appropriate more new technology to support their strategies and operations. However, the good news story about innovation needs to be tempered because this study demonstrates that many organizations lack sufficient capacity to benefit fully from innovations. The root of the problem lies in the stimulus to implementing IT tending to originate from external factors (such as relationships with other firms) rather than internal visions. This can mean that innovations fail to take into account organizational capacity, which can result in excessive demands on their resources, hindering future innovation.

There are two important requirements of organizational change, if the positive aspects of innovation are to outweigh the negative: effective leadership and learning. As the authors state, 'the vision of the CVB directors and their willingness to support learning are instrumental to the success of all IT implementation efforts'. This is particularly important because although IT changes how organizations position themselves relative to their competitors, it does not 'automatically level the playing field'. Bureaus need to exploit the value chain as they use IT, and 'the most enduring challenge is to transform information into knowledge'. And, at the same time, the most effective bureau directors realize that technology cannot be simply copied; instead, they as leaders, and their organizations, need to be able to adapt or modify technology.

Source: After Yuan *et al.* (2006: 339–40).

This is vividly borne out by Sigala *et al.*'s (2004) study of IT adoption and utilization in the UK medium-scale hotel sector (Box 3.2) (see also Sigala and Mylonikis 2005).

Box 3.2 The selectiveness of IT innovations: UK three-star hotels

IT is often referred to as a homogenous set of hardware and software but is in fact a highly heterogeneous category, as Sigala *et al.* (2004) indicate in a study of UK hotels. They demonstrate that there are considerable variations in the types of IT utilised, both within and between functions such as property management, web sites, and data storage. There were also considerable differences in the extent to which three star hotels in the UK (mostly small to medium scale establishments) had innovated in respect of different IT opportunities. In general, innovation take up levels were much higher for low-level than for high-level IT in relation to property management and the web. There were also some IT fields where very few, or even no, hotels had innovated.

Percentage take up of IT technologies: function and sophistication

	(IT sophistication ranked on an ascending five-point scale)	
	Sophistication of technology	*Percentage of respondents*
Property management system		
Automate front-office operations	1	96.2
Automate back office operations	1	88.5
Communicate and share information	3	44.9
Collect and store data	3	71.8
Analyse data and/or produce reports	5	65.4
Platform enabling other applications	5	50.0
Web site		
Information provision	1	96.6
Links to other sites	1	63.6
Online bookings	3	30.7
Customer communications	3	64.8
Collect customer information	5	34.1
Provide customized content	5	18.2
E-mail		
Automate front-office operations	1	n/a
Automate back-office operations	1	n/a
Store information	1	n/a
Make room reservations and bookings	3	81.3
Conduct transactions with suppliers	3	38.5
Enable external communication	5	52.7

Intranet		
Automate front-office operations	1	20.0
Automate back-office operations	1	20.0
Store information	1	70.0
Make room reservations and bookings	3	36.7
Conduct transactions with suppliers	3	20.0
Enable internal communication	5	76.7
Enable external communication	5	26.7
Extranet		
Automate front-office operations	1	0.0
Automate back-office operations	1	0.0
Store information	1	0.0
Make room reservations and bookings	3	40.0
Conduct transactions with suppliers	3	20.0
Enable internal communication	5	0.0
Enable external communication	5	60.0
Customer data warehouse		
Automate tasks of front- and/or back-office staff	1	59.7
Automate tasks of sales and marketing staff	1	61.2
Enable staff of different departments to access customer information	3	44.8
Develop personal customized promotions/ sales offers	3	76.1
Deliver customer relationship management activities	5	22.4
Plan the hotel strategy	5	29.9

Source: After Sigala *et al.* (2004: 184).

Tacit knowledge: knowing more than can be made explicit

There has been a tendency to assume that because of increasing electronic transfer of knowledge (or perhaps, more accurately information), tacit knowledge has become less important. Instead, it is contended that individuals can use the internet to send data, reports, assessments and commentaries around the world in nano seconds. This is, of course, a travesty because some types of knowledge are highly specific to persons or contexts and cannot easily be codified, if at all. This leads Maskell and Malmberg (1999) to argue that, in fact, precisely because there is, what they term, the 'ubiquitification' of some forms of (codified) knowledge, tacit knowledge – which is not so easily reproducible – has become even more important to the competitiveness of firms. The same point was made by Manyika (2006) in the *Financial Times*, in an article entitled 'The coming imperative for the world's knowledge economy':

> This new frontier of studying tacit interactions is interesting not only because it is virgin territory but also because successful management

techniques are hard to copy. In contrast to transformations and transactions which can be mapped and codified, tacit interactions depend on complex mixtures of judgment, problem-solving and information exchanges, often involving group behaviour that is difficult to replicate. However, to get the most from workers involved in tacit interactions, managers must abandon much of what they think they know about strategy, organisation and information technology. For example, since the days of Alfred Sloan, former president and chairman of General Motors, companies have resembled pyramids, with a handful of tacit workers (managers) at the top co-ordinating armies of workers engaged in transformations and transactions. This model needs to be rethought when tacit workers make up a large proportion of the workforce both deep inside the company and on its boundaries, interacting with customers, suppliers and partners.

Polanyi (1958, 1966) provided the classic definition of tacit knowledge as personalized knowledge that was difficult, if not impossible, to express in words or in explicit form. This definition has subsequently been refined and extended, notably by Blackler (2002) whose review of research in this area identified four main types of tacit knowledge:

- *Embrained* knowledge is dependent on conceptual skills and cognitive abilities, which allow recognition of underlying patterns, and reflection on these. The individual mindset is a key influence on learning.
- *Embodied* knowledge results from experiences of physical presence (for example, via project work). This is practical thinking rooted in specific contexts, physical presence, sentient and sensory information, and learning in doing.
- *Encultured* knowledge emphasizes that meanings are shared understandings, arising from socialization and acculturation. Language, stories, sociality and metaphors are mainsprings of knowledge.
- *Embedded* knowledge is embedded in contextual factors and is not objectively pre-given. Moreover, shared knowledge is generated in different language systems, (organizational) cultures and (work) groups.

While these distinctions are analytically useful, it must be recognized that in practice they tend to overlap (Figure 3.1). There has been increased recognition of these different types of tacit knowledge because of the changing organization of work, notably greater emphasis on so-called 'soft' skills of communication, problem solving and creativity (Ng and Li 2003). However, the four types provide contrasting definitions of tacit knowledge, with different implications for innovation. Whereas embrained and embodied knowledge focus on the personal knowledge held by individuals, encultured and embedded knowledge emphasize that knowledge is socially situated.

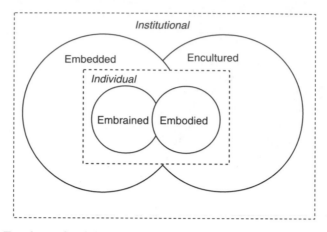

Figure 3.1 Typology of tacit knowledge.

Source: Based on typology suggested by Blackler (2002).

They represent relational knowledge, grounded in the institutionally specific relationships between individuals.

This typology of tacit knowledge provides useful perspectives on tourism. Tourism workers, especially those involved in front-stage work, bring embrained and embodied knowledge to their encounters with tourists – their ability to understand patterns, and to perform key tasks bodily, whether as receptionists or ski instructors, for example. Although manuals can be written about how to perform both jobs, their performance also involves high levels of tacit knowledge acquired through learning from others, or from experience. But their knowledge is also encultured, having developed in a particular social context. Hence, a receptionist in an American hotel may have excellent knowledge about the expectations of American guests, but very little knowledge about the expectations of Japanese guests. Similarly, the ski instructor who understands very well how to do his/her job in Europe may lack the encultured knowledge to perform the same role effectively in a Japanese resort. Embedded knowledge is also highly specific, for example, knowing how a particular organization functions, and is not always transferable across organizations.

The nature of embedded knowledge also raises important issues about individual versus collective knowledge. Whilst knowledge is clearly individual, there is also a view that a great deal of knowledge is produced and held collectively (Brown and Duguid 1998). It involves 'know-how' that is embedded in work practice, and is created through experiences at work. The key point here is that most work is not individual but involves cooperation between individuals so that it is shared amongst work groups and is therefore collective. In such situations – whether working as part of an entertainment group, or a team servicing a restaurant – the sum of the tacit knowledge of individuals is less than the total tacit knowledge of the team, because they also share collective knowledge. The challenge for organizations is to identify the tacit knowledge held by individuals or collectively by groups of workers, and to transfer this to the organizational level, so that it can be: (1) redistributed to other workers; and (2) becomes part of the organizational resource base, and is not lost when individual workers leave the company. This is also part of the challenge for becoming a learning organization, which is geared to trying to maximizing the capacity to learn of all workers and of the organization as a whole (Pfeffer 2002). However, this is particularly challenging in the tourism industry, especially in those sub-sectors characterized by high levels of staff turnover or seasonality (Hjalager 2002: 470) – in other words, where conditions are less favourable for inter-personal transfers of tacit knowledge. The next section addresses these and other issues related to the transfer of knowledge within and between organizations.

Inter- versus intra-organizational knowledge transfers

One of the greatest challenges facing any firm is the management of knowledge transfers. Pyo (2005: 584) expresses the essence of this challenge when writing about the requirements for knowledge management systems in tourism destinations:

> Knowledge management systems attempt to capture, store and disseminate an organization's know-how and intellectual assets. Knowledge management is a systematic process for acquiring, organizing and communicating the knowledge of employees so that other employees may make use of it to be more effective and productive in their work.

The management of knowledge creation and of knowledge transfers are also critical to innovation, which is essentially about ideas generation, evaluation, development and testing, as part of a process of commercialization (Kotler and Armstrong 1997). Fundamentally, knowledge may come from either within the organization or from without. Internal knowledge is classically thought of as being generated by R&D. Larger companies will have dedicated R&D sections, although this is less formalized in tourism and in most service activities than in manufacturing. R&D has two main functions: to develop new products and also to enhance learning capacity (Fischer 2001: 204). However, firms may also rely on more informal means of harvesting knowledge within the firm, for example via unorganized inter-personal communication. But knowledge can also be sourced externally to the organization (for examples from customers, competitors or suppliers), and smaller firms are likely to be relatively more dependent on these mechanisms of knowledge transfer. However, in practice, both intra- and inter-organizational knowledge transfers are likely to be intertwined in complex ways. Moreover, the sources of knowledge are constantly changing, and the challenge for the tourism firm is to adapt to new sources of knowledge, and learning how to harvest and apply these effectively. Firms respond to this challenge in diverse ways, as for example Claver-Cortés *et al.* (2006) demonstrate in their study (of hospitality in Alicante, Spain) of different types of corporate approaches to business strategies for addressing competitiveness. They identified four main types of resources, each of which has different implications for the approach of firms to knowledge management and innovation:

- *Passive strategies.* These give relatively little attention to intangible resource management (including knowledge), and to improvement goals. Typically these are independent and small hotels.
- *Strategies based on resources and capabilities.* These hotels, which tend to be at the luxury end of the market in terms of services and facilities, generally place less stress on improvement goals but have invested in high levels of computerization.
- *Strategies based on specialization.* These are mostly hotels in the lower categories in terms of facilities, and their survival strategies are based on specialization rather than improvement goals.
- *Strategies based on improvement.* These include the largest hotels, with above average services and facilities. Their strategies are focused on quality and on improvement goals.

Knowledge management and innovation are approached differently by each of these hotel types. However, it is notable that the study found relatively low levels of association between this typology and the performance of the hotels as measured in terms of occupancy or profits. There are a number of reasons for this including differences in their operating environments, but also because there are many different approaches to knowledge management, not all of which can be encapsulated within formal corporate strategies. The most effective firms in any setting or industry are likely to be those that have a broad-based approach to knowledge management. This is symbolized by the notion of the 'learning organization', defined by Garvin (1993: 80) as

> an organisation skilled at creating, acquiring and transferring knowledge, and at modifying its behaviour to reflect new knowledge and insights. New knowledge creation can occur as a result of insight or inspiration from within the organisation; additionally it can also be provoked from external influences by expanding and/or relaxing organisational bound-aries. Whatever their source, such new ideas form the foundation for organisational improvement and learning. Nevertheless, they alone can-not create a learning organisation unless there are accompanying changes to the manner in which the organisation and its members behave.

In other words, a learning organization is one that has 'learnt to learn' (Pedler *et al.* 1991). It has a learning approach to strategy formation, encourages the participation of employees in decision-making, shares knowledge within the firm, studies the impacts of its actions and learns from these, has supportive reward systems, a flexible organizational structure, and a willingness to learn from other organizations and companies. Above all, this implies a culture that values shared learning, and encourages self-development. This is an ideal type, of course, and far easier to discuss than to realize.

Bayraktaroglu and Kutanis (2003: 151), in a rare study of learning organizations within tourism, have stressed the centrality of knowledge management to their operations and strategy. They have a capacity for systematic problem solving, experimentation (actively seeking and testing new knowledge), drawing on collective and individual memory and past experiences, for learning from and with others, for effective communication and for constant evaluation and adaptation of management and organizational activity. This is, of course, an idealized tourism type, but nevertheless provides an useful benchmark against which to evaluate the performance of particular organizations. Their case study of the Polat Renaissance Hotel in Istanbul provides an example of how one company has sought to become a learning organization (Box 3.3). In the following sections, we examine in more detail the issues relating to intra- and the inter-organizational transfers of knowledge.

Box 3.3 The Polat Renaissance Hotel, Istanbul: learning and knowledge

The five-star Polat Renaissance Hotel in Istanbul was opened in 1993. The company's vision and mission, as expressed in both corporate documents and interviews with managers, are:

1 All employees are members of the same team and the customers are also members of that team.
2 Customers' perceptions of the services provided, and especially the image of the hotel, are important.
3 The aim is to satisfy the customer not only in what is said but also through employee behaviour.
4 The staff are well trained and the company is committed to continuous improvement.
5 All staff have a shared vision of responsibility.
6 Employees consider it to be a privilege to be a member of the staff in the organization.
7 Customers are addressed by name as a sign of consideration.
8 There is a transparent service policy.
9 The priority is the security and well-being of guests and staff.
10 Every single person in the organization knows exactly what the overall targets are.

11   The company considers and supports the creative ideas offered by the staff.

12   Motivating the employees and maximizing their morale is a priority.

These are, of course, an idealized set of goals, but they reflect some of the characteristics of a learning organization, especially in terms of valuing and empowering employees, effective communication and knowledge harvesting and transfer. This is underlined by the identification of the following keys to the successful operation of the hotel, emphasizing decentralized management, learning and employee empowerment:

- mental transformation within the organization, that is flexibility of organizational format;
- providing support for the innovative ideas of staff;
- developing an organizational culture that encourages individuals and teams of workers to challenge established ways of working and thinking;
- supporting the development of individuals, and creating a learning atmosphere.

Source: After Bayraktaroglu and Kutanis (2003: 151).

Internal knowledge: intra-organizational transfers

Nonaka and Takeuchi (1995) provided a classic statement on the nature of knowledge management within firms, which they conceptualized in terms of the need to transfer knowledge between individuals and the organization, and also between tacit and explicit forms. This gave rise to their well-known fourfold typology (Figure 3.2). The transfer of tacit knowledge to tacit knowl-

	Tacit *to*	Explicit
Tacit	Sympathized knowledge *Socialization*	Conceptual knowledge *Externalization*
from **Explicit**	Procedural knowledge *Internalization*	Systemic knowledge *Combination*

Figure 3.2 Tacit–explicit knowledge conversions.

Source: Nonaka and Takeuchi (1995).

edge (for example, via conversations between individuals) is 'socialization'. The transfer of tacit knowledge to explicit knowledge involves identifying the personal knowledge held by individuals and groups and codifying this in reports, manuals or guidelines that can be disseminated more widely within the company; this is 'externalization'. The reverse process, or 'internalization' involves converting explicit knowledge into tacit knowledge; for example, where an individual works from a manual or other codified knowledge, and adds this to his/her other stocks of personal knowledge, thereby transforming and adapting it to the individual's capacity and particular working environment. Finally, 'combination' involves converting one form of explicit knowledge into another form of explicit knowledge, for example a paper-based database into an electronic one. Nonaka and Takeuchi stress that the focus of organizational knowledge creation is the group; however, the organization also facilitates knowledge creation via its institutions and business practices (see also Williams 2007).

The challenge for the organization is how to utilize the most effective combination of different types of knowledge transfer or conversion, that is how to manage organizational learning (Senge 1990). This may mean the application of IT systems to organize and analyse databases, but above all it is about 'connecting people with other knowledgeable people and with information, enabling the conversion of information to knowledge, encapsulating knowledge to make it easier to transfer and disseminating knowledge around the company' (Jones 2002: 138). Codified or explicit knowledge is important, but cannot be effectively understood, analysed and applied without the tacit knowledge of individuals and groups. How should managers ensure that they maximize knowledge creation and transfers within an organization? Clearly

> adhocracy is not enough. Disaggregated groups must be stimulated to outperform the world's best competitors toward focused strategic goals. Creative groups cannot be driven to such ends: they must be led. They must see themselves as active participants in the company's vision, genuine resources in its strategy, and drivers toward 'figure of merit' targets that define winning. . . .
>
> (Quinn *et al.* 2002: 11)

In practice that means implementing the necessary mechanisms to support knowledge creation and transfer. In part, this is about effective reward systems, although it also carries the danger of short termism, and exclusive focus on selective goals (Shipton *et al.* 2005: 119). But reward systems are not sufficient to ensure effective knowledge creation and transfer. There is also a need 'to give voice' to employees within the organization (Stamper and van Dyne 2003: 35). In other words, it means making it possible for employees to make suggestions about innovations or about how to improve practices within the organization. Examples in restaurants include suggesting new menu items, or commenting on the lack of freshness in some ingredients. In effect, giving voice to employees is about empowering them, giving them partial responsibility for the success of the business, by incorporating them into knowledge management and decision-making. This can be conceptualized in terms of 'organizational citizenship', although in practice this notion can be problematic in an industry where there are high levels of part-time and casual employment (Box 3.4).

Empowerment, or organizational citizenship, is a key ingredient in knowledge creation/transfers within the firm, and in innovation. The benefits of empowerment are considerable (Brown and Lawler 2002: 245): more rapid responses to customer needs during service delivery or to dissatisfied customers during service recovery; making employees feel better about their jobs; encouraging employees to interact with customers with more warmth and enthusiasm; and – critically – harvesting the service ideas held by empowered employees. Empowerment is particularly important where business is differentiated, customized and personalized, or where it involves managing a relationship as opposed to simply performing individual transactions. This very much applies to the tourism industry, although it is variable. Whereas, say, Disney employees relate to visitors via thousands of brief encounters, an

---

Box 3.4 Organizational citizenship: part-time versus full-time employees in restaurants in the US

This case study of organizational citizenship is based on a survey of 257 employees and their managers in six restaurants (two large chain restaurants, one large destination resort, and three small family-owned restaurants).

One of the findings of the study was that not only were there relatively low expectations of giving voice to employees in general, but that this applied equally to both part-time and full-time employees. One explanation centres on the idea that making suggestions is perceived as risky, because it can be seen to imply that current practices are problematic; this could be understood as criticism of management or of co-workers. Another explanation relates to the prevalence of employees in entry-level positions, with relative little formal training or previous experience, who may therefore consider that they lack the expertise or authority to recommend changes. And in some types of restaurants, based on high-volume turnover, standardized server routines may provide little scope for employees' suggestions. In contrast, both part-time and full-time workers who work in less bureaucratic and standardized formats, have much greater discretion in relation to their work.

Source: After Stamper and van Dyne (2003).

escorted tour involves close relationships with a limited number of tourists over a period of days, if not weeks (Brown and Lawler 2002: 254). As would be expected, it may be difficult to empower workers in a tour operator or hotel reservations call centre, where the individual employees are working to closely written scripts when dealing with customers.

In summary, then, an innovative organization will have a well-designed system of knowledge management that encourages internal knowledge creation and transfer. This will have a number of characteristics (Chell 2001: 47):

- sound employee relations practices, where accountability is combined with empowerment;
- a flexible organizational structure, which is informal and has a relatively flat hierarchy; and
- an organizational culture that stresses creativity, and welcomes change as an opportunity rather than a threat.

Firms with such characteristics have the basis for a virtuous circle, whereby the growth and development of the organization attracts other able and committed individuals to work for it. This can be conceptualized in terms of enhancing the entrepreneurial function within the firm, that is encouraging workers to be 'intrapreneurs'. However, effective innovation requires more than just a favourable environment within the company. As Sundbo (1998: 123) writes, intrapreneurs 'do not exist in isolation in . . . large organizations; they form part of internal networks and organizational relationships'. Innovation also requires effective external linkages to enhance learning and knowledge transfer, and these are considered in the following section.

External knowledge sources: inter-organizational relationships

Recent writings on the nature of the firm have stressed that it should be seen as having blurred boundaries, and constituted of flows of knowledge across these boundaries, rather than as a discrete entity. Asheim and Coenen (2006: 164) express this in terms of 'a transition from an internal knowledge base of firms to a distributed knowledge base of value systems of firms or value chains of products'. Arguably, the ability of firms to develop effective external linkages, and to absorb the knowledge that they acquire in this way, is critical in shaping innovations, and in determining their competitiveness.

These flows of knowledge across the boundaries of the firm, or organization, can be either planned, for example, via contracts with suppliers or collaborative agreements, or they can be unplanned knowledge spillovers. Knowledge spillovers occur in various ways: via observation, by espionage, through interchanges within communities of association (Wenger 1998), through 'buzz' or professional gossip, through purchases of services and equipment but, above all, through the movement of personnel between firms (discussed in more detail later in this chapter). Kingston (2004) refers to this as knowledge seepage, but also emphasizes the need to differentiate between those situations where there is knowledge sharing (a new party gains access to knowledge, which may or may not weaken the position of the original user of this knowledge, in relative terms) and absolute knowledge loss (where one firm's gain is another's loss). An example of the latter would be the movement between clubs of an 'irreplaceable' top entertainer.

Planned knowledge sharing via collaboration is widespread in many industries, particularly where high development costs are involved, or it is possible to collaborate on more basic research in the earlier stages of the innovation process. Collaboration may take many different forms (Tidd *et al.* 2002) including:

- *subcontracting* – the classic Japanese model is based on long-term relationships with suppliers who become active collaborators in developing new products;
- *technology licensing* – which offers advantages to the 'collaborator' in terms of speed of access, but limited control over its use;
- *research consortia* – working together on relatively well-specified projects, usually in the earlier stages of innovation;
- *strategic alliances* – agreement between two or more firms to co-develop a new technology or product, and likely to involve nearer the market stages of innovation than research consortia;
- *joint ventures* – involving either contracts, or setting up ventures with joint shares;
- *innovation networks*, such as characterize learning regions.

Particular attention has been given to new forms of collaboration rather than simple trading between firms and their suppliers, which can provide mutual interdependence and more effective knowledge coordination than is associated with more adversarial supply-chain relationships (Roper and Crone 2003: 340). Collaboration also results in reduced costs in acquiring knowledge, and of innovation. However, firms also incur transaction costs when collaboration, that is the time devoted to fostering and developing partnerships, as well as the dangers of enhanced knowledge seepage (Tidd *et al.* 2002: 169). These costs can be minimized where the collaborators have a degree of mutual trust and shared knowledge bases.

Many of these forms of collaboration are rare in tourism, compared to, say, the manufacturing sector, where most academic research has been focused. However, tourism organizations do collaborate in various ways, for example, joint marketing between airlines and hotel chains. Tourism also sources external knowledge through purchases of technology (for example, IT software) which, frequently, has been developed for use in other sectors originally (Ioannides and Petersen 2003: 413). In contrast to relatively low levels of planned knowledge sharing in tourism, knowledge seepage or unplanned knowledge overspills are commonplace in tourism (see Chapter 2). This reflects the importance of tacit knowledge in the industry (moving with people), and the difficulties of establishing exclusive ownership rights over innovations.

Even where firms are effective at tapping or capturing external sources of knowledge, there are considerable variations in their capacity to absorb and use this effectively. To some extent, their effectiveness depends on the knowledge complementarity between the partners (Roper and Crone 2003), which depends on both their existing stocks of knowledge and the effectiveness of their knowledge sharing coordination. Furthermore, Roper and Crone (2003: 342) identify three types of complementarity:

- *additive complementarity*: knowledge sharing yields immediate gains;
- *sequential complementarity*: knowledge sharing leads to further knowledge seeking behaviour; and
- *complex complementarity*: the knowledge possessed by each partner is of value to the other partner, leading to reciprocal knowledge transfers.

Two other factors also influence the effectiveness of knowledge absorption (Roper and Crone 2003). First, the willingness of the partners to collaborate in knowledge sharing, which is partly dependent on management orientation and partly on the perceived profitability (as opposed to the costs) incurred. Second, the size of the knowledge gap between the collaborators. If the knowledge gap between a firm and supplier is beyond a certain size, the recipient will be unable to assimilate all the knowledge transferred to it. Finally, Autio *et al.* (2000) argue that the absorption of new knowledge is negatively affected by the amount of 'unlearning' of old knowledge that is required. This task is made problematic by the values that tend to be attached to 'old' knowledge, especially where it is embedded knowledge developed jointly by groups of workers within an organization, who collectively are reluctant to jettison it in favour of new knowledge.

The tourism industry generally does not perform strongly in respect of knowledge absorption and knowledge management. First, there is an unimpressive record of 'capturing knowledge', apart from a few leading organizations such as British Airways and Singapore Airlines (Cooper 2006: 53). Second, tourism destination competitiveness relies on the absorptive capacity of a multitude of SMEs, and these have a poorer record of knowledge management than larger firms (but see Box 3.5 on how variable this is). Third, there has been a narrow and selective over-dependence on bought-in information technology, as a source of innovation. While not denying that this has a role to play, such IT imports have often been characterized by imperfect systems and a tendency to manage information rather than to generate more complex but more useful knowledge (see the first section of this chapter). Some of the tourism data warehousing projects from the 1990s exemplify this point (Cooper 2006: 54): these complex but poorly designed operations were mostly under-utilized by the tourism industry (Pyo *et al.* 2002).

Box 3.5 Absorption capacity in the Australian tourism industry

The Cooperative Research Center for Sustainable Tourism in Australia has researched the absorption capacity of the tourism industry. The project was based on a survey of a range of tourism firms, which identified their generation and use of knowledge and information, and the transfer mechanisms involved. Three main sub-sectors were surveyed: regional organizations and public sector bodies related to tourism; trade associations; and private companies.

The survey demonstrated that the two main sources of variation in absorption capacity were the size and the sector of the organizations. The findings also revealed that the most commonly used type of research output is tourism statistics (tourist surveys, demographics and marketing information). However, the private sector's use of such research is tightly focused on marketing and demographics, compared to the trade associations and the public sector which trawl more widely for knowledge and information. Tourism statistics and demographics were often considered to be the most useful types of information by smaller tourism firms, while marketing information was more prized by larger organizations.

In terms of sources, the private sector is again more narrowly focused on a limited range of sources, mainly government bodies, internal sources, industry bodies and trade magazines. In contrast, the other organizations used a broader range of sources. There is generally an increasing reliance on electronic transfers of information, although several accommodation providers also stressed the importance of hard copies, while seminars/workshops were important for tour operators.

As would be expected, respondents were more likely to adopt knowledge and information that is relevant, easy to access and uncomplicated to read.

Source: After Cooper (2006: 57–8).

Finally, it is also important to note that international economics suggests that transnational firms have knowledge advantages compared to firms operating within a single country. This has two dimensions: the re-use of existing knowledge from the 'home' country, and the acquisition of new knowledge in the 'host' country. First, the model for the re-use of existing knowledge within the transnational company dates from some of the earliest industrial organization writings on the multinational enterprise (Hymer 1960; Kindleberger 1969). This argues that the transnational company enjoys an absolute ownership-specific advantage over host country firms. In this model, production is organized vertically, with knowledge creation concentrated in the home country and being distributed to the host country. Such strategies of re-using knowledge are optimal when the firm's business strategies are primarily based on replicating existing products or services in new markets (Hansen *et al.* 1999). This is facilitated by the codification of knowledge, where possible, for ease of transfer and access. Second, and in contrast, if a firm aims to develop new and more differentiated products in the host country, taking into account national differences in how markets are constructed, then a knowledge creation strategy is required, and this is more likely to involve tacit knowledge exchanges. Transnational companies also have greater capacity to harvest new sources of knowledge in the countries they invest in, especially where such knowledge is nationally specific. That is, they can access, and transfer such knowledge across borders to their other branches, more effectively, which implies a more decentralized model of knowledge management (Morgan 2001).

Transnational companies are also more likely to have the absorptive capacity to utilize knowledge more effectively. There are, of course, differences in the forms of foreign ownership, ranging from direct and exclusive ownership, to various forms of partnerships and mixed ownership, and franchises. These have contrasting knowledge transfer and absorptive capacities. The importance of transnational ownership is exemplified by the experiences of transnational Balearic companies operating in Latin America (Box 3.6).

Box 3.6 Transnational Balearic tourism companies in Latin America: proprietary knowledge advantages

Balearic hotel chains internationalized rapidly in the 1990s, following initial overseas investments by Barceló Hotels & Resorts in 1985. By 2003, these chains owned some 780 hotels, and more than half were located outside of Spain, with about half of these in Latin America and the Caribbean. This expansion has been underpinned by ownership advantages related to their quality reputation, and organizational and management knowledge. These outweigh the potentially higher operating costs of expanding into foreign markets.

A case study of their hotels in Mexico and the Dominican Republic suggests that the Balearic chains have been more innovative in new, non-Spanish markets than in their mature home markets. The average number of innovations recorded in these foreign branches, in 2000–2, was 14.3, somewhat higher than the 13.9 recorded in the Balearics. In fact there was a consistently high level of innovation across the foreign hotels: 72 per cent recorded 10–15 innovations, while 28 per cent recorded more than 15 innovations.

The level of innovation is also influenced by the size of the hotels, which may be related to the range of services and facilities offered, and to the available resources at the local level. However, the relatively similar mean values also suggest that there may be a chain-wide innovation effect, with innovations being managed and distributed across the group.

Number of rooms	Mean number of innovations
100 or fewer	13.0
101–250	13.8
251–500	14.4
Over 500	14.7

In both the Balearics and in Latin America and the Caribbean, process innovations were recorded most frequently, followed by product innovations and, at some distance, organizational innovations. Process innovations were far more important than product innovations in Mexico and the Dominican Republic, compared to the Balearics, but there is no obvious reason for this. Finally, within process innovations, those related to the production of services were several times more numerous than those related to the delivery of services.

Technological innovations were important throughout the chain but highly selective. In Mexico and the Dominican Republic, for example, 59.6 per cent of technological innovations were in the realm of IT, followed by environmental innovations (23.5 per cent), and security (5.5 per cent).

Source: After Jacob and Groizard (2004).

In the next section, we consider further some of the mechanisms for knowledge transfer.

Knowledge channels

As discussed in the previous section, firms or organizations acquire knowledge both internally and externally. The latter are either obtained via direct inter-firm linkages, for example via partnerships or from suppliers, or constitute extra-firm linkages, for example to local or professional knowledge communities. In this section we consider, in more detail, some of the mechanisms through which such knowledge transfers are effected, noting features that are distinctive to tourism. Six main channels of knowledge transfer are identified below (see also Figure 3.3):

Imitation/demonstration/observation. New products or processes can be imitated, through observation. This is the classic view put forward in the North–South technology transfer literature (Findlay 1978). The scope of the

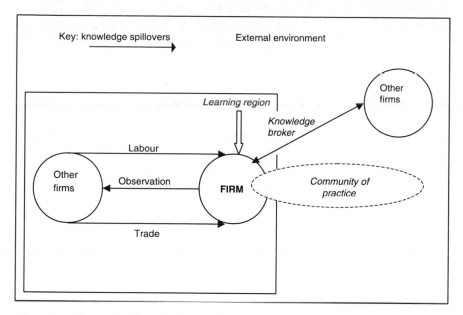

Figure 3.3 Channels of knowledge transfer.

demonstration effect is considered to be dependent on the technical complexity of the product and the process. In tourism, the front-stage processes are highly visible, and the level of technology is relatively unsophisticated (with a few exceptions such as air travel). It is therefore relatively easy for competitors to observe changes in service delivery or in the facilities introduced into hotels or restaurants. However, as many of these service quality innovations are dependent on tacit knowledge, there are constraints on learning and imitation through observation.

Labour mobility. If tacit knowledge is a key to imitation, then (skilled) labour mobility will be critical to realizing this. Effectively, knowledge is transferred by the physical movement of workers that have been exposed to working in organizations with superior knowledge and technology bases. This mobility may be localized, where there are cost advantages for the workers who do not have to change residence when changing employer. This is particularly significant where there are clusters of related industries, forming knowledge communities. In such clusters, high levels of knowledge spillovers via labour turnover may be accepted as a shared mutual benefit, being a mechanism that raises overall knowledge levels within the community, and its overall competitiveness (Henry and Pinch 2000). Alternatively, labour mobility may be realized via migration. In some cases, this may be based on inter-firm moves, as when a manager moves between hotels in different regions. In other cases, the mobility may be extra-firm (Williams 2006, 2007), as when tourist-workers move between regions, without specific jobs to go to, driven as much by tourism as by employment goals. For example, a ski instructor may aim to be in the European Alps and New Zealand's Southern Alps in their respective winter sports seasons, rather than moving to a particular job for career progression reasons.

There is considerable evidence that labour turnover is often the most important channel for knowledge spillovers in manufacturing (Djankov and Hoekman 2000), but we know far less about tourism. However, tourism is characterized by relatively high levels of labour turnover because of relatively low entry barriers into jobs: this is characterized as a situation of weak internal and strong external labour markets (Riley *et al.* 2002). Where such workers bring with them skills and experiences learned in other relevant work settings, this can be an effective channel of knowledge transfer. But, in practice, the casualization of the tourism labour supply, and the structural and socio-psychological features of the labour market (Riley *et al.* 2002), suggest that knowledge transfers via labour mobility may be relatively less significant in tourism, compared to other sectors. There is, however, an important exception to this. Tourism markets are mobile, by definition. Given the internationalization of tourism, this means that large and increasing numbers of tourists seek services in countries where their language is not spoken, and the cultural norms are unfamiliar (Williams 2005). Tourism firms may therefore be willing to pay a premium for workers who possess such knowledge, as Aitken and Hall (2000) record in New Zealand. For example, large hotels that regularly host touring parties of Korean visitors, may seek to employ Korean migrant workers.

Inter-firm exchanges: collaboration and suppliers. These constitute planned knowledge spillovers or exchanges, as firms work together at particular stages in the production chain, as discussed earlier in this chapter. Firms collaborate with their suppliers, or with intermediaries (for example, hotels with tour operators), or with potential competitors (for example, destination-wide marketing campaigns). Such collaborations involve various forms of formality and ownership of the joint venture, but they also involve knowledge sharing. This is realised via 'project ecologies' (Grabher 2001) whereby individuals from the different partners are brought together to work jointly for a fixed time period. In manufacturing, this may mean assembling a team to work on a new product over a period of one or two years. In tourism, it is more likely to involve setting up a joint committee that meets regularly to coordinate a set of activities, often related to marketing. But, in both cases, these project ecologies are designed to facilitate knowledge interchanges, and creation of new knowledge.

Another form of inter-firm knowledge linkage, and one that is particularly important in tourism, is via purchases from suppliers, notably of technology. The hotel and restaurant sectors are both dominated by suppliers, compared to many other economic sectors (Pavitt 1984), which is fairly typical of the less knowledge-intensive services. In other words, they innovate by buying in R&D embodied in technology rather than undertaking R&D within the company (Sirilli and Evangelista 1998). Such innovation is particularly notable in respect of hardware and computers facilities, and kitchen and restaurant equipment. To some extent, this reflects the lack of direct inter-action with tourists in these operational areas (Orfila-Sintes *et al.* 2005: 862), that is, they 'can be automated with no loss of the service's personal component'.

Learning regions and/or geographical clustering. Learning regions are terri-torial spaces where there is a strong, positive environment that is conducive for collective learning. Proximity facilitates the development of strong levels of trust and shared values, which leads to high levels of mutually beneficial knowledge exchanges. These are both formalized in the form of inter-firm linkages and partnerships (involving other knowledge creating bodies such as universities and government agencies) and informal, based on 'buzz' or the exchange of work-related gossip in different settings within the region (Bathelt *et al.* 2004). There is little specific research on the notion of learning regions in the tourism literature, although a small but growing literature on the related concept of geographical clustering (see Chapter 6).

Communities of practice. Communities of practice (Wenger 1998) is a well-established concept that emphasizes that individuals are bound together by shared meanings and understandings, and the practices that emerge from networking. Such communities can be facilitated by spatial proximity, and so overlap in part with learning regions, but this is not a necessary condition. Indeed, some commentators (such as Amin 2002) argue that relational prox-imity (achieved via communities of practice) is increasingly likely to outweigh spatial proximity as electronic communication eliminates spatial friction in knowledge exchanges. Others (such as Gertler 2001) contest this, arguing that spatial proximity remains critically important in tacit knowledge exchanges. Communities of practice are influential in knowledge transfer in tourism, as in all economic sectors. For example, hotel managers or accountants tend to belong to professional associations, or meet up with similar professionals at conferences or other venues, where they can and do exchange knowledge.

Brown and Duguid (1991) argue that communities of practice are critical to knowledge transfers into and within companies. Being at the interface of the organization and its external environment (whether local or at a distance), they play a key role in innovation: 'the process of innovation involves actively constructing a conceptual framework, imposing it on the environment, and reflecting on their interaction' (Brown and Duguid 1991: 53). However, they caution that communities of practice tend to be more effective in informing incremental than radical innovation. The latter requires the disembedding of 'old' knowledge within an organization and work groups, and therefore tends to be more likely to occur at the interstices of communities of practice. In other words, while they constitute powerful channels of knowledge sourcing and transfer, they may also be blinkered by the limitations of their shared world view. There has been little research on this subject in tourism but the general principles, outlined by Brown and Duguid, can be expected to apply.

Knowledge brokers. Knowledge brokers are influential individuals who operate within and across company boundaries, that is, they are instrumental in intra- and inter-firm knowledge transfers. Brokers are those individuals who act as bridges for knowledge transfers between different communities. Wenger (2000) identified a number of different types of brokering. 'Boundary spanners' (Tushman and Scanlan 1981), take care of one specific boundary over time, and are exemplified by say Chinese American investors in tourism facilities in the US, who shuttle to and fro between these locations (Lew and Wong 2002). 'Roamers' travel from place to place, creating connections and creating or transferring knowledge. They are exemplified by the potential of some tourist workers (Uriely 2001) to act as brokers in this capacity, although this depends on the individuals and the receptiveness of the companies that employ them. Finally, 'outposts' bring back news from 'the forefront', while exploring new territories: for example, the representative of a multinational hotel chain who has been seconded for a period to work with a new supplier in a country new to the company's production chain, and learns from this experience.

Consultants constitute one example of the highly institutionalized broker, although they have variable practices in relation to knowledge transfer and creation, depending on how they view their relationships with their clients (see Box 3.7).

Box 3.7 Three models of consultancy

A study of the role of consultants in the tourism industry identified three main models of consultancy practice:

1   Consultants who consider themselves to be experts who transfer knowledge to their clients as a means of resolving the particular problems they face. This type of consultant would view his or her role as an advisor or as a problem solver. They and their clients expect them to share their expertise, and it is precisely such expertise which has attracted the client to employ them rather than rival consultants. It is also their expertise that is the key to successful resolution of the challenges facing the client.
2   Consultants who consider they are the client's service-oriented partner aim to create a helpful relationship with the client, based on attending to the clients' needs across a range of both major and minor issues. Their self-image constitutes being the client's helper, friend or ally and they believe that it is their client-service skills, and the level of attention they give to their client, which differentiate them from rival consultants. Their success is based on their management of the partnership with the client, and in this sense it is an unequal partnership.

3   Consultants who consider they are 'empowering experts' see themselves more as coaches to their clients. Their main objective is to ensure that their clients achieve the goals they have set themselves. Their self-image emphasizes creativity in feeding ideas to the clients, but above all their close focus on understanding and empowering clients via behind the scenes coaching.

Empirical findings in the US suggest that approximately half of the consultants consider themselves to be experts (type 1), approximately a third consider they are service oriented partners (type 2), and a smaller residue consider they are empowering experts (type 3).

Source: After Walsh (2002: 41–3).

The tourist, knowledge and innovation

Two distinctive aspects of innovation and knowledge are considered here, related to the roles played by tourists as both producers and consumers: that is, seeing tourists as innovators, and as sources of information about consumption that influence innovation by other agents, such as tourism firms and organizations.

First, we consider *tourists as innovators* in their own right, that is as having an active role in creating new tourism products and processes. This has implications for our overall understanding of tourism. Howells (2003: 3–4) provides a generic starting point for this discussion, arguing the need to recognize that competences are built up around the consumption process, requiring 'a whole set of attributes in investment, knowledge and enterprise in the consumption process'. He sees this as being associated with the notion of the 'enterprising consumer' (Earl 1986: 53–84) and the development of 'consumption knowledge' (Metcalfe 2001: 38). Armed with such skills and knowledge, the consumer becomes an active agent in innovation, not least because he and she is the real expert on their individual consumption needs.

This is particularly evident in tourism where production and consumption are closely intertwined. Tourists are 'dynamic social actors, interpreting and embodying experience, whilst also creating meaning and new realities through their actions' (Selby 2004: 191). No tourist is ever a totally passive recipient of tourism experiences, but rather – to varying degrees – is an active agent in creating these for himself/herself and others. The tourist who points out a particular historic aspect of a building to another tourist is, in a sense, contributing to innovation in the realm of the tourism experience. That is why tourist destinations do not have given meanings. Instead, these are negotiated by a group of actors, which includes tourists as well as tourism firms and others (Selby 2004: 191). Negotiation blurs into innovation, especially when we consider, for example, the way that tourists construct their own itineraries around particular tourism sites and destinations.

Moreover, the role of the tourist as innovator also has ramifications further back in the tourism production chain. Tourists are becoming increasingly active in planning and booking their holidays, effectively becoming miniscule-scale tour operators. Although determined individual travellers have always been able to play such roles, this has been enhanced by the internet. In other words, the conjunction of post-Fordist tourism consumption, whereby tourists seek more individualized tourism experiences, combined with shifts in the economics of tourism production, have created greater scope for tourists to become innovators in producing as well as consuming tourism experiences. This is particularly marked for those individuals who take the lead in organizing holidays for groups of family and friends. Moreover, in fulfilling these roles, tourists draw on a stock of knowledge accumulated through previous experiences of tourism consumption/production.

Second, tourists are also a critically important *source of knowledge to other agents of tourism innovation*. This is, of course, logical and obvious: any firm that ignores its customers' experiences (knowledge) runs a risk of producing services for which there is no demand. Successful businesses are those that actively and routinely seek either to acquire information about their customers or, better still, see tourists as sources of knowledge, which can feed through into innovation – whether incremental or radical. The challenge for the firm or tourism organization is how best to capture the tacit knowledge that tourists possess. The significance of this should not be under-estimated and Poon (1993: 272), for example, argues that

> perhaps the most important source of learning is from consumers . . .
> Travel consumers today know the world of travel. Their collective experience is a source of tremendous wealth; their collective desires are a source of tremendous information for those seeking to satisfy them.

There are different ways in which tourism firms and organizations can seek to capture this knowledge. The simplest means are questionnaire surveys administered at different points during or after a holiday or visit. However, as Von Hippel *et al.* (2001: 35) argue: 'All processes designed to generate ideas for products begin with information collected from users. What separates companies is the kind of information they collect and from whom they collect it.' One strategy used by some of the more progressive companies is to seek to harvest the knowledge held by 'lead users'; whiles some of these 'lead users' may be intermediaries (for example, tour operators for airlines), others are individual consumers. Various forms of networking, discussion groups and in-depth interviews can be utilized to tap the knowledge of these unusually reflexive and creative individuals. For example, in the world of electronic games, Sony created a web site to support hackers who wished to develop new types of games that could be played on the Sony Playstation (Von Hippel *et al.* 2001). It attracted more than 10,000 participants, a vast, diverse and potentially creative set of innovators. In tourism, perhaps the most obvious comparable example is the way in which tourism companies have responded to the increased awareness of environmental issues amongst tourists, learnt from them, and have innovated by designing holidays products that seek to integrate sustainable tourism practices. Ecotourism is a particularly fertile area of such innovation.

Creativity and creating tourism

While we have mostly discussed knowledge transfer in this chapter, there is also a distinctive although linked process of knowledge creation. Depending on whether this has incremental or radical dimensions, it involves different degrees of creativity. This section will review our understanding of creativity, a process that also links to entrepreneurship (Uljin and Brown 2004: 5), as discussed in Chapter 8.

'Creativity is a necessary (but not sufficient) factor enabling innovation' (Carayannis and Gonzalez 2003: 587), and indeed these are often confused as being identical – which they are not. Rather, '[c]reativity is the ability flexibly to produce work that is novel (i.e. original, unexpected), high in quality, and useful, in that it meets task constraints' (Sternberg *et al.* 2003: 158). This is also the view set out in Harvard Business Essentials (2003: 82–3): 'Creativity is not a state of mind nor a form of personal "wiring" . . . Instead, creativity is a process of developing and expressing novel ideas for solving problems or satisfying needs.' Therefore, creativity is not so much about talent as being a goal-oriented process that generates innovations.

But stressing that it is goal-oriented should not obscure imagination being a critical ingredient of creativity: 'Creativity is related to the capacity to imagine, since it requires the creator to perceive future potentials that are not obvious based on current conditions' (Carayannis and Gonzalez 2003: 588). Another way to approach this is to understand creative individuals as being those who are able to think outside the box, or who can think laterally. Amabile (1998) provides an useful framework for combining these different perspectives on creativity, arguing that it has three key components:

- *Expertise*: Technical, procedural and intellectual knowledge.
- *Creative-thinking skills*: How people approach problems, which is a function of personality and work style.
- *Motivation*: Intrinsic (internal passion or interest) has a greater impact on creativity than does extrinsic.

Whether an individual can be considered to be creative depends on the context in which that individual works (Sternberg *et al.* 2003: 158). Moreover, creativity is rarely an individual act; rather it tends to be sparked by interactions amongst individuals, particularly within their key work (or other) groups. Inter-personal interactions, tapping the tacit knowledge of individuals, are a fruitful source of fresh perspectives and novel thinking, which of course is also consistent with the view expressed earlier that the work group is the key unit in the transfer of knowledge within workplaces. Design and R&D teams are deliberately constructed in such a way as to maximize group creativity, which means drawing on diverse perspectives, but also on open and flexible thinking. This is notoriously difficult in practice, but Harvard Business Essentials (2003: 84–5) gives some guidance on the key features of creative groups:

- individual differences produce a creative friction that sparks new ideas amongst group members;
- diversity of thought and perspective is a safeguard against 'groupthink', or the tendency for individual thought to converge, for social reasons (socialisation, desire to avoid conflict, dominant individuals etc.) around a particular point of view;
- diversity of thought and skills gives more opportunities to develop good ideas.

In practice, a delicate balance is required between divergent and convergent thinking if group creativity is to be maximized. The creative process is likely to begin with divergent thinking, when one or more individuals break away from familiar or established perspectives and practices. Convergence, which includes the process of convincing others about these new ideas, is an important check that the idea has potential.

Creativity is as central to innovation in tourism as in any other economic sector. Major tourism attractions, for example, may set up temporary or semi-permanent project teams whose role is to think imaginatively about how to create new, or enhance existing, attractions. And it is also clear that individuals such as Thomas Cook epitomize creativity. Nevertheless, there has been little systematic research on creativity in the tourism industry.

One of the most influential strains of recent thinking about creativity originates in the work of Richard Florida (2002), particularly his ideas and empirical research about 'creative cities'. As Peck (2005) explains, for Florida creativity has become the 'defining feature of economic life' because 'new technologies, new industries, new wealth and all other good economic things flow from it' (Florida 2002: 21). Creative cities are able to generate, attract and retain an effective combination of talent, creative people in the arts and cultural industries, and key elements in this are diverse ethnic, racial and lifestyle groups. This is reinforced by the views, outlined above, of Harvard Business Essentials (2003) concerning the role of diversity.

There are a number of critiques of Florida's work, relating to its elitism, failure to recognize the discrimination faced by minorities in even the most diverse and tolerant communities, and a myopic view of cosmopolitanism (Williams 2006: 601–2). Peck (2005) provides an extensive critique of Florida's work, which he considers to be poorly theorized, based on flawed empirical indicators, and strongly although opaquely infused by neo-liberal ideologies:

Discourses of urban creativity seek to normalize flexible labor-market conditions, lionizing a class of workers that can not only cope with, but positively revel in, this environment of persistent insecurity and intense, atomized competition ... This is achieved, in part, by the suggestive mobilization of creativity as a distinctly positive, nebulous-yet-attractive, apple-pie-like phenomenon: like its stepcousin flexibility, creativity preemptively disarms critics and opponents, whose resistance implicitly mobilizes creativity's antonymic others – rigidity, philistinism, narrow mindedness, intolerance, insensitivity, conservativism, *not getting it*. . . . The cities that grow will be those with cool people in them, and cool people will only go to cool cities. But 'what makes a city cool?'

(Peck 2005: 764–5)

In other words, while creativity is important, it is not a necessary condition for innovation and growth, and it does not unfold any more in the rather myopic social environment described by Florida, than in an economic vac uum (you should not ignore the active role of capital and of management). But despite this note of caution, Florida's ideas have gained credence with a swathe of policy makers in urban governance, and have influenced   to varying degrees – the strategies pursued by particular places. These strategies may invoke tourism as an instrument in creating the desired social environment that supports creativity, as evident in Providence, in the US (Box 3.8).

Box 3.8 Providence's call to action as inspired by Florida's ideas about creativity

Providence's economic strategy, which was significantly inspired by Richard Florida's work on creativity and creative cities, was based on five 'arching strategies'. Some of these have a direct bearing on leisure activities, conservation, understandings of 'authenticity', design, and arts and cultural activities. In turn, although only implicitly, these will feed through into tourism activities, while the latter can also be used a source of income generation to fund social and economic innovations.

   Arching Strategy 1: To position Providence as the authentic creative hub in the Southern New England Region:

   This involves promoting the 'Providence story of creativity' as the central focus of the strategy, characterizing the city as open-minded and authentically quirky, as evident in its eclectic mix of design, biomedical science, technology, and arts and cultural activities.

Arching Strategy 2: To build a creative community that attracts and retains creative people:

This involves fostering a culture of creativity, diversity, art and science for all its people, reducing brain drain and attract new talent to the city. Projects include a cultural audit, producing a calendar of events, developing more artist-owned work/living spaces, and connecting young people to creative companies and 'authentic' neighbourhoods.

Arching Strategy 3: To grow the creative economy with emphasis on the design and business innovation, and biomedical research:

Projects include helping diverse types of entrepreneurs to build companies of different scales throughout the city, including a jewellery district.

Arching Strategy 4: To build an integrated infrastructure to support economic development and foster an entrepreneurial climate:

This involves fostering an entrepreneurial climate composed of diverse investors, entrepreneurs and innovative business-building practices.

Arching Strategy 5: To build quality and authentic places for creative people:

The aim is to connect creative people to the sense of place in particular neighbourhoods as a way of retaining authenticity and minimizing displacement. Particular projects involve connecting creative people to the outdoors and enhancing the city's bikeway system.

Source: After Peck (2005: 750).

Conclusions

Knowledge and learning lie at the heart of innovation. The problem is that knowledge remains an elusive term, and knowledge management is similarly an ill-defined exercise, which can often be compared to 'fumbling in the dark' or 'chasing shadows'. Codified knowledge is concrete enough, and the two most relevant forms for recent tourism innovation have been IT applications and the creation of electronic databases. These technologies tend to be bought in, rather than developed through in-house R&D, in common with much of the service sector, enhancing the role of the supply chain.

Far more elusive than codified or explicit knowledge is tacit knowledge. This is often held up as the key to competitive advantage for two reasons. First, because it is essential for unlocking the full potential of codified knowledge or technology, and second because it is more difficult for competitors to imitate. Herein lies one of the distinctive features of tourism innovation, or indeed of service sector innovation generally, namely the difficulties of protecting intellectual property rights. This makes it even more difficult for firms and territories to engage effectively with innovation – even if they acknowledge the advantages of innovation, they also know that the above average rent or profits that accrue to first movers are often short lived.

However, despite these reservations, the most progressive and most innovative firms do seek to maximize knowledge transfers and learning within the firm, while seeking to minimize knowledge seepage to competitors. This requires attention to both the intra- and inter-firm level and to a variety of knowledge channels, over which firms can exert varying degrees of control. Some of the key points in this are how to combine locally sourced and externally sourced knowledge, how to harvest the creativity of key workers, and how to turn the tourist from a mere customer, or even co-producer of services, to a partner in innovation. These issues cannot be addressed, let alone answered in terms of abstract social space, rather, there is also a need to recognize that institutions play a key role in shaping innovation, and this is the subject of the next chapter.

4 The state and tourism innovation

Institutions, regulation and governance

Introduction

In the public and business psyche, the notion of innovation is often tied to the role of the private sector, partly in response to the notion that government is a barrier to innovation and enhanced productivity. This attitude is, perhaps, personified by the statement of Ronald Reagan, at his first inaugural address as president of the US in 1981, that 'government is not the solution to our problem; government is the problem'. Such a perspective equates government's capacity to innovate with the necessities of bureaucratic decision-making, and is akin to what Williamson (1975) referred to as a 'program persistence bias' with a supposedly inherent 'anti-innovation bias'. Programme persistence refers to the funding of programmes beyond levels that can be sustained on their merits, and follows from the influence of programme advocates in the resource allocation process (Teece 2000). Such a pattern of bureaucratic behaviour can have the countervailing effect of reducing funds available to new programmes, which are unlikely to be as well represented in decision-making processes. This perspective on public decision-making was strikingly expressed by Downs (1967: 160) when commenting that

> the increasing size of the bureau leads to a gradual ossification of operations – since each proposed action must receive multiple approvals, the probability of its being rejected is quite high – its cumbersome machinery cannot produce results fast enough and its anti-novelty bias may block the necessary innovation.

However, despite the continued prominence in policy circles of neo-conservative and neo-liberal articulations of the role of the state as being 'the problem', the reality is that the state is a major direct and indirect agency in innovation, and tourism innovation in particular.

This chapter examines the role of the state in innovation, an area that is regarded as a significant weakness in understanding systems of innovation (Edquist 2001). It is divided into three main sections. The first examines the nature of the state and discusses how it is of significance to innovation. Second, it discusses the institutional dimension of innovation. Finally, it highlights the significance of multi-layered governance for innovation systems. Throughout the chapter a public policy perspective is utilized with the chapter setting a framework to contextualize the following chapters on the different scales at which innovation systems are directed and in which tourism firms are embedded.

The state and innovation: a continuing but changing role

Although the state and its agencies are important determinants in any system of innovation, a weakness of the systems of innovation approach is the lack of a component or 'theory' that engages with the role of the state (Edquist 2001: 17):

> A component about the role of the state in the SI approach should include the mechanisms through which the state influences the innovation system (e.g. through innovation policy), but also how the rest of the system – and of the society at large   influences the state.

There are competing conceptualizations of the state. It can be conceptualized as a set of officials with their own preferences and capacities to effect public policy within a political system or, in more structural terms, as a relatively permanent set of *political institutions* operating in relation to civil society (Nordlinger 1981). The term 'state' encompasses the whole apparatus whereby a government exercises its power within a given territory. It includes elected politicians, the various arms of the bureaucracy, unelected public/civil servants, and the plethora of rules, regulations, laws, conventions and policies that surround and constitute government and private actions. In the influential Weberian sense, the state refers to that organization that has a monopoly on legitimate violence within a specific territory in order to provide legal order (Weber 1994). The main institutions of the state include: the elected legislatures, government departments and authorities, the judiciary, enforcement agencies, other levels of government, government-business enterprises and corporations, regulatory authorities, and a range of para-state organizations, such as labour organizations (Hall and Jenkins 1995). Although the boundaries of the state are becoming increasingly blurred in many jurisdictions, as increasing emphasis is placed on the creation of public–private partnerships and reducing government intervention in the economy, the state still sets the regulatory framework within which public and private activity occurs (Dredge and Jenkins 2007).

The state via its actions and inaction has both direct and indirect effects on innovation. According to Breznitz (2006, 2007) initial state action to develop innovation-based industrial development is required more in less-developed economies than in developed ones, as private firms are not willing or able to incur the risks that R&D activities entail. Nevertheless, regardless of the development context, state decisions with respect to innovation have substantial implications, as indicated by a number of key decisions.

1   Decisions by the state on how to acquire the necessary R&D skills influence which organizations, private or public, conduct industrial R&D. In turn, the location of such R&D activities has substantial influence over the innovation capabilities of private firms.
2   Decisions by the state over the level of control exerted on the technological development path of industry, including decisions of how, and whom, to finance, as well as whether, and how, to induce investors to finance the industry, have a significant bearing on both the R&D resources available to the industry, and the scope of R&D activities taken.
3   State decisions toward developing leading national companies – sometimes referred to as 'national champions' – have long-term consequences for industry's opportunity structure.
4   State decisions regarding foreign firms and investors, within and outside its national borders, affect the resources and information the industry receives from its main customers, as well as the diffusion and development of specific innovative capabilities. Of particular importance are decisions taken as to whether to enhance specific relationships between local and foreign companies, investors, and financial markets (Breznitz 2006).

Although these 'decisions' are more effective as encapsulations of R&D in manufacturing than of innovation in services, they usefully capture something of the scope of state influence with respect to the latter.

In terms of direct intervention, the state has long been recognized as having a critical role to play in tourism through a range of different functions. These include coordination, planning, legislation and regulation, entrepreneurship stimulation, promotion, social tourism and interest protection (Hall 2008a). Each of these aspects of government intervention in tourism may have a bearing on innovation (Table 4.1). However, the relative significance of these aspects varies from jurisdiction to jurisdiction, just as their importance has also changed over time. The state also has a number of indirect influences on tourism innovation. This refers not just to policy actions in other policy arenas that may affect tourism in some way (e.g. a foreign policy decision may have an unintended consequence for international travel flows that creates new opportunities for, or undermines innovations) but also to the overall structural context of institutional arrangements, political culture and economic behaviour. The combined structural and agency influences of the state can clearly have an important role for systems of innovation at a variety of scales (Nelson and Rosenberg 1993; Fuchs and Shapira 2005). Therefore, in the same way that innovation needs to be understood within specific contexts (Chapter 1), so too does the operation of the state, and policy and decision-making, with respect to innovation.

Table 4.1 Innovative dimensions of the state's roles in tourism

Role	Examples
Coordination	New forms of government institutions may be developed so as to provide improved knowledge transfer between public, private and non-government sectors. These are often described under the umbrella term of public–private partnerships.
Planning	New forms of planning philosophies and practices may be adopted. An example is the development of stakeholder-oriented planning approaches so as to provide for improved problem solving.
Legislation and regulation	Implementing new regulatory regimes that may reduce costs to industry or may provide new forms of regulatory protection for tourism resources. For example, regulation may support the development of carbon trading schemes for the transport sector.
Entrepreneur	State-sponsored development of new infrastructure, such as stadia or transport routes. Such developments may sometimes involve state ownership or may take the form of direct grants.
Stimulation	New forms of intervention in order to develop tourism such as supporting knowledge transfer to the tourism industry and workforce, the development of tourism clusters and networks, or direct funding schemes such as tax incentives or the provision of cheap land. A number of European Union (EU) regional development schemes seek to stimulate tourism both directly and indirectly by developing new networks in order to leverage intellectual capital for peripheral areas.
Promotion	New marketing campaigns, branding strategies, target markets or the use of new distribution channels.
Social tourism	Although not as significant a role of the state as is it once was, the provision of tourism opportunities for disadvantaged groups in society is itself innovative in some jurisdictions.
Interest protection	The state may find new means of providing equity in tourism related policy and decision-making.

One way in which the role of the state with respect to tourism innovation can be represented is indicated in Figure 4.1. Specific state-initiated tourism innovation policy and support structures are embedded within broader innovation policies and policy settings (Table 4.2). Moreover, different policies have different speeds of impact, and spread of impact with respect to the distribution of societal benefits (Figure 4.2), with such factors often being significant influences on policy demands and choices.

Although the state clearly plays a formative role in shaping what could be termed 'total tourism innovation policy', its role in direct tourism policy tends to be far more limited. Tourism innovation policy can usually be characterized as a subset of industry policy, in which industrial R&D activities are highly subsidized in most developed countries (Hall 2008a). Tourism rarely features prominently in such policies and, in a number of circumstances, may possibly not even qualify as being part of a country's innovation policy field at all (for example, see Kotilainen 2005). In contrast, a broader understanding of innovation policy can be defined as state or quasi-state action

> that influences technical change and other kinds of innovations. It includes elements of research and development . . . policy, technology policy, infrastructure policy, regional policy and education policy. This means that innovation policy goes beyond science and technology . . . policy, which mainly focuses on stimulating basic science as a public good from the supply side. Innovation policy also includes public action influencing innovations from the demand side.
>
> (Edquist 2001: 18)

Such a conceptualization of innovation policy and the nature of state intervention is important because the specific tourism innovation programmes that are established by states around the world represent only a relatively small proportion of overall government actions that impinge on tourism, with other sector specific or general innovation programmes being much more

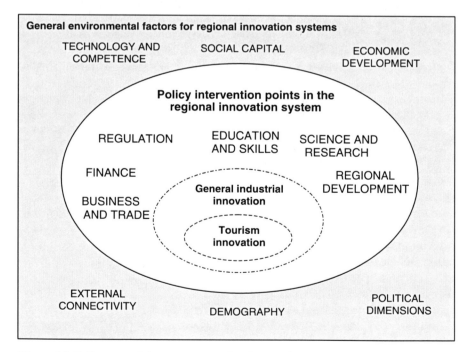

Figure 4.1 Influences of the state on tourism innovation.

Table 4.2 Levels of engagement of state policy with innovation systems

State influence	Policy dimension
Contribution to structural factors of innovation	Institutional arrangements.
Overall policy settings, behaviours and actions	Conscious decision-making and policy setting in order to improve the quality of innovation systems, e.g. education policies, migration policy, macro and microeconomic policies. There are also unintended consequences of policy decisions that are significant for innovation capacity.
General industrial policy	General industrial policies with respect to industry that will influence innovation systems. Will also often include a subset in the form of sector specific or multi-sector policies, i.e. service industries. For example, industry education and training policies are often set generally as well as having some specific sectoral targets. Similarly, the degree of openness that an industrial sector has with respect to international trade will influence the innovative capacities of that sector.
Innovation policy	Innovation policy is often, though not always, a subset of industrial policy.
Tourism policies and interventions	Tourism specific innovation policies and programmes.

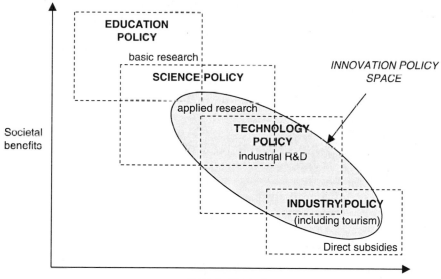

Figure 4.2 Relative positioning of the effectiveness of state innovation policies.

prominent. This can be illustrated, for example, by the Canadian Industrial Research Assistance Program (Box 4.1). Nevertheless, such programmes will still have significant implications for tourism and tourism innovation, possibly greater in some cases than tourism specific policy measures.

Box 4.1 The Canadian Industrial Research Assistance Program (IRAP)

The Canadian National Research Council (NRC) IRAP is one of the longest serving policy programmes for SMEs (less than 500 employees), having been established almost 60 years earlier. According to the NRC: 'It is a vital component of the NRC, a cornerstone in Canada's innovation system, regarded world-wide as one of the best programs of its kind.' IRAP is explicitly mandated to support SMEs directly in the development of technology, enhancing competitiveness and growing businesses. The programme has a number of functions:

1   providing R&D guidance to SMEs through the stages of an innovation cycle, ranging from the early stage of development to the pilot stage;
2   as a working partner in building innovative clusters and promoting collaboration;
3   coordinating international technology missions (including match-making assistance by linking SMEs with foreign partners);
4   providing information and technology transfer services to SMEs (in association with Federal Partners in Technology Transfer); and
5   working as connection points for external organizations, such as venture capital, HRSRC on internship programmes and DFAIT on trade issues.

IRAP delivers its activities via carrying out projects and providing advice, with innovation assistance being provided to over 12,000 firms each year. The budget for IRAP for the financial year 2006/7 was CDN$127 million, with CDN$80 million allocated to project funding and CDN$27 million to advice and support. The subsidy is shared in principle. For consultants, 50–75 per cent of cost is paid by NRC–IRAP, and as for subcontracts, up to 50 per cent of total or 80 per cent of salary costs, whichever is applicable. From the CDN$80 million project funding, CDN$14 million is a repayable contribution. The size of project varies from less than CDN$15,000 to a maximum CDN$1 million with the aim being to enhance innovation capabilities through training and improving problem solving capacities.

IRAP-funded projects cover a number of sectors although are primarily taken up by IT, professional service and manufacturing process firms, with just over 5 per cent being taken up by service sector businesses. IRAP selection criteria are:

- level of technical and commercial risk;
- economic benefit to Canada;
- management quality;
- increase of company R&D capability through the project;
- level of commitment;
- consistency with national priorities;
- social benefit to Canada;
- contribution to regional development; and
- advancement of scientific knowledge.

Tourism has benefited from IRAP in direct and indirect ways In terms of innovation, there has been flow-on effects from improvements to shipping access in Arctic Canada, as well as the development of new technologies used in museums and other tourist attractions. For example, Calgary-based company CleanPix Corporation developed a web-based digital asset management service with IRAP support. The company's clients are primarily from tourism and travel firms and organizations. CleanPix converts and stores each of the client's uploaded image files into all of the required file formats, from high-resolution print-quality files to low-resolution web ones. When a file request comes in, the client simply points the requester to the online file, which can be accessed from anywhere with an internet connection. Between 2002 and 2006 the company handled over a million requests for images and other digital files. CleanPix reduces costs for clients and increases their marketing and public relations reach. Up to a third of the marketing costs for many companies is in their physical brand management, such as burning and shipping CDs with promotional materials. Prior to using CleanPix, the City of New York Tourism Bureau couriered about 1,500 CDs a year to magazines and others. Using CleanPix they respond to 2,000 media requests a month, with downloads of up to 60 megabytes, from the CleanPix site. However, tourism has also been integral to the process because of the extent to which the programme utilizes regional events to bring current and potential innovation network partners together.

Source: Derived from NRC Canada – IRAP, http://irap-pari.nrc-cnrc.gc.ca/main_e.html.

The above discussion on the role of the state should not be interpreted as suggesting that innovation capacity, even at the national level, is solely determined by the state. Far from it. The terrain of thinking with respect to the role of the state in ensuring economic competitiveness has changed dramatically so that the social model of state-led private sectors has passed. The state can no longer maintain full control of the market domain, even where innovation districts are directly driven by state initiatives (Millar *et al.* 2005). Instead, contemporary conceptualization of the role of the state in innovation and competitiveness tends to emphasize public–private sector cooperation and partnerships in inter-territorial economic competition (Larédo and Mustar 2001). This perspective is portrayed for example, in an APEC (Asia Pacific Economic Cooperation) innovation briefing on SMEs, which have particular importance in tourism innovation (see Chapter 8):

> While the private sector has to place efforts in survival and development by itself, the state has to abandon the idea of being a controller of businesses and instead transform itself into a facilitator of businesses. Indeed, the state has to focus on the creation of an environment that supports and fosters the flexibility, agility, and network capacity of SMEs.
>
> (Lee 2006)

Moreover, the policy exemplars with respect to innovative capacity have themselves changed (Breznitz 2006, 2007; Ebner 2007). In the late 1980s, the innovation systems of Germany and Japan, where carefully devised institutions for vocational training, workplace learning and technology dissemination contributed to industrial improvements, were seen as models for other countries to follow (Nelson 1993). In the 1990s, with the IT economic boom the United States, and particular Silicon Valley, with characteristics of a vibrant capital market, an advanced system for intellectual property protection, university-centred knowledge transfers, and academic entrepreneurship assumed the role of innovation policy exemplar (Larédo and Mustar 2001). More recently there has been greater emphasis on the regionalization of innovation policies, and a greater role for the local state at the potential expense of national policies, as a result of shifts in European innovation systems as well as recognition of the federal characteristics of the Canadian, Australian and US innovation systems. There is a lack of such icons in tourism innovation policies, but it is possible to identify shifts over time, from exemplars such as state-led resort development in the Mediterranean, to tourism-led urban regeneration programmes in places such as Baltimore or Boston, to outdoor activity tourism policies in places such as South Island, New Zealand.

Innovation policy transfer is enacted at many different levels, including the inter-firm, but the government-to-government level is particularly important for many types of innovation policies. Recognizing the changing focus of government-to-government innovation policy transfer is important in understanding the fluidity of the theoretical and political lens through which innovation systems are examined. Unfortunately, an over focus on copying or imitating exemplars, rather than on learning, has meant many regions have been treated with off-the-shelf, 'best-practice' cluster or regional innovation system solutions, drawn 'from the experience of successful regions or some expert manual' (Amin 1999: 371) without due regard for their specific place context and circumstances: innovation has to be understood as being socially situated. What works in Baltimore may not work in European or Latin American cities, and what works in Asia may not work in Africa. These arguments are taken up in more detail in the following two chapters that look specifically at national and regional innovation systems.

Despite the reservations expressed above, a key theme in recent research is the central role of the state and its institutions as a facilitator and enabler of innovation. For example, with regard to the political process of industrial development, Breznitz (2006) contends that in successful cases of rapid innovation-based industrial development, state agencies first create a set of firms and industrial actors (organizations that are involved in the industry but are not private firms) and then seek to develop a deeply meshed network amongst firms, and between firms and the state. The state also helps to embed firms into international financial and production markets and networks.

Breznitz's (2006, 2007) findings, with respect to innovation systems in Ireland, Israel and Taiwan, are that in successful cases of rapid innovation-based industrial development, the state's initial role is as a key actor in the creation of a networked polity (Ansell 2000). In such an innovation system, the state at first creates a hierarchical network. Then, in the course of a co-evolutionary process (that is, a process in which two or more parties influence the development of each other), according to Breznitz, the network becomes denser as well as more egalitarian and international, with the state gradually moving from a position of power and control into a position of centrality. Consequently, the state becomes more of a 'facilitator organizer and less of an overall commander' (Breznitz 2006: 677). However, even in its role as a facilitator, the state is seeking to gain a return from its initiatives with respect to innovation by keeping firms 'in place' rather than have them become mobile and move elsewhere beyond its territorial domain. Therefore, in seeking to understand the role of the state in innovation systems we need to address the way that the state may seek to 'govern' innovation systems as well as the institutions that contribute to the system. Many of these institutions are economy wide, rather than tourism specific, although the particularities of the tourism industry (see Chapter 1), mean that their influences on tourism innovation are necessarily contingent.

The institutions of innovation: cornerstones or shackles?

Institutions are an important component of the innovative systems approach although the term is often used in a 'fuzzy' manner by different authors, referring to both organizational actors and as a set of institutional rules (Edquist 2001). Institutions are a set of social rules that may be explicit and formalized (for example, constitutions, statutes and regulations), or implicit and informal (for example, organizational culture, rules governing personal networks and family relationships). Edquist and Johnson (1997: 49) define institutions as 'a set of common habits, routines, established practices, rules or laws that regulate the relations between individuals or groups'. More recently, Edquist (2006) has equated institutions to 'the rules of the game' within which innovation is undertaken. In this context, institutions are best viewed as a filter that mediates and expresses the play of conflicting social and economic forces in society. The institutional framework mediates conflict by providing a set of rules and procedures that regulates how and where demands on public policy can be made, who has the authority to take certain decisions and actions, and how decisions and policies are implemented. Institutional arrangements are not static, however, and the institutions and relationships comprising the state system also reflect and adapt to the broader evolution of social and economic forces. Although institutional arrangements have been recognized as one of several important factors in the tourism public policy process (Hall and Jenkins 1995), they have not been a specific focus of research on tourism innovation.

Institutional arrangements are of importance for tourism and industry policy processes as 'policy making is filtered through a complex institutional framework' (Brooks 1993: 79). In the short run, institutions 'place constraints on decision-makers and help shape outcomes . . . by making some solutions harder, rather than by suggesting positive alternatives' (Simeon 1976: 574). As the number of check points for policy increases, so too does the potential for bargaining and negotiation. In the longer run, 'institutional arrangements may themselves be seen as policies, which, by building in to the decision process the need to consult particular groups and follow particular procedures, increase the likelihood of some kinds of decisions and reduces that of others' (Simeon 1976: 575). New government departments may be established as part of the growth in the activity and influence of government, particularly as new demands, such as environmental concerns, national competitiveness or national security, become a high priority on the political agenda. All of these potentially shape the role of the state in innovation. As Mercer (1979: 107) observed: 'The setting up of entirely new government departments, advisory bodies or sections within the existing administration is a well established strategy on the part of governments for demonstrating loudly and clearly that "something positive is being done" with respect to a given problem.' At the same time, as noted earlier, the nature of what 'is being done' in the name of the state, is also changing (see Box 4.2).

As well as being fundamental to understanding policy making, institutions and organizations are cornerstones of the systems of innovation approach (Chapter 1). Institutions exert considerable influence over the behaviours of firms and organizations by establishing constraints or providing incentives

Box 4.2 Changing role of government innovation agencies

Changes in the pattern of innovation, for example with respect to glob-alization, public–private cooperation and user based innovations, are reflected in the organizations that are responsible for innovation sup-port. The role of innovation agencies, whether at the national or regional level, is becoming more of a partner than that of a regulator. Agencies are acting more like investors than as public finance providers (Figure 4.3). According to Kotilainen (2005: 78–9): 'In most cases this is a radical change. It often requires changes in legislation and, even more so, in the mindset of people working in administration. A businesslike attitude is required.'

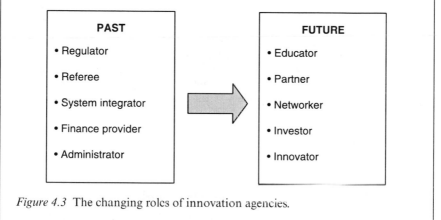

PAST	FUTURE
• Regulator	• Educator
• Referee	• Partner
• System integrator	• Networker
• Finance provider	• Investor
• Administrator	• Innovator

Figure 4.3 The changing roles of innovation agencies.

for innovation through a wide range of mechanisms. Edquist and Johnson (1997: 51) suggest that institutions perform three basic sets of significant functions in relation to the innovation process:

1   reducing uncertainty by providing information;
2   managing conflicts and cooperation; and
3   providing incentives.

Given that formal institutions are, in large part, an outcome of state action, government policy making and decision-making becomes fundamental in ensuring that institutional settings are favourable for desired policy outcomes with respect to innovation and competitiveness. Government involvement in innovation is important as it underlies a number of activities within systems of innovation that act to reduce the levels of uncertainty felt by private actors, particularly with respect to innovation in new fields. Table 4.3 outlines a number of state activities that may be undertaken within innovation systems

Table 4.3 State activities in innovation systems

Activity	Example
1 Provision of research and development and the creation of new knowledge	State support for the creation of new knowledge primarily occurs in science and technology sectors such as engineering, health and medicine and the natural sciences. In tourism, market research may be supported by the state.
2 Competence building through the provision of education and training, creation of intellectual and human capital	Often primarily focused on the supply of labour for innovation, and R&D activities, but may also be broadly focused on education, skills and training systems.
3 Formation of new product markets	Governments are often involved in supporting marketing initiatives. Tourism is an economic activity in which marketing is supported by the state at a number of different scales.
4 Articulation of quality requirements	National and international standards may be developed with respect to quality. In tourism the relative quality of accommodation and attractions is often expressed through government supported accreditation systems or via national regulation.
5 Creating and changing organizations	Undertaken by programmes and policies designed to enhance entrepreneurship and intrapreneurship, R&D organizations and policy agencies. For example, creation of regional marketing boards to support national tourism offices.
6 Networking	Support for the development of networks and clusters so as to encourage learning between different organizations
7 Establishing and changing institutions	Creating and revising laws with respect to intellectual property rights, tax, R&D investment, health and safety and the environment.
8 Incubating activities	Through provision of access to facilities and administrative support. For example, by conveying knowledge about incubation spaces, government activities and support, and matching firms with potential partners.
9 Financing of innovation processes and other activities	Financial support may be utilized so as to encourage commercialization of innovations and encourage adoption of 'bright ideas'.
10 Consultancy services	Services may include advice on technology transfer, commercialization, market information and legal advice.

(Edquist 2006). Such activities contribute to four main areas: provision of knowledge inputs to the innovation process (1, 2); demand-side factors (3, 4); provision of constituent elements of the innovation systems (5, 6, 7); and providing support services for innovating firms (8, 9, 10). The interaction between state activity and the components of innovation systems (institutions, firms and people) provides the foundation for innovation policy. However, in examining innovation policy Edquist (2006) emphasizes that the systems of innovation approach is focused on the determinants of innovation processes rather than their consequences. Despite the undoubted desire of many actors in government and industry, an ideal innovation system cannot be specified as 'innovation processes develop over time and involve the influence of many factors and feedback processes' (Edquist 2006). This observation is significant because, although it highlights the importance of undertaking comparative analyses of innovation systems, their highly contextualized and evolutionary character means that it is inappropriate to develop a 'copycat' model of innovation. There is no magic formula for the replication of innovation systems, precisely because these are rooted in specific sets of institutions. Instead, each nation, region or firm needs to understand the specificity of processes in other contexts, in order to develop systems appropriate to their particular situation.

Edquist (2001, 2006) argues that there are two reasons for policy intervention in a market economy with respect to innovation. First, private actors and markets must have failed in achieving the objectives that have been formulated, i.e. a policy problem must exist. 'This is in line with the principle that innovation policy should complement firms and markets, not replace or duplicate them' (Edquist 2001: 18). Second, public actors must have the capacity to mitigate the problem. This is not to argue that the state has a monopoly on the 'solutions' to such problems, and it should be noted that 'there are many other factors than knowledge and rationality that may influence the state in its role of pursuing innovation policy' (Edquist 2001: 19). Rather, Chaminade and Edquist (2006) observe that the policy discussion at each point in time should focus upon changes in the division of labour between the public and the private sectors or upon changes in those activities already carried out by public agencies. This includes adding new public policy activities as well as terminating others with the latter being regarded as 'not least important' (Edquist 2006). Given the particular features of tourism – being a composite industry, host–tourism relationships and strong environmental impacts, amongst others (see Chapter 1) – it is likely that both of the reasons for intervention noted by Edquist (2001, 2006) are likely to hold: that is the failure of markets to deliver desired outcomes, and the state having a capacity to intervene.

The scope of change in the innovation system is integrally related to the extent to which it builds on, or challenges, prevailing institutions. Boschma (2005) provides useful insights, distinguishing between two types of innovation policy: evolutionary and revolutionary, which although originally applied at the regional level can refer to innovation policy settings at a number of scales

(Table 4.4). Evolutionary innovation policy takes the specific internal context (national, regional or local) in terms of both institutions and industrial structure as the starting point. It is a fine-tuning policy that aims to strengthen the connectivity between the elements of the innovation system. In these circumstances, policy makers have few degrees of freedom, yet, according to Boschma (2005) they are more likely to be successful if their actions are localized, that is, focused on reproducing and strengthening the existing structures and institutions. The internal environment determines, to a large extent, the available options and probable outcomes of innovation policy.

In contrast, the goal of a revolutionary innovation policy is the restructuring of the social and institutional framework by constructing new national and regional innovation systems, increasing diversity and a high degree of openness regarding the flow of labour, capital and knowledge within and across state boundaries. In these circumstances, policy makers have more degrees of freedom, but at the cost of a higher degree of uncertainty regarding the actual outcome of innovation policy making, and its success. Since path dependence is less relevant, it is less meaningful to account for the location-specific context as a starting point for innovation policy. According to Boschma (2005), radically new trajectories of industrial development build on generic conditions because the existing actors and institutional environment are unlikely to provide the specific stimuli. But, extending the metaphors of evolutionary economics further, we would contend that as even revolutionary innovation policies cannot be constructed in a social vacuum, these are better characterized as path-dependent path-creating (Nielsen *et al.* 1995), rather than path-creating processes. In other words, echoing the title of this section of the book, are institutions cornerstones or shackles for (tourism) innovation?

For Boschma (2005) the paradox of state innovation policy is that it can be very effective and successful in conserving existing economic activities by means of evolutionary policies, yet it has difficulty triggering, and sometimes even opposes, the new economic activities required for long-term development. However, this does not mean that evolutionary and revolutionary policies are mutually exclusive. Policies in existing sectors may bring about

Table 4.4 Evolutionary and revolutionary types of innovation policy

Evolutionary	Revolutionary
Location-specific policy	Generic policy
Fine-tuning	Restructuring of institutional framework
Strengthening existing connectivity	Stimulating new connections
Benefiting from specialization	Stimulating diversity
Few degrees of freedom	More degrees of freedom
Less uncertainty	More uncertainty

Source: Adapted from Boschma (2005).

incremental innovations while simultaneously the generic conditions for revolutionary change are being developed. However, as Boschma (2005) notes, such a multiple policy approach is challenging and requires subtle and holistic policy making, because policies designed to achieve one set of objectives may work against the achievement of others. Such a 'happy mix' of innovation policies is difficult to achieve, particularly as it has to both draw on and reshape institutions simultaneously.

One way to combine policy settings is to encourage the creation of new industrial trajectories, whether new sectors or new technologies, by building upon the existing competence base of firms, employers and employees. Such a policy approach captures the importance of creating 'related variety' in a region, thereby broadening a region's sectoral base, while encouraging knowledge spillovers between sectors (Frenken *et al.* 2005). As Levinthal (1998) emphasizes, revolutionary or punctuated technological innovation may stem from the combination of existing technologies or activities in entirely new ways. For example, the rise of an environmental sector after the decline of the mining industry in the Ruhr area of Germany can be interpreted in such a fashion (Boschma 2004); by extension, the development of mining museums, which use knowledgeable ex-miners as guides, also provides some such spillovers. Some proponents of sustainable tourism may also regard the development of nature-based tourism products in highly urbanized or industrial districts as a revolutionary technological innovation, although nature-based tourism is usually an evolutionary progression from existing product offerings. Instead, the emergence of 'new' cross-sectoral tourism products such as various forms of industrial tourism (e.g. many food and wine tourism activities) provide a better example of the capture of related variety; these have been able to encourage new industrial trajectories through agro-diversification in a number of regions (Clark 2005).

Regardless of the nature of innovation policy an increasingly important concern is the political level at which policy is developed and enacted. Most of the original work on innovation systems focused on the national level and on the actions of the national state. Many of these studies highlighted the significance of country-specific capabilities, knowledge and skills in effecting technological change (Nelson 1993). Perhaps unsurprisingly, it was found that countries differed in their methods of adopting innovations, in sectoral strengths, and in their capacity to produce change (Archibugi and Michie 1995). A number of 'imperfections' or 'failures' have been identified in national innovation systems (Woolthuis *et al.* 2005), and it is notable that institutions feature prominently amongst these:

- Infrastructural failures: physical infrastructure.
- Transition failures: failure to adapt to a new technology.
- Lock-in/path dependency failures: inability to adapt to new technological paradigms.
- Hard institutional failures: related to the legal systems and regulations.

- Soft institutional failures: related to social institutions such as political and social values.
- Strong network failures: 'blindness' that evolves if actors have close links and they miss new outside developments.
- Weak network failures: lack of linkages.
- Capabilities failures: lack of learning capabilities.

Institutional weaknesses are not confined to the national level – which is not surprising, given that these are articulated at different levels (discussed below in relation to multi-level governance). For example, Anderson *et al.* (2006) in discussing systematic failures in national innovation systems in a report to the Council of Science and Technology Advisors to the Government of Canada (CSTA) argued that:

> In federal states the national system of innovation is the sum of several regional systems. These regional systems of innovation are often weak because of a need for leadership – the technological future appears to depend more on social than on technological processes. Thus regional innovation systems are fragile because they are weakly institutionalized; the federal innovation system provides the leadership required.

Nevertheless, there was a remedy at hand for such a situation, with Anderson *et al.* going on to refer to a report of the CSTA that stated:

> We are convinced that, through linkages, the government can engage the full capacity of the national science and innovation system, and draw on the most appropriate expertise, experience and resources wherever they reside, in order to more effectively identify, address and resolve national issues.
>
> (CSTA 2005, cited in Anderson *et al.* 2006)

Notwithstanding Anderson *et al.*'s somewhat unusual assessment of state capacity at the national scale in federal systems, which in itself illustrates Edquist's (2001) above observation on the lack of an adequate understanding of the role of the state in systems of innovation, the comments in relation to the Canadian federal system do illustrate the extent to which the reshaping of national systems of innovation is now a major concern to many countries (Anderson *et al.* 1998). However, they also evidence a need to have a multi-scalar framework with which to assess state involvement in systems of innovation. This is particularly so because while all countries have examined issues of innovation at a national level, some have focused significant attention at the subnational level while others have also concentrated on supranational and multinational initiatives. Similarly, others have focused on the sectoral level, while others have sought to implement more multi-sectoral innovation strategies. Furthermore, the different scales of innovation systems are not mutually exclusive; rather, they interact with each other in ways that reinforce the need to understand the state as multi-scalar, and therefore the need for an improved understanding of governance of innovation systems. Box 4.3, for example, illustrates some of the layers of innovation policy within the Baltic States (Estonia, Latvia, Lithuania) of the EU.

Box 4.3 Innovation policy in the Baltic States

The Baltic transition economies of Estonia, Latvia and Lithuania provide an example of both multi-layered innovation systems and differences between national systems of innovation. Following their independence from Russia in the early 1990s, the Baltic States sought to embrace European-style economic policies and development models. Although all three states had developed national innovation policies by the end of the twentieth century their capabilities to implement these was poor as a result of relatively poorly developed economies and a wide range of competing social and economic demands on government resources and policy attention. All three countries had relatively low levels of expenditure on research and development, being approximately 0.4–0.7 per cent of GDP, while there were also significant gaps between the research and business communities, and weakly coordinated techno-logical transfer activities (Egle 2006). However, the accession of the Baltic states to the EU in 2004 marked a dramatic change in their national innovation systems as it provided for enhanced EU support for national innovation programmes and knowledge transfers. This has been undertaken via the availability of EU structural funds and other EU programmes, many of which are regionally focused. In the case of Latvia for example, it is estimated that, for the period 2002–9, there will be as many financial resources available for research from various EU funds as there will be from the Latvian public budget (Egle 2006).

Table 4.5 illustrates the EU programmes that are being utilized to support innovation activities and also indicates some of the national programmes that are underway. The national programmes also high-light the different trajectories that different countries can take with respect to innovation as there are three countries with similar geographies, economic structures and population sizes, all within the EU, yet having different emphases in innovation. However, common issues with respect to innovation programmes are recognized, in part emphasizing underlying institutional similarities.

At the national level this includes (Egle 2006):

- lack of administrative capacity of public institutions for managing public funds;

- substantial levels of bureaucracy, with overly long evaluation and decision-making processes;
- lack of flexibility in supporting projects;
- unclear criteria for selecting projects in open calls for proposals;
- possible distortion of competition between companies by state aid programmes;
- overlapping of different programmes and activities;
- experienced people being involved in too many projects of different programmes.

In contrast, at the European level, perceptions include:

- growing levels of bureaucracy;
- long delays in cash flow to projects;
- lack of risk sharing for innovation projects.

Despite these constraints, the rapid development of national innovation systems in the Baltic after accession to the EU coincides with a period of rapid economic growth in the countries' economies (Egle 2006). Although it is too early to establish causality between these, this example does illustrate the way in which levels can become 'folded-in' on each other (Amin 2002), with the EU innovation policies informing the national ones, and vice versa.

Table 4.5 Layers of innovation policy in the Baltic States

Scale	Innovation actions and policies

Supranational	**EU**
	 • EU Framework programmes FP 5, FP 6, FP 7
	 • Competitiveness and Innovation Framework Programme (CIP)
	  – IT support services: Innovation Relay Centres (IRC) network
	  – Initiatives: e.g. PRO INNO Europe; Networks of Innovating regions in Europe (IRE); Support to innovative start-ups (PAXIS); Europe INNOVA, Gate2Growth
	 • Networking on innovation issues through European projects
	  – Regional innovation strategies (RIS Latvia, RIS Estonia, RIS Lithuania)
	  – InterReg projects, e.g. 'Hansa Passage'

National	**Estonia**	**Latvia**	**Lithuania**
	• Estonian Innovation Fund; Estonian Small Business Loan Fund; Estonian Export Support Fund • Creation of Enterprise Estonia	• Market oriented research programme	• National 'Innovation in Business' programme (includes innovation support measures, grants for companies for innovative projects, development of innovation assistance network)
Regional	Urban and regional government		

Development of innovation policies in some local governments, particularly in larger urban centres but little domestic public funds for policy action.

Significant involvement in EU regional innovation strategies that encourage innovation and knowledge transfer:

• Regional innovation strategies (RIS Latvia, RIS Estonia, RIS Lithuania).
• InterReg projects.

Governance and a multi-layered approach to innovation

Arguably one of the most significant dimensions of globalization has been the transformation of political and regulatory practices. As Anderson *et al.* (1998: 5) commented:

> Although the nation-state and national economy are, and will continue to be, central actors in systems of innovation, the emergence of large-scale, supranational, regional trading blocs and the growth of international interdependence inevitably raise questions about the development of innovation systems above the national level.

As a result of, and as an expression of, political and economic globalization, state authority, power and legitimacy have ceased to be bounded on the strict territorial basis that has been the basis for sovereign governance for most of the past 200 years (Hall 2008a). Instead, under conditions of 'postsovereign governance', the governance of some key economic and financial issues is increasingly being handled by the transfer, whether temporary or permanent, of goal-specific authority from national states to regional or multilateral supranational and international organizations, as well as to the local or sub-national state. Under this set of conditions the governance of a number of policy and planning areas, including the innovation policy field, is being maintained not just by territorial state-bounded authorities, as in much of the past two centuries, 'but rather by a network of flows of information, power and resources from the local to the regional and multilateral levels and the other way around' (Morales-Moreno 2004: 108). Similarly, the tourism policy field is also being maintained in the same way, particularly through the actions of the UN World Tourism Organization and the World Travel and Tourism Council at the supranational level (Coles and Hall 2008).

In this context there is a need to examine not only the role of the national state in tourism and innovation, but just as importantly, the roles and inter-actions of international and supranational bodies, private actors such as transnational corporations and non-governmental organizations, and the important role of the local state in regional innovation systems (Cooke *et al.* 1997). These policy actors along with the regulatory mechanisms of the national state are contributing to the development of a new multi-layered governance architecture (Peters and Pierre 2001) for numerous policy and issue areas including innovation and tourism. This is establishing, therefore, a multi-layered and co-evolutionary set of innovation systems in which firms and other actors are embedded (Hall 2005) (Figure 4.4).

The term 'governance' has a number of meanings (Rhodes 1996, 1997; Kooiman 2003), and has often come to imply changes in the public sector that minimize the role of formal governmental actors and give a greater role to the private sector and to non-government organizations. For example, Kooiman (1993: 6) argues that governance has become an inter-organizational phenomenon, and that it is best understood through terms such as 'co-managing, co-steering and co-guidance', all implying more cooperative methods for identifying and achieving policy goals. Kooiman (1993: 258) defines governance as: 'The pattern or structure that emerges in a socio-political system as a "common" result or outcome of the interacting interven-tion efforts of all involved actors. This pattern cannot be reduced to one actor or group of actors in particular.' Indeed, Kooiman's observations on govern-ance with respect to structure has a direct relationship to the concept of a system of innovation used throughout this book, as an innovation system constitutes a particular type of socio-political system with a specific set of actors and institutions with a relatively common set of interests.

Multi-layered governance implies more than decentralization. Although not denying the importance of decentralization, Peters (1996, 1998) neverthe-less emphasizes that governance implies 'steering', or the employment of some mechanism(s) of providing coherent direction to society by national-state governments or, in the present case, the efforts of the state and its agencies to steer the trajectories of innovation systems for reasons of com-petitiveness and productivity. This theme is also picked up by Morales-Moreno (2004: 108–9) who argues that, 'we could define governance as the

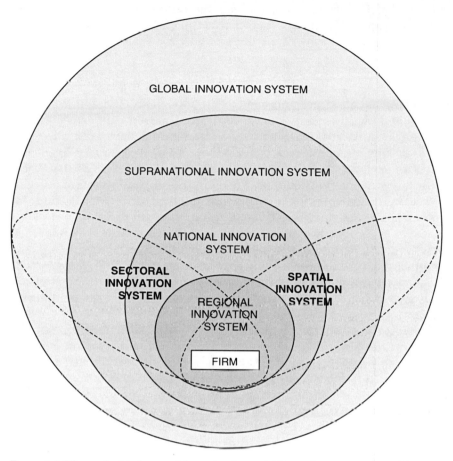

Figure 4.4 The embeddedness of firms in the multi-layered governance architecture of innovation systems.

capacity for steering, shaping, and managing, yet leading the impact of transnational flows and relations in a given issue area, through the inter-connectedness of different polities and their institutions in which power, authority, and legitimacy are shared'. The identification of transnational rela-tions here is significant as there are many issues that are not transnational and that are clearly the domain of territorial-based state sovereignty. Tourism and innovation are both areas that are marked by substantial transnational flows and relations, whether through people, economic capital or the transfer of knowledge and intellectual capital. However, while the policy significance of innovation diffusion is generally understood by policy makers, the contribution of tourism as both an agent of diffusion and as a foci of innovation has often not been fully appreciated (Hall 2005, 2008a; Coles and Hall 2008), particularly in context of multi-layered governance.

Conclusions

Governance does not mean the end of state sovereignty, even if it is necessarily diminished. Sovereignty still resides in the hands of national-states who clearly remain the main actors in the international sphere, especially when some states do not fully ascribe to the notion of a multi-levelled polity. States may join supranational and international agreements, such as the World Trade Organization (WTO) or the World Tourism Organization, but they can also leave. In the case of the EU, which is often used as an example of supranationalism, it may even be argued that the power of the state has been increased as a result of integration rather than eroded, since the tendency does appear to be for the supranational EU to supplement the role of the national-state in those functions which the state performs less well under contemporary conditions of globalization, for example, innovation-related areas such as the regulation of international trade – including that of tourism services, competition and labour mobility (Majone 1996; Hall 2008b). The notion that the state is finished or is a 'hollow' vessel is therefore substantially premature (Rhodes 1994). Of course, as Peters (1998) observes, the capacity of states to behave as a unitary actor is sometimes greatly overstated or misinterpreted in the 'state' literature as well, 'but it still appears easier to begin with that more centralized conception and find the exceptions than to begin with a null hypothesis of no order and find any pattern'. However, there is no disputing the tremendous transformation of sovereignty that has occurred and that points to the formation of a multi-levelled polity (Peters and Pierre 2001), which has a number of implications for tourism innovation at various scales that will be examined in the following chapters.

5 Tourism within national innovation systems

Introduction

The national innovation system (NIS) approach has been one of the most influential in seeking to understand the innovation trajectories of countries (Lundvall *et al.* 2002). It is recognition that innovation needs to be understood as part of a broader social, economic, technological and political system. The concept emphasizes that while globalization and 'external international connections are of growing importance, the influence of a country's education system, industrial relations, technical and scientific institutions, government policies, cultural traditions and many other national institutions is fundamental' (Freeman 1995: 5). However, this notion is not new, and as some of the more influential authors on the concept (e.g. Lundvall 1992; Lundvall *et al.* 2002) acknowledge, the idea actually goes back at least to Friedrich List's conception of the *National System of Political Economy* (1856 [org. 1841]). The latter 'advocated not only protection of infant industries but a broad range of policies designed to accelerate, or to make possible, industrialisation and economic growth. Most of these policies were concerned with learning about new technology and applying it' (cited in Freeman 1995: 5), which would now likely be termed 'The National System of Innovation'. Freeman (1968: 58) himself used the term in 1968:

> The rate of technological change in any country and the effectiveness of companies in world competition in international trade in goods and services, does not depend simply on the scale of their research and development . . . It depends on the way in which the available resources are managed and organized, both at the enterprise and national level. The national system of innovation may enable a country with limited resources . . . to make progress through appropriate combination of imported technology and local adaptation and improvement.

NISs are constituted by 'interconnected agents' that interact influencing the execution of innovation in the national economy. These interactions occur in a specific context and under certain shared norms, routines and established practices (Nelson and Rosenberg 1993). NISs may therefore be styled as segmented layers of institutions and production modes that integrate national, regional and local ensembles of actors, institutions and resources that pose particular issues of governance and the role of the state (see Chapter 4). These elements are illustrated in Figure 5.1. The key characteristics of an NIS can be summarized as:

- firms are part of a network of public and private sector institutions whose activities and interactions initiate, import, modify and diffuse new technologies (and more generally, knowledge);
- an NIS consists of linkages (both formal and informal) between institutions;
- an NIS includes flows of intellectual resources between institutions;
- analysis of NISs emphasizes learning as a key economic resource, and that geography and location matter (Holbrook and Wolfe 2000).

The innovation systems framework therefore consists of analysing the existence of actors in a given territory (institutions, universities, industries), their main competences, and their interactions in innovation-informing networks (Lundvall 1992; Lundvall *et al.* 2002; Pyka and Küppers 2002), providing policy makers with a tool that allows the construction of more competitive and efficient innovation systems. For example, the Organisation for Economic Co-operation and Development (OECD) noted that the study of NISs offers new rationales for government innovation policies, particularly with respect to technology, that go beyond policies focused on market failures to policies that can identify systemic issues in innovation (OECD 1997, 2000). Over time, a number of different areas of influence on innovation policy and practice have therefore developed as a result of attempts to articulate and operationalize the NIS approach (CSTA 2005):

- The design of innovation policy needs to be realized in a consistent and coherent manner, that is, individual policies have to share a common goal, to improve national innovation performance. The idea is not to propose stand-alone policies, but to design a portfolio of policy instruments, in order to enhance not just individual elements of the NIS but the system as a whole.
- Policies need to be designed to provide effective linkages between the supply and demand sides by attempting to make innovation activities technically and commercially successful.
- Innovation policies need to be embedded in a broader socio-economic context. This requires the interaction of science, technology and innovation policy making with other areas, such as trade, taxation and macro-economic policy.
- The diversity of levels of analysis within the NIS approach is one of its strengths. Understanding the meso and micro analytical levels (see

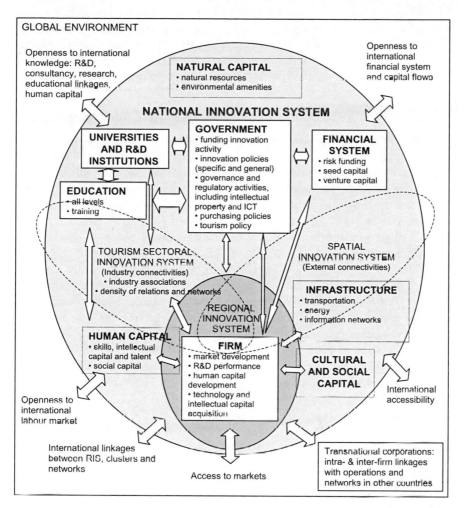

Figure 5.1 Elements of NISs.

Chapters 6 and 7) are not only legitimate but also necessary. They broaden and deepen understanding of NIS and highlight the policy constraints of national policies (Lundvall *et al.* 2002).

- There is a need to work on systems failures, and not just on market failures, and particularly the process for identifying the causes of lock-in, thereby eliminating bottlenecks so as to enable innovation and economic progress both at the firm and system level (Woolthuis *et al.* 2005).

This chapter provides a review of a number of NISs using the scope of formal national innovation strategies as a mechanism to identify both the focus and processes of innovation policy, but also the role of tourism within these. However, comments are also provided about the extent to which other government policies, for example with respect to tourism, that often lie outside of formal innovation policy, as well as various institutions and actors, all contribute to tourism within NISs. One of the most significant findings is that tourism is hardly noted at all within national innovation policy, with the significance of this being discussed in the final section of the chapter.

Australia: *Backing Australia's Ability*

> This Government believes that innovation – developing skills, generating new ideas through research, and turning them into commercial success – is key to Australia's future prosperity. Innovation is not only the province of new or high tech industries, but also essential to the future of many of our traditional sectors such as agriculture, manufacturing and mining. The Howard Government is determined to ensure that innovation drives growth and we capitalise on the enormous potential of the new millennium.
>
> (Commonwealth of Australia 2001: 7)

The *Backing Australia's Ability* strategy was introduced by the Australian national government (the Commonwealth government) in 2001 to promote science and innovation. Initially a five-year AUS$3 billion plan, funding support was boosted in 2005 to constitute a ten-year, AUS$8.3 billion funding commitment stretching from 2001 to 2011. The strategy targets 'the three key elements of the innovation system' (Department of Education, Science and Training 2005):

* strengthening Australia's ability to generate ideas and undertake research;
* accelerating the commercialization of ideas;
* developing and retaining skills.

According to the national government the strategy represents a commitment to:

* pursue excellence in research, science and technology;
* build a more highly skilled workforce;
* increase opportunities for taking new ideas to market.

The plan covers six main areas:

* building up the knowledge infrastructure;
* strengthening linkages in the innovation system;
* building critical mass and focus;
* strengthening commercialization of public sector research;
* improving the situation for business R&D;
* strengthening the skills base.

Table 5.1 Citations of tourism in the Australian government innovation report

Report	Tourism as primary focus	Tourism as secondary focus
2005–6	–	–
2004–5	–	During 2003–4, the Australian Biological Resources Study (ABRS) supported research on algae and fauna of marine and freshwater waterways. 'This increasing knowledge base will assist in monitoring the health of our waterways and the related sustainability of water related industries such as irrigation farming, fishing, oyster farming and tourism' (Commonwealth of Australia 2005: 94).
2003–4	–	Geoscience Australia's 2002–3 revision of 513 revised map sheets at 1:250000 scale, covering the entire continent, 'will be used by researchers across disciplines, in areas as diverse as emergency management, exploration investment, immigration, defence and land use assessment and planning, and tourism' (Commonwealth of Australia 2004: 57).
2002–3	–	–
2001–2	–	–

Source: Commonwealth of Australia (2002, 2003, 2004, 2005, 2006).

To oversee the implementation of *Backing Australia's Ability*, a high-level committee comprising the prime minister, the minister for industry, tourism and resources, the minister for communications, information technology and the arts, the minister for education, science and training and the minister for finance and administration was established. Although tourism is based within one of the departments responsible for the innovation strategy (the Department of Industry, Tourism and Resources) tourism is not a focal point for national innovation. In fact, tourism is hardly mentioned at all. In an analysis of Australian government reports of the innovation strategy from 2001 to 2006, tourism is only cited twice (Table 5.1), and this is only in terms of projects that may have value for tourism rather than being tourism specific projects. However, the Cooperative Research Centre (CRC) for Sustainable Tourism is mentioned in the list of CRCs in all sectors at the rear of the report (see Box 5.1).

Innovation is mentioned in Australia's national tourism strategy: 'The strategy is based on expectations of a highly competitive international environment requiring flexibility, innovation and responsiveness at all levels of the Australian tourism industry' (Australian Government 2003: xiv). It also 'envisages a strong and vibrant Australian tourism industry which ... embraces innovation and ongoing improvement and adopts appropriate

Box 5.1 Sustainable Tourism Cooperative Research Centre (STCRC)

The STCRC was established under the Australian government's CRCs programme to underpin the development of a dynamic, internationally competitive, and sustainable tourism industry. The STCRC is a not-for-profit company owned by its industry, government and university partners (Table 5.2).

Table 5.2 STCRC partners in Australia

Tourism companies	Industry bodies	Government	Educational institutions (universities)	Other educational institutions
Qantas Airways Voyages	Australian Federation of Travel Agents Australian Tourism Export Council Tourism Task Force Australia	*Commonwealth* Tourism Australia *State tourism agencies* Australian Capital Tourism Northern Territory Tourist Commission South Australian Tourism Commission Tourism New South Wales Tourism Queensland Tourism Tasmania Tourism Victoria Tourism Western Australia *State non-tourism agencies* NSW Department of Environment and Conservation Parks Victoria Western Australia Conservation and Land Management *Local government* Gold Coast City Council	Curtin University of Technology Edith Cowan University Griffith University James Cook University La Trobe University Monash University Murdoch University Charles Darwin University Southern Cross University University of Canberra University of New South Wales University of Queensland University of South Australia University of Tasmania University of Technology Sydney Victoria University	Technical and Further Education (TAFE) NSW

Source: STCRC (2005).

OUR VISION is innovation driving a dynamic, internationally competitive and sustainable tourism industry.

OUR MISSION is the development and management of intellectual property to deliver innovation to business, community and government enhancing the environmental, economic and social sustainability of tourism – one of the world's largest, fastest growing industries.

Activities are focused on research, education and commercialization and extension. Spin-off companies include:

- Decipher – A tourism business knowledge company.
- EarthCheck – A company that develops benchmarking and sustainability improvement systems for commercial application.
- Green Globe Asia Pacific – A joint venture company providing global certification and sustainability services for enterprises and destinations.
- Sustainable Tourism Services – Provides extension and commercial research capabilities.
- Sustainable Tourism Holdings – Dedicated to commercializing innovations developed from STCRC intellectual property.

International operations include:

- APEC International Centre for Sustainable Tourism – A multilateral sustainable tourism research consortium established to facilitate new levels of cooperation between APEC member economies.
- Sustainable Tourism Development Consortium (STDC) – A joint venture between STCRC and GRM International. STDC provides teams of experts for public and private sector sustainable tourism consulting and development projects throughout Asia Pacific.
- International Centre of Excellence in Tourism and Hospitality Education – Works directly with partners to develop world-class educational programmes for tourism and hospitality. THE-ICE builds recognition for Australia as a world-leading quality supplier of sustainable tourism and hospitality education and training.

Associate centres include:

- Qantas Chair in Tourism Economics;
- University of New South Wales Centre for Regional Tourism Research;
- Southern Cross University Centre for Small Tourism Enterprise and Innovation;
- Victoria University;

* University of South Australia.

Source: Derived from STCRC (2005) and http://www.crctourism.com.au.

---

technology'. Later the document notes: 'The tourism workforce must comprise skilled professionals who are able to contribute to enterprise innovation and are also able to enjoy attractive career opportunities within the industry' (Australian Government 2003: xv). Under the heading of 'growing high-yield tourism', the tourism strategy notes:

> Like other market sectors, tourism customers are attracted to the diverse range of new and innovative products and experiences provided by the market. Such innovation and improvement is the basis of growth and success. Australia needs to be at the forefront of such innovation, with a focus on developing high-yield market segments.
>
> (Australian Government 2003: 29)

Innovation is not mentioned again in the strategy. However, the strategy's implementation plan (Australian Government 2004) does note: 'The White Paper outlines a whole-of-government approach to tourism, aimed at removing duplications, maximizing opportunities and facilitating partnerships and innovation' and goes on to indicate:

> The government is achieving the whole-of-government approach through a range of new collaborative mechanisms, including
>
> * a new Intergovernmental Arrangement between the Australian Government and the states and territories;
> * the annual Tourism–Industry Government Forum; and
> * the Industry Implementation Advisory Group.
>
> (Australian Government 2004: ix)

However, that is the only time that the document explicitly refers to innovation. There are therefore no explicit connections made between national tourism policy and national innovation policy. This is not to suggest that sections of either the national tourism strategy or its implementation plan are not relevant to innovation. Increasing collaboration can clearly be of benefit for innovation, while there is a section on 'enhancing research and statistics' that, most importantly with respect to knowledge transfer, stated that Tourism Research Australia would develop an information dissemination strategy (Australian Government 2004: 27). However, what neither the national innovation strategy nor the national tourism strategy address is actually *how* tourism is going to be strengthened in terms of either specific tourism innovation policies, for example relating to skills, entrepreneurship and new product development, or generic policies, such as immigration, foreign investment or taxation (the significance of the latter is explored in Box 5.2). There is therefore a substantial difference between mobilization of the various elements of the Australian NIS in relation to targeted sectors such as biotechnology, pharmaceuticals and IT, and the governance of the NIS with respect to tourism.

Box 5.2 Tax breaks boost Australian R&D spend

Australian SMEs have invested record amounts in R&D since changes to tax concessions in 2001. A report released by Industry Minister Ian Macfarlane, in July 2007, showed that expenditure on R&D reached a record AUS\$8.4 billion in 2004–5 (Australian Government 2007). According to the minister: 'This represents a \$2.5 billion increase since the introduction of the Howard Government's 175 per cent premium and tax offset' (Macfarlane 2007). The offset provides a tax concession for additional R&D expenditure above a three-year average to encourage companies to increase their spending on innovation and R&D. Mr Macfarlane said changes to the testing for the concession were expected to increase R&D spending by AUS\$1 billion over the next four to five years. The evaluation report also found the tax offset was proving to be an incentive to innovate, with an extra 1,000 small companies investing in R&D based on previous trends. The measure had boosted R&D spending by about AUS\$310 million a year, representing a doubling of expenditure by start-up companies although this may be an over-estimate as it assumes new firms would not have conducted R&D before the offset. The tax offset also helps start-up ventures overcome the challenges of obtaining finance for R&D by enabling companies in tax loss to cash out their future deductions under the tax concession. According to the Australian Government (2007: 24): 'The increase supports the policy rationale for establishing the Offset – that small technology firms are significantly limited in R&D investment because they lack access to available capital.'

Unfortunately, the report does not specify tourism as a separate category in analysing R&D expenditure. Although it does report that all sectors are using the new elements:

> Most differences in usage is [*sic*] due to the size of the firm, with small firms more likely to use the offset and large firms, whose base R&D funding dominate [*sic*] the R&D, more likely to use the premium. Mining companies, utilities and non-metallic minerals are strong users of the basic 125% Concession.
>
> (Australian Government 2007: 12)

As with all SMEs, those in tourism face significant barriers to innovation in terms of access to capital (see Chapter 8), particularly in the growth stage. This scheme therefore has considerable potential for boosting tourism innovation, although the question remains as to whether such a generic policy adequately addresses the distinctive features of the tourism industry (see Chapter 1), including seasonality, and the significance of tacit rather than codified knowledge.

Canada: *Achieving Excellence*

Canada's innovation strategy was launched in February 2002, with the release of two companion documents: *Achieving Excellence: Investing in People, Knowledge and Opportunity* (Government of Canada 2002) and *Knowledge Matters: Skills and Learning for Canadians*. Both focused on what Canada must do 'to ensure equality of opportunity and economic innovation in the knowledge society'. According to the Government of Canada (2002) *Achieving Excellence* focused on the need to consider excellence as a strategic national asset: 'It focuses on how to strengthen our science and research capacity and on how to ensure that this knowledge contributes to building an innovative economy that benefits all Canadians.'

Both documents highlighted goals, milestones and targets for improving innovation, skills and learning in Canada, particularly with respect to the Canadian government's goals to boost the economy by nurturing a more knowledge-based workforce, and to build a strong scientific and research environment by 2010. If the goals are met, investment in R&D will have doubled and venture capital investments per capita will match US and EU levels. However, while the US acts as a benchmark for Canadian innovation policy because of its proximity, Canadian institutions are strongly oriented towards creating benefits for Canada and this is a clear criterion for public funding (Kotilainen 2005).

Unfortunately, tourism is not mentioned in the Canadian national innovation strategy. As noted in Chapter 4 Canada has long had national government programmes which aim to promote SME-related technological and science innovation (see Box 4.1) and there is a substantial set of institutional arrangements relating to science and technology, education, industry, defence, health, agriculture and fisheries that have innovation as a focus. For example, the NRC and the Canadian IRAP have provided support for SMEs to develop technology, enhance competitiveness and grow business as well as support the development of clusters in different regions. Although the tourism industry has been a beneficiary of the government initiatives in terms of the amount of human mobility that is related to knowledge transfer, partnership and venture development, very few tourism firms have been the beneficiaries of innovation assistance. Similarly, Industry Canada (2007) has only one programme, the Regional Ontario Development Program, which mentions tourism. The

National Science and Engineering Research Council has a range of programmes that support technological and scientific innovation, including an Industrial Research Chair Programme but tourism has not been a direct beneficiary of these programmes. Although not generally regarded as being specifically a part of the Canadian innovation policy framework (Kotilainen 2005), the Social Science and Humanities Research Council of Canada has funded a limited number of tourism-related research projects. Similarly, the Canadian Research Chairs Programme to establish 2,000 research professorships in universities across Canada by 2008 has funded one tourism specific chair (at the University of Waterloo in the area of tourism and climate change).

As in the Australian institutional arrangements, tourism is a part of the industry portfolio. Canada's national tourism strategy (Canadian Tourism Commission 2006) identified six priority areas where federal, provincial and territorial governments can collaborate more closely with each other and with industry to improve industry competitiveness and enhance growth. The priorities include: border crossings; transport infrastructure; product development; human resource development; tourism information and statistics; and tourism marketing. Innovation is only noted once in the strategy where one of the 'key principles' that guide the strategy is to promote federal, provincial and territorial government 'interventions that are research-based, and lead to action and innovation in product development and marketing' (Canadian Tourism Commission 2006: 3). As part of the background to the strategy, a report was produced in 2003 with respect to the Canadian federal government's commitment of resources to tourism. This indicated that CDN$7.8 million was allocated to research and statistics, and CDN$90.8 million to product and business development (Canadian Tourism Commission 2003). This represented 1.5 per cent and 25.9 per cent, respectively, of total federal government resources to tourism. No information is available, however, as to the extent this actually represented investment in, or support for, different types of innovation.

Elsewhere, there is more evidence of the existence of some elements of an NIS for tourism. Tourism Canada (Canadian Tourism Commission), the lead national agency for tourism, has product innovation and enhancement listed as one of its core functions in its strategic plan, 2007–11. Its 2007 budget allocated just over CDN$1.5 million to product development, CDN$1.2 million for R&D, and a further approximate CDN$3 million for research, including industry contributions. By 2011 Tourism Canada expect Canada to have international tourism revenues of almost CDN$20 billion (Canadian Tourism Commission 2006).

In Canada, as in Australia, tourism does not feature prominently – indeed, hardly at all – in the NIS. This did not change significantly with the introduction of a revised national innovation strategy in 2007 (see Box 5.3). In part this reflects the narrow conceptualization of what constitutes the 'knowledge economy', and a focus on science and technology as opposed to service industries such as tourism. Nevertheless, the national tourism policy does pay some limited attention to innovation, and funds are channelled into

Box 5.3 Change of government, change of strategy, change of
         institutions

The mandate of the Canadian Council of Science and Technology
Advisors (CSTA) concluded on 17 May 2007 with the release of the
government of Canada's science and technology strategy, *Canada's
New Government: Mobilizing Science and Technology to Canada's
Advantage* (Government of Canada 2007). The science and technology
strategy announced the government's intention to create a new Science,
Technology and Innovation Council as part of a broader effort to
consolidate external advisory committees in order to strengthen the
role of independent expert advisors. The new council will provide the
government with policy advice on issues referred to it by the government and will release regular state-of-the-nation reports that track
Canada's science and technology performance and progress against
international benchmarks of success. Tourism was not mentioned in the
report.

Industry Canada, the government department whose mandate is
'to help make Canadians more productive and competitive in the global
economy, thus improving the standard of living and quality of life
in Canada' (Industry Canada 2007: 5) also underwent organizational
change. The previous policy sector is being restructured to create a
more focused strategic policy group, and a new science and innovation
group that will focus on innovation policy in its broadest sense. The
previous operations sector was also split into the small business and
marketplace services sector and the regional operations sector following
a reorganization of Industry Canada's operational agenda. With respect
to machinery of government changes that affected Industry Canada,
a secretary of state (small business and tourism) was appointed in
January 2007. The secretary of state will be responsible for small business and tourism, 'including outreach to key stakeholders and business
associations such as the Canadian Federation of Independent Business
and the Tourism Industry Association of Canada. Industry Canada
will support the Secretary of State in his endeavours to address key
priorities pertaining to small business and tourism' (Industry Canada
2007: 54). However, Industry Canada's (2007) report on plans and priorities had no specific tourism programme or sub-programme noted,
although the tourism industry did warrant two paragraphs that were
dedicated to the 2010 Olympic Winter Games in Vancouver and the
national tourism strategy.

tourism innovation, particularly product development and innovation. However, although innovation in tourism marketing and product development is recognized in the national strategy there are no specific mechanisms identified as to how this will actually be realized.

New Zealand: *Growing an Innovative New Zealand*

A New Zealand Vision
A land where diversity is valued and reflected in our national identity
A great place to live, learn, work and do business
A birthplace of world-changing people and ideas
A place where people invest in the future
The Economic Objective
To return New Zealand's per capita income to the top half of the OECD rankings and maintain that standing.
Enhancing the role of government
Government will be proactive in supporting growth, will work co-operatively with other sectors to achieve that, and will emphasise the importance of sustainability.

(Clark 2002: 6)

On 12 February 2002, Prime Minister Helen Clark released the government's policy framework for economic transformation, *Growing an Innovative New Zealand* (Clark 2002). This Growth and innovation framework (GIF) was designed to pursue the long-term sustainable growth necessary to improve the quality of life of all New Zealanders. The framework builds on what was perceived as New Zealand's economic strengths: a stable macroeconomic framework, an open and competitive microeconomy, sound infrastructure, a modern society, a healthy and relatively skilled population, and sound environmental management. According to Clark (2002) the GIF reflects a growing understanding of the value of policies that impact directly on innovation and recognizes the government's role in:

- addressing barriers to exporting and fostering deep links with international firms and markets;
- attracting foreign direct investment (FDI) that contributes to the development of the local economy;
- supporting innovation in firms;
- building a strong and capable workforce with sound generic and applied skills;
- engaging with industry sectors and regions to address barriers to growth;
- promoting institutions and practices that forge stronger links between industry, education providers and public sector researchers.

These clearly address many of the issues that we have already noted as being critical in knowledge transfers (Chapter 3), particularly the contended inherent knowledge advantages of foreign capital, skills and quality, as well as the need for an institutional framework that facilitates innovation (Chapter 4). According to Clark (2002: 6), government policies would be aimed at sustaining:

- a stable macroeconomic framework;
- an open and competitive microeconomy;
- a modern cohesive society;
- a healthy population;
- a highly skilled population;
- sound environmental management;
- a globally connected economy;
- a solid research, development and innovation framework.

Again, much of this agenda is relevant to tourism innovation, particularly the importance of extra-firm and extra-regional connections to facilitate knowledge transfer (Chapter 3), but also the fact that the quality of the environment lies at the heart of the national tourism product. In order to build effective innovation the strategy stated that government would be concentrating its policies and resources in four areas (Clark 2002):

- enhancing the existing innovation framework;
- developing, attracting and retaining people with exceptional skills and talents who are able to innovate and so contribute to increasing overall productivity;
- increasing global connectedness to overcome the tyranny of distance;
- focusing innovation initiatives in areas where their impact will be maximized.

All four areas, of course, are potentially important for tourism. In fact, tourism was commented on within the GIF but only in marketing and imaging terms:

> In the past most of our international publicity has been focused around our environment and/or our sport. While this has been successful in attracting tourism, it does not necessarily encourage entrepreneurial migrants.
>
> (Clark 2002: 43)

> By showcasing New Zealand scenic locations, skills and talent, large budget [film and television] productions can generate significant benefits for our tourism sector and for other high-value added industries.
>
> (Clark 2002: 47)

> Offshore perceptions of New Zealand are outdated. While there is some

awareness internationally of our 'clean green image', from a tourism point of view there is too little awareness of New Zealand as an innovative country at the leading edge of knowledge.

(Clark 2002: 48)

The requirements for marketing ICT are very different to those associated with primary products or tourism, and the challenges arising from our distance to market need to be recognised in government assistance packages.

(Clark 2002: 61)

Perhaps the association of tourism with image rather than innovation lay behind the sector not being selected as a business area 'which can achieve the biggest impact' (Clark 2002: 49) and where government effort would be directed. In May 2002, the government established four taskforces for biotechnology, IT, design, and screen production (film and television). These are areas which were, and to an extent still are, a focal point of government innovation activity (Ministry of Economic Development 2005), reflecting the conventional focus of innovation policies on the so-called 'knowledge economy', or high tech sectors. However, the marketing of New Zealand as an innovative country does not appear to have changed (Box 5.4).

Box 5.4 'Innovative' Rugby Ball Venue to showcase New Zealand

New Zealand is to build a giant Rugby Ball Venue close to the Eiffel Tower during the final stages of the 2007 Rugby World Cup in order to showcase New Zealand tourism and trade to international audiences. The 12-metre high and 25-metre long structure, which will cost NZ$4.6 million to construct and operate, will stand on the Champs de Mars, and over 40,000 people are expected to experience a 'virtual' New Zealand. In the day time, the venue will be open to the public, promoting New Zealand tourism, businesses, culture, lifestyle, food and wine, and technology. In the evenings, it will become the hub for New Zealand-hosted trade and industry events, exhibitions, big screen viewing, functions and meetings, 'taking the best of NZ Inc. to the world'. According to Prime Minister Helen Clark:

> This is a bold and innovative move; an example of New Zealand's new thinking, and an example of a small country out to make a big impression. Just as we have leveraged off Lord of the Rings, the America's Cup regattas and Team New Zealand for the benefit of our trade and tourism and the overall New Zealand brand, so a similar programme will be taking place alongside the Rugby World Cup in France as the All Blacks compete . . . The eye-catching venue – in the shape of a giant rugby ball in central Paris enables us

> to showcase New Zealand's world-class talent for innovation and creativity.
>
> (Clark 2007)

According to Trevor Mallard, the minister for the Rugby World Cup, sport and recreation and industry and regional development:

> The Rugby Ball Venue is the first part of a four year build-up programme and co-ordinated cross-government strategy of leveraging activities as we work to maximise the benefits for New Zealand when we host the Rugby World Cup in 2011. All the events that will be held there will be aimed at increasing trade and tourism revenues, and attracting new investment partners and highly skilled foreign migrants, while other activities will look to celebrate New Zealand culture and sporting success.
>
> (Clark 2007)

The promotional approach with respect to the Rugby World Cup remains substantially at odds with the direction of the growth and innovation framework that was launched just five years earlier. As noted above, Prime Minister Clark stated then that '[o]ffshore perceptions of New Zealand are outdated. While there is some awareness internationally of a national "clean green image" from a tourism point of view, there is little awareness of New Zealand as an innovative country at the leading edge of knowledge' (Clark 2002: 48). The fact that New Zealand had reverted to a more traditional promotional strategy suggests at the difficulties in overcoming the legacies of previous readings of innovation and imaging campaigns, as well as the difficulties in promoting the intangibles of innovation compared to those of sport.

In March 2006 there was a shift in government policy with the focus moving towards 'economic transformation'. According to the economic development minister this is a strategy for securing New Zealand's future prosperity and forging a unique New Zealand national economic identity:

> The aim of the economic transformation agenda is to raise living standards for all Kiwis. To do so we need to carve out a New Zealand approach that will give us a New Zealand economy that is more productive, innovative and export-led – one that plays to our strengths and delivers high-value products and services for businesses and consumers around the world.
>
> (Mallard 2006a)

Economic transformation is a cross-departmental effort led by the Ministry of Economic Development. It comprises five themes: growing globally competitive firms; world-class infrastructure, innovative and productive workplaces; Auckland as an internationally competitive city; and environmental sustainability. The Cabinet Paper on Future Prosperity (Mallard 2006b) stated that, at the broadest level, economic transformation is about

creating a better life for all New Zealanders. Much of what New Zealanders value and desire in life is underpinned by a strong, healthy economy. A high-value, innovative and creative economy will mean:

- a great place to live, learn, work and do business;
- a country where its people enjoy higher incomes and more leisure;
- a country that has strong connections and relationships with the rest of the world;
- a socially cohesive place where diversity and ideas are valued;
- a country that provides quality health and education services; and
- a country with a healthy and sustainable environment.

Economic transformation is about ensuring that the economy is better able to continuously adapt and lift its performance. We need to be able to discover and capitalise on new opportunities and respond to threats to existing activities. Achieving this on a sustainable basis will make New Zealand more internationally competitive.

(Mallard 2006b: paras 13, 15).

Again tourism did not feature explicitly in the economic transformation strategy even though the Ministry of Tourism is a semi-autonomous body within the industry and regional development branch of the Ministry of Economic Development. However, the infrastructure theme is closely connected to issues surrounding the provision of transport infrastructure, while the theme of Auckland as an internationally competitive/world-class city also has potential implications for tourism, given that the city is the major international gateway into the country. The focus on Auckland, which is the largest population centre, may have longer-term implications for the economies and innovation capacities of other significant urban centres such as Christchurch and Wellington.

In New Zealand tourism is located in a separate ministry within the Ministry of Economic Development, which is also responsible for a number of other portfolios and areas, including regulation and competition, economic development and strategy, international trade, energy and resources, consumer issues, radio, IT and business services. Innovation was noted in the first New Zealand Tourism Strategy (2001) as one of the values that 'describe the characteristics that those involved in tourism in New Zealand are likely to exhibit. They contribute to making the New Zealand experience unique and also to how visitors feel about the experience' (Tourism Strategy Group 2001: 15). This was expanded to suggest:

- innovation in product development;
- free thinking to differentiate product and delivery;
- innovation in the way we manage the sector.

The only other time that innovation was mentioned in the document was with respect to partnerships. 'New areas for public–private co-operation are likely to be in technological innovation, policy making and legislative issues, and hosting of mega-events' (Tourism Strategy Group 2001: 20).

In 2007 the Ministry of Tourism launched a draft of a new national tourism strategy. Under the heading of 'tourism is at the forefront of a globally competitive and sustainable New Zealand' the strategy states that its core is 'increasing the value of tourism' (Ministry of Tourism 2007: 14). Again, innovation is not mentioned in the document. However, it does note that '[r]einvestment and new investment is crucial to maintain product, innovate and complete globally' (Ministry of Tourism 2007: 21) or in relation to the role of innovative products in the regional benefits of tourism (Ministry of Tourism 2007: 49).

New Zealand's 2006 Economic Transformation strategy acknowledges many strands of recent thinking about innovation, including global connections, social diversity and cohesion, and creating a social and environmental setting that will attract and retain creative, knowledgeable workers. Its failure to engage more with the tourism sector is a failure to acknowledge the importance of the sector to the national economy, or that – even given the sector's economic performance – its level of innovation is below the New Zealand average (Statistics New Zealand 2007). In either case, this stands in stark contrast to the high profile innovations in much of the New Zealand tourism industry in the areas of adventure tourism and culture (see chapters 8 and 9). Alternatively, it may herald the difficulties of shaping an effective national tourism innovation system, given the complex and composite nature of the industry.

Norway: 'a vision for the future'

The Government's vision
   Norway shall be one of the most innovative countries in the world, where resourceful and creative enterprises and people are given opportunities for developing profitable business. Norway shall be in the lead internationally in important areas, in terms of knowledge, technology and wealth creation.

(Ministry of Trade and Industry 2003: 5)

The overarching objective of the government's innovation policy is to facilitate increased wealth creation across the country so as to provide Norwegian society with the resources needed to achieve overarching welfare policy objectives. Increased wealth creation requires increased innovation on the part of Norwegian industry, particularly as current oil-wealth is regarded as standing in the way of an appreciation of the need for adaptation in much of the Norwegian economy. According to the Ministry of Trade and Industry (2003: 5):

> Innovation policy must be comprehensive, and adopt a long-term approach. This plan will contribute to a more coordinated and targeted effort, across various policy and administrative areas. We will at the same time improve cooperation between private and public sector players, and across different levels. Only in this way can we lay the foundation for high growth regions, future employment, and welfare.

The Norwegian government has defined the following objectives to ensure this:

- favourable and predictable conditions for trade and industry, offering a good overall foundation for innovation and wealth creation;
- an outstanding system for learning and education, offering industry access to people with relevant knowledge of a high quality;
- more research-based industry;
- more new start-ups with a potential for growth;
- an electronic and physical infrastructure promoting effective interaction between businesses, markets, knowledge centres and public authorities;
- a new administrative practice that facilitates the development of an effective, dynamic and comprehensive innovation policy (Ministry of Trade and Industry 2003).

It is a progressive vision for the future, which recognizes external connections, learning, human capital and institutions as being critical for innovation and economic development. More specifically, government measures to facilitate the development of an effective, dynamic and comprehensive innovation policy, include:

- appointment of a government committee for the development and coordination of policy design at the national level;
- inviting business representatives, and other key players within the innovation community, to regular contact meetings to improve cooperation between public authorities and private players for purposes of furthering policy design and implementation;
- identifying organizational solutions that ensure improved coordination between public administration levels and sectors;
- adopting performance measures and the development of indicators within key areas of importance to innovation, and develop systems for policy design evaluation and learning (Ministry of Trade and Industry 2003).

In order to achieve its innovation goals, Norway has reorganized the institutional arrangements surrounding innovation. The most significant initiative has been the establishment of Innovation Norway, which has merged ten previously separate organizations. Its main functions are regional development through funding of companies and individuals, providing guarantees for companies, running an international network of industrial and trade attachés (export council), promoting tourism, encouraging investment in Norway, developing competence, advisory activities, network development and support, assisting inventors and working with the Norwegian Research Council (Kotilainen 2005). The mission of Innovation Norway is 'to promote private and socioeconomic profitable business development throughout the country, and to release the commercial opportunities of the districts and regions by encouraging innovation, internationalisation and image building' (cited in Kotilainen 2005: 46). In addition to being able to access many of Innovation Norway's programmes, tourism is integrated into its activities as a means of providing visibility via city tourism, marketing and various campaigns, as well as being an enabler of innovation via providing study tours for representatives of tourism businesses and agencies.

As with other countries Norway's national innovation strategy does not specifically mention tourism. However, the Ministry of Trade and Industry, and the Department of Industrial Development and Internationalisation, which is a part of the Ministry, explicitly recognizes tourism as an integral part of the NIS. It notes: 'The promotion of Norway at home and abroad, innovation and the establishment of new enterprises, cooperation, quality control and an increase in the level of knowledge are all central elements for the travel and tourism industry' (Ministry of Trade and Industry 2007). By the end of 2007, it aims to have developed a national tourism strategy that will concentrate on the following areas:

- The profitability in the travel industry depends upon the ability to develop products that meet the demands of tourists. Therefore, innovation is essential. In relation to other businesses, the travel industry is characterized by low levels of innovation.
- Tourists want more knowledge and information from industry providers, resulting in a need for more investment in expertise knowledge.
- Cooperation between actors in the Norwegian travel industry is invaluable since tourists are increasingly requesting multiple-activity trips (Ministry of Trade and Industry 2007).

The Norwegian innovation system has undergone significant change since the end of the twentieth century. Although Norway still has substantial national financial reserves as a result of oil-wealth, with the anticipated decline in these revenues there is a recognized need for the economy to diversify, particularly into the services area. Therefore, Norway has substantial revised and expanded the capacity of the institutional arrangements for innovation.

Unlike several countries, tourism is explicitly connected into national innovation policy. As with the Australian, Canadian and New Zealand innovation systems, Norway's tourism strategy and lead agency is institutionally connected to a trade and development ministry. However, unlike these other countries, Norway recognizes tourism as an important component of its innovation strategy. The reasons for this are unclear. Norway's population size and environmental assets are similar to those of New Zealand, for example, yet Norway has appeared to have recognized the role of tourism as a potential means to leverage economic value from those assets in a much more sophisticated way than New Zealand. Moreover, the overall cultural basis for innovation policy in Norway creates some significant differences. For example, the development of women's role in business is explicitly recognized in programme terms, as are cross-sectoral relations. A final observation is that, although nationally funded, the innovation strategy is very strongly focused on the regions and on developing existing traditional sectors such as fishing and agriculture that also have a strong regional dimension. It is therefore possible that such an emphasis has made it more likely that tourism is drawn into discussion of the various development competencies and possibilities of each region as well as recognizing the role that tourism has in assisting the accessibility of such regions.

Taiwan: 'responding to future challenges'

In May 2002, Taiwan launched a six-year national development plan called Challenge 2008. Its vision was to develop Taiwan into a 'green silicon island' that balances the needs of environmental protection and economic development. The development plan was anticipated to cost an estimated NT$2.6 trillion (approximately US$75 billion) and to have the following outcomes:

1   Expanding the number of products and technologies which meet the world's highest standard.
2   Doubling the number of foreign visitors.
3   Increasing R&D expenditures to 3 per cent of the GDP.
4   Reducing the average unemployment rate of the next six years to less than 4 per cent.
5   Increasing the average economic growth rate of the next six years to over 5 per cent.
6   Increasing the number of broadband internet users to over 6 million.
7   Creating approximately 700,000 jobs (Government Information Office 2002).

Major reforms will focus on three areas: government, banking and finance. Investment will be directed toward four broad areas:

•   cultivating talent;

- encouraging research, development and innovation;
- improving international logistics;
- creating a high quality living environment.

The strategy of economic development includes:

- 'economy first, investment first, Taiwan first' to assist in cultivating a Taiwanese identity;
- economic liberalization and internationalization so as to meet the challenges of globalization and entry into the WTO;
- upgrading technological innovation and R&D to transform Taiwan into a high value-added manufacturing country;
- developing a global logistics management system to maximize geographic location and labour force advantages;
- promoting government efficiency.

Perhaps not surprisingly, these strategies reflect Taiwan's manufacturing-led drive for economic growth. The strategic industries selected within industrial technology policy are traditional industries with high value added such as high tech textiles, health food and care products, high-end materials, electro-optics, chemical materials, light metals, light high-efficiency electrically powered vehicles and sport/recreation products. However, services such as R&D services, information applications, logistics and care services are also being developed. Finally, so-called 'green industries' are also under consideration for development support, including resource sorting, green regeneration/utilization, and resource chemical engineering assistance (Kotilainen 2005). Perhaps the interest that different innovation related ministries attach to the development of environmentally related industrial sectors may be one reason why tourism is a named component of the national development plan. According to the Government Information Office (2002).

> The competitiveness of the tourism industry relies on innovations to develop, grow, and attract visitors . . . In order to increase the number of foreign visitors to five million, necessary breakthroughs include, discovering areas in Taiwan with tourist potential; establishing a mechanism which provides incentives for holding international meetings, conventions, and exhibitions in Taiwan; unifying interdepartmental efforts to promote international tourism; and coordinating with the private sector in advertising and promotion.

The economy of Taiwan, as with that of Norway, is undergoing rapid change. Norway has been seeking to buffer the loss of oil revenue while Taiwan is attempting to compensate for the loss of electronics manufacturing jobs to China, even though the final product is still being sold as Taiwanese. Interestingly, in both cases tourism is being recognized as a potentially significant component of an NIS, even though the primary focus of Taiwanese innovation is still technology oriented. Importantly, with respect to the wider relationship between tourism and mobility, the Taiwanese Science and Technology Policy Research and Information Centre, which is a government think-tank for innovation policy, has identified human resources and mobility as one of its major research themes (Kotilainen 2005). Furthermore, there is also some evidence that the innovation trajectory of Taiwan has been strongly influenced by particular social and economic factors, such as the necessity to utilize international networks for economic development post-1949 and the ongoing central role of the state in innovation and R&D, and that these have led to accumulated innovation capacity (Yim and Nath 2005). In the case of Taiwan there therefore appear to be several important structural dimensions that have increased the likelihood of actor recognition of the role of tourism as part of an integrated innovation strategy, compared to its neglect in several western countries.

United Kingdom: *Building a Knowledge Driven Economy*

The innovation challenge has been a clear theme of UK national government policy making since 1997. In that time the Department of Trade and Industry has published a number of White Papers on the issue including *Our Competitive Future – Building a Knowledge Driven Economy* (1998); *Excellence and Opportunity – A Science and Innovation Policy for the 21st Century* (2000); and *Opportunity for All in a World of Change – Enterprise, Skills and Innovation* (2001). In 2003 the Department of Trade and Industry produced *Competing in the Global Economy: The Innovation Challenge* which was, in effect, a national innovation strategy, and which defined innovation as 'the successful exploitation of new ideas' (Department of Trade and Industry 2003: 8).

The UK government envisions the United Kingdom as a key knowledge hub in the global economy, with a reputation for world-class scientific and technological discovery, and as a world-class model for turning that knowledge into new and profitable products and services. The innovation strategy identifies seven success factors for innovation performance:

- sources of new technological knowledge;
- capacity to absorb and exploit new knowledge;
- access to finance;
- competition and entrepreneurship;
- customers and suppliers;
- the regulatory environment;
- networks and collaboration.

Tourism is not mentioned in *The Innovation Challenge* although there was recognition that there is a need to increase the level of innovation in service industries if we are to meet the challenges posed by the outsourcing of low – value added administrative jobs to developing nations. Services accounted for 56% of GDP in 1981 and 72% in 20012. Our productivity in services is no better than in manufacturing when compared with our major competitors.

Technology is being used increasingly in areas such as retail banking and computer games to improve business processes and customer service, while almost a fifth of business Research and Development (R&D) expenditure today takes place in services.

(Department of Trade and Industry 2003: 9–10)

Box 5.5 Innovation and university research in the UK, 2007

The break up of the Department of Trade and Industry (DTI) was widely predicted before Gordon Brown announced his reorganization of British government, but what would fill the vacuum was unclear. One important change was directed at the research councils that are one of the two main sources of funding for research in higher education. Whereas these used to be sponsored by the Office of Science and Innovation, which was part of the DTI, after June 2007 they were overseen by the newly created Department of Innovation, Universities and Skills (DIUS), with a new minister for science and innovation. The creation of the new department was considered a significant shift in the UK's (formal) institutional landscape. The title of the department recognizes the almost totemic importance of science, human capital, and university–private sector knowledge transfers as lying at the heart of an innovative economy with a sustainable, skilled and creative workforce for the economy (see Tables 5.3, 5.4). Indeed, the official policy line from the new department is that it aims to 'make Britain one of the best places in the world' for research and innovation. There was also explicit recognition of the role of creativity and the creative industries, in the comments of Philip Esler, chief executive of the Arts and Humanities Research Council one of the research councils affected by this new institutional set up:

> Innovation is core to the research community, and we hope DIUS will be taking a broad perspective on this. The creative economies green paper, to be published in autumn, is a tremendous opportunity to put the role of the creative industries – about 10% of the UK economy – centre stage.
>
> In explaining our role, one of the challenges for arts and humanities communities has been a tendency for the government to converge 'technology transfer' with 'knowledge transfer'. Arts and humanities research does not necessarily create 'things', but it can offer a broader, more complex role in the creative economy.

Interestingly, in the same speech he went on to emphasize that academic training makes a key contribution to the need for a flexible and knowledgeable workforce in a knowledge-driven economy in a globalized world. He also identified three priorities, which tell us much about the competitive nature of innovation and innovation policies.

1   Defence of the protected allocations to science in the national budget.
2   Maintenance of the public support that he argues has given UK research an unrivalled dynamism, as evident in the fact that although the population of the US is five times larger than the UK, it only produces two and a half times as much science as the UK.
3   The importance of focussing on innovation in the service sector, which accounts for 80 per cent of the economy, especially the creative industries and financial services.

Table 5.3 Characteristics of top-500 universities in the Shanghai ranking, on a country basis

Good performers	Poor performers
• High budget per student • Wage setting by the university (except Belgium, Germany and the Netherlands) • High wages • Hiring is controlled internally by the university • Low rigidity in wages (measured as same seniority same wage; except in Switzerland) • High independence in setting curricula • Low percentage of tuition fees in the budget (except in the UK)	• More public universities • Low budget per student • High level of endogamy (university employment of its own graduates) (except in Finland) • Wage setting by the state (except in Finland) • High rigidity in wages (measured as same seniority same wage; except in Ireland) • State approves the budget (except in Italy) • Low percentage of competitive funds for research in the budget (except in Finland)

Source: Derived from Aghion (2007).

Of course, these are partisan views, reflecting partial interpretation of the innovation gap between the UK and the US, and the defences of particular forms of public spending in support of that. However, it also signals growing recognition of the importance, if not of tourism, at least of the culture industries, which are a near relative of the former (Cheshire and Malecki 2004).

Table 5.4 Shanghai academic ranking of world universities by country and region, 2005

Country/Region	Number of universities in top 100	Number of universities in top 500
US	53	168
UK	11	40
Japan	5	34
Germany	5	40
Canada	4	23
France	4	21
Sweden	4	11
Switzerland	3	8
Netherlands	2	12
Australia	2	14
Italy	1	23
Israel	1	7
Denmark	1	5
Austria	1	6
Norway	1	4
Finland	1	5
Russia	1	2
China	–	18
Spain	–	9
South Korea	–	8
Belgium	–	7
New Zealand	–	5
Brazil	–	4
South Africa	–	4
Ireland	–	3
Poland	–	3
India	–	3
Singapore	–	2
Hungary	–	2
Greece	–	2
Turkey	–	2
Mexico	–	1
Argentina	–	1
Czech Republic	–	1
Chile	–	1
Portugal	–	1
North and Latin America	57	198
Europe	35	205
Asia/Pacific	8	93
Africa	–	4

Source: Derived from Institute of Higher Education, Shanghai Jiao Tong University, Academic Ranking of World Universities 2005, http://ed.sjtu.edu.cn/rank/2005/ARWU2005Statistics.htm.

In 2007, a change of prime minister, with Gordon Brown replacing Tony Blair, signalled a significant change in the institutional landscape of formal innovation policies, if not of the NIS (see Box 5.5). However, despite a clear shift in national policy direction for innovation, tourism policy still remains the 'Cinderella' at the innovation ball. Tourism policy in the UK is highly fractured on regional lines with different regions adopting different structures and strategic directions. England, Scotland and Wales have adopted three quite different approaches to public involvement in tourism. In England, the government has decided that devolving most of the responsibility for tourism development to the regional level will provide the best return on its expenditure – largely abandoning a *national* tourism policy, let alone a national tourism innovation strategy. In Scotland the area tourist boards have now been brought under the control of the national tourist authority, VisitScotland, signalling a counter move to greater centralization. Wales has combined national coordination with independent tourism development at the regional level. The Welsh Department of Enterprise, Innovation and Networks has strengthened its control over tourism marketing and development by taking over the Wales Tourist Board, while setting up four Regional Tourism Partnerships to develop and implement regional tourism strategies (Janson 2006).

The outcome is blurred policy responsibilities, fragmentation and substantial policy confusion. At the time of writing, VisitBritain, the national tourism agency, had no tourism strategy. The web page of VisitBritain's Tourism Strategy and Government Policy revealed a list of 35 government departments and agencies with their web addresses. Although this does reflect the extent to which tourism potentially diffuses through national policy systems – the very essence of a national innovation strategy for tourism – and why the state often acts to coordinate tourism policy (see Chapter 4), this simply underlines the lack of such a strategy in England. In contrast Scotland and Wales have well developed tourism strategies both of which place substantial emphasis on innovation. Scotland's strategy notes that as part of an action plan for the future,

> [t]here needs to be a culture of enterprise and innovation across the industry to drive continual investment in new products and services that build on Scotland's tourism assets and deliver fresh, engaging and distinctive visitor experiences which reflect modern consumer interests; and we need to harness new technology to deliver those products and services effectively.
>
> (Scottish Executive 2006a: 16)

In order to enhance innovation, a tourism research network and a tourism innovation group, which will foster greater collaboration between operators, are being established. However, it is interesting to note that the Scottish Executive has drawn substantial distinctions between what the state would pay for with respect to innovation and what they believed should be a private sector responsibility. For example, in comments on the draft strategy, suggestions as to the need for a Skills Challenge Fund and an E-Commerce Challenge Fund (training and skill development programmes that would be paid for by the state) met with the following response:

> No. The public sector will support the industry by developing and delivering training provision. However, there will often be a cost to take up this training. Nevertheless, having the right skills will enhance your business and therefore your bottom line. Investment in training is therefore an investment in your business.
>
> (Scottish Executive 2006b: para. 40)

The Welsh tourism strategy also places substantial emphasis on innovation with the vision for 2013 being '[a] customer responsive, innovative, sustainable and profitable industry which makes an increasing contribution to the economic, social, cultural and environmental well being of Wales' (Welsh Assembly Government 2006: 9). One of the four strategic aims also refers to '[a]ccepting that there is a value to be gained from doing things differently to our competitors through innovative ways of working' (Welsh Assembly Government 2006: 9). Reference to innovation occurs many times in the document. It is too early to tell what differences this will make to the Welsh tourism industry but there is a clear attempt to connect Welsh tourism with the Welsh innovation system, although there is no connection with the UK NIS. The innovation connection probably comes about at least partly through formal institutional influences, as tourism is the responsibility of the minister for enterprise, innovation and networks within the Department for the Economy and Transport. In addition, the regional innovation dimension has been strategically targeted as the tourism strategy was revised in order to coincide with the European Structural Funds Programme scheduled for 2007–13 (Welsh Assembly Government 2006: 6) – an example of the multi-layered nature of the governance and government of tourism innovation policies.

Conclusions

This chapter has provided an overview of NISs by examining countries whose innovation systems are often referred to as exemplars in the international research literature in innovation (e.g. Lundvall *et al.* 2002; Kotlainen 2005). Some clear conclusions can be drawn from the discussion:

- Tourism is generally ignored as a target sector in national innovation policy, which generally has refocused from the manufacturing sector to tightly delimited notions of 'the knowledge-based economy'.
- Tourism firms or organizations receive only miniscule amounts of direct financial support from national innovation funding in relation to its supposed economic and employment significance. This is not restricted to

the countries reviewed above. For example, an analysis of the 12,222 projects involving SMEs funded across the EU's Fourth (FP4), Fifth (FP5) and the Sixth Framework Programmes (FP6) found that only 89 – less than 1 per cent – mentioned tourism in their project descriptions and, of those, not all were tourism related (Tables 5.5 and 5.6).

- Tourism is poorly connected with NISs where this is expressed through either national innovation policy or tourism policy. Moreover, these two policy arenas, surprisingly, are also mostly poorly connected with the notable exceptions of Norway and Taiwan.
- As a result of the growth in its relative economic importance, the service sector is gradually becoming recognized as an area of innovation opportunity. However, this is mostly in relation to advance business and producer services, such as finance and design, and does not usually refer to tourism services or, indeed, most consumer services.
- Even where national tourism policies do acknowledge the importance of tourism, these rarely extend beyond aspirations, usually related to product and market innovation. Only exceptionally do they address other types of innovation, such as process or organizational (see Chapter 1). Furthermore, there is generally a failure to specify how these broad goals, or aspirations, can be encouraged or achieved, and the role of the state in this, whether directly or indirectly. Dedicated tourism innovation programmes are rare, which is no less than astounding given the links between innovation, productivity and competitiveness (see Chapter 2). Tourism strategies and policies are also poorly connected with innovation policies.

Some of the potential reasons for the disconnection between tourism and innovation systems have been noted in earlier chapters. However, the critical factors are likely to be related to the overall perception of tourism as a weak basis for sustainable economic development and value creation. In part this

Table 5.5 Key word citation in projects involving SMEs funded across FP5, FP6 and FP7 in the EU, 1998–2008

Citation term	Projects
Technology	7,974
Innovation	4,533
Information technology	2,930
Health	2,832
Environment	2,353
Transport	1,934
Food	915
Biotechnology	750
Tourism	89
No. of projects	12,222

Source: After CORDIS (Community Research and Development Information Service), http://cordis.europa.eu/en/.

Table 5.6 Analysis of tourism-related projects involving SMEs funded across FP5, FP6 and FP7 in the EU

Focus of project	Tourism focused	Benefit to tourism
ICT	29	17
Environment	–	16
Energy	1	7
Planning, evaluation and strategy	3	5
Education and training	2	–
Health	–	3
Transport	–	2

Source: After CORDIS, http://cordis.europa.eu/en/.

perception may also be related to the tourism industry's failure to influence policy agendas in developed countries (Hall 2008a), which is rooted in the weak and fragmented organization of tourism interest groups (Shaw and Williams 2004: chapter 2), as well as a lack of understanding in both tourism and innovation policy circles of the potential enabling role that tourism plays in innovation *across* the economy.

Where innovation and tourism are better connected there appear to be strong institutional elements at work. The example of the Welsh Assembly government being a case in point with respect to political institutions where tourism is relatively effectively tied into broader ministerial and departmental foci on innovation. Being a sub-section of Ministries of Trade or Economic Development, as in the case of Australia or New Zealand, does not necessarily provide for linkages with innovation policies either. In fact, having a separate Ministry for Tourism although potentially being perceived as giving a policy profile to the industry (Hall and Jenkins 1995), may only serve to create policy silos in which different policy networks, such as those related to tourism and innovation, operate. It is also possible that there is greater potential for recognition of the role of tourism in some of the institutions that support regional rather than NISs.

Several reasons can be suggested why this may be so. There is greater potential recognition of tourism's economic contribution, or at least influence on policy makers in the local state. This would potentially be the case in Wales, Scotland and, to an extent, Norway. However, it does not explain the case of New Zealand where although tourism is often cited as one of the largest industries, and is tied in with national branding campaigns, it was not considered an element of innovation or economic change strategy. Additionally, it can be argued that national innovation policy is dominated by global level discourses, driven by bodies such as the OECD or the World Bank. The dominant discourses, as for example that on the knowledge economy, are informed by current understanding of what drives economic performance (and innovation) in the most advanced countries. It is difficult for tourism to gain entry into such discourses. Indeed, it is notable that countries such as

Norway and Taiwan are arguably less influenced by global-level discourses because of their substantial capacities for greater economic, cultural and political independence in some key respects, and as such are charting more of an independent direction.

In contrast, although the same international discourses permeate the local and regional levels, these are also more open to the interests of local business elites, and have to turn policy rhetoric into concrete measures that engage with the realities of economic activity – including tourism. The lack of recognition for tourism in NISs may also reflect a longstanding (mis)perception that tourism is not a 'serious industry', does not significantly add value, and is not a driver of economic development – none of which are tenable as generalizations, of course – and is therefore only given 'lip-service' in policy terms (Hall and Jenkins 1995). It may also reflect a situation in which economies that imitate the neo-liberal global innovative and competitive discourse, whether at the national or regional scale, may have different institutional settings than innovative ones. This is an issue that we will address in more detail in the next chapter.

6 The regional innovation system

Territorial learning, regions and cities

Introduction

The notion that territorial agglomeration provides the optimum context for an innovation-based learning economy promoting localized learning and endogenous regional economic development has become well established in the innovation literature (Asheim 2002; Asheim and Coenen 2004). From such a perspective, innovation is 'an intrinsically territorial, localized phenomenon, which is highly dependent on resources which are location specific, linked to specific places and impossible to reproduce elsewhere' (Longhi and Keeble 2000: 27), so that the regional and local levels are also important sites for innovation. Such perspectives have been closely allied with two key related concepts: regional innovation systems (RISs) and clusters. As Asheim and Coenen (2004: 2) emphasized: 'Even though both concepts are closely related, they should not be conflated.' This is an error which has been common in the relevant tourism literature on the subject (Michael 2006). Indeed, the failure to distinguish between the two concepts is a reflection of the capacity of policy makers and their advisers, to utilise 'off-the-shelf', 'best-practice' cluster, regional innovation or competitiveness solutions drawn 'from the experience of successful regions or some expert manual' (Amin 1999: 371).

This chapter focuses on the regional innovation system. First, it focuses on the development of the concept and the reasons why innovation systems are regarded as having a meso or regional dimension. Three particular features are identified: the collectivity that defines a region, the so-called 'soft' aspects of economic activity, and the extralocal or spatial innovation system. A typology of RISs is then provided that highlights different categories of RIS with respect to aspects such as sectoral diversity, sectoral innovation, and competitive strategies. The typology draws on the discussions in earlier chapters to highlight the differences between imitative strategies and 'genuine', or more precisely, disruptive or radical innovation in learning regions. Tourism is often prominent in imitative or low-road strategies but this is not necessarily the case, as tourism can make a substantial enabling contribution to RISs.

The regional innovation system

The concept of an RIS first appeared in the 1990s (Cooke 1992, 2001), several years after the development and application of the NIS concept by Freeman and Lundvall (see Chapter 5), with the RIS also drawing parallels with concepts such as the innovative milieu (Aydalot and Keeble 1988; Camagni 1991) and technology districts (Saxenian 1994). Both NIS and RIS draw on the notion that systems of innovation are systems of dynamic and complex interactions between actors in networks, with particular institutional features. However, there are differences as to the scale of territorial analysis, in part reflecting different institutional settings and innovation needs, as well as the specific social situations within which innovation systems operate. Given the substantial focus on regional economic and governance systems in the EU, as opposed to the more centralized economic decision-making context of Japan, in which Freeman (1987) first applied the concept NIS, it should not be surprising that European scholars, and those within federal systems, have focused substantial attention on RISs. Indeed, Lundvall *et al.* (2002: 226) recognized that a weakness of the system of innovation approach, 'is that it is still lacking in its treatment of the power aspects of development', including the relative distribution of power within the institutional arrangements of state systems.

As noted in Chapter 5, the NIS approach focuses on the role of nationally-based institutions and interaction between actors in explaining the difference in innovation performance and economic growth between countries. However, in many national systems, the distribution of decision-making power in a number of innovation-related policy areas can be best understood at a meso or regional scale. Furthermore, the meso level is crucially where non-proprietary and intangible higher order industrial capabilities are developed and maintained by the interactions among firms (Oinas and Malecki 2002). This does not undermine the importance of the NIS but rather reinforces one of the key themes of the book – that innovation is highly contextualized and should be understood as being embedded within various, but inter-folded, economic, political and cultural scales. The development of the capabilities crucial for innovation, as well as innovation itself, is a relation specific process. As Lundvall and Borrás noted in their report to the EU (1997: 39): 'the region is increasingly the level at which innovation is produced through regional networks of innovators, local clusters and the cross-fertilising effects of research institutions'.

There are a number of reasons therefore why innovation systems need to be understood as having a regional dimension. Drawing in part on Tödtling and Kaufmann (1998), these include:

1   Important preconditions for innovation such as the qualification of the labour force, and the availability of educational institutions and research organizations are tied to specific regions. Research organizations may

even be located deliberately so as to assist in regional development, thereby giving some regions an innovation advantage over others.

2   Clusters are often highly localized, giving rise to networks between firms and public organizations at the regional level. Often these networks go beyond the mere exchange of goods and services and include 'untraded interdependencies' whereby, for example, information relevant for innovation is shared.

3   Interactions between knowledge providers and firms such as university–industry links, knowledge spillovers and spin-offs are often localized since they work through the mobility of persons within local labour markets, and through face to face contacts between actors. Under certain conditions this may lead to high tech development in specific regions.

4   Regions have taken a more active and stronger role in innovation policy in recent years. Many regions, for example Wales and Scotland (see Chapter 5), have developed innovation policies and plans and have become active in supporting technology transfer and innovation activities. Often these concepts included strengthening particular industrial clusters in the region. In Europe, these efforts have developed in parallel with EU innovation policy (e.g. the Framework Programme) leading partly to joint (regional–EU) support programmes. For example, the Welsh tourism strategy had been deliberately synchronised with the availability of funding for European regional programmes (Chapter 5). These are illustrations of multi-layered governance (Chapter 4). In the European context, as well as other semi-federal, or full federal systems where a reallocation of central government funds to regional innovation programmes is possible, for example Australia and Canada, some regions may have strong financial incentives to foster formalization of RISs. It should be noted, however, that there is considerable controversy as to the extent to which RISs can be designed or imposed via strategies, as opposed to growing organically.

5   Due to the interactions between firms, knowledge providers and policy actors, a common organizational culture may develop in a regional production system that, under certain conditions, supports collective learning and innovation, thereby contributing to a specific trajectory of development and innovation. However, in some cases it is possible that systems may become too closed and networks too rigid and 'lock in' may occur leading to a failure at absorb new firms or ideas – especially those external to the region – and a subsequent reduced capacity to adjust to new challenges, and prevent a slow slide into collective decline.

6   Within many countries, 'specific regions tend to bring about a large share of the outcomes which, in the NIS framework, would be regarded as the accomplishments of national systems of innovation' (Oinas and Malecki 2002: 105).

Because of the ways that scales are folded together (Amin 2002), regions obviously are shaped by and shape the national level. However, they also have scope to 'go their own ways', and to contest global challenges differently, thereby diverging from national averages with respect to the configuration of the facilitators of innovation, such as the education and training systems, scientific and technological capabilities, industrial structure, interactions within the innovation system, and openness to external factors (Oinas and Malecki 2002). As the UK Ministry of Trade and Industry commented:

> There are considerable regional differences as regards the focus on devel-opment, growth and innovation. Differences in terms of industrial struc-ture and distances to important markets and relevant knowledge centres may also translate into different innovation capabilities. In addition, con-tinued conversion from capital- and labour-intensive industries to more knowledge-intensive industries may result in a lower level of economic activity in rural areas.
>
> (Ministry of Trade and Industry 2003: 8)

To this we can also add Hudson's (1999) telling comment that too many easy assumptions are made about the ways in which 'learning region' or other such models are transferable between regions. In particular, he poses the question of how regions with poor learning records can unlearn as a precursor to becoming more innovative.

Definitions of the RIS vary, but central to them is the notion of how the institutional and cultural environment of a region interacts with the activities of private firms to influence the innovation process (Holbrook and Wolfe 2000). Nauwelaers and Reid (1995: 13), in a review of European regions, provided an influential definition of an RIS as: 'the set of economic, political and institutional relationships occurring in a given geographical area which generates a collective learning process leading to the rapid diffusion of know-ledge and best practice'. As with the NIS, regions differ quite strongly in their ability to develop an effective innovation system. Tödtling and Kaufmann (1998) suggest three factors that may be responsible for such variations in the European context:

- Firms in a region differ in their ability to innovate due to their sectoral specialization, as well as their functional and organizational charac-teristics.
- Firms in a region differ in their propensity to interact depending on the existence of clusters, networks and the attitude of actors towards cooperation.
- Regions differ in their capacity to construct relevant institutions (for example, in research, education, training, technology transfer) and in their 'governance model', which is dependent on their decision-making powers, financial resources and their policy orientation.

As a result of these differences, it can be expected that 'some regions have no or a weak innovation system while others have systemic interaction to a higher degree' (Tödtling and Kaufmann 1998: 5).

The concepts of 'cluster' and RIS are closely related but are different. An RIS may include several sectors from the regional economy (although sectoral RISs also exist). In fact, as long as there are firms and knowledge organizations that interact systematically, an RIS can be said to exist. This can be contrasted with the definition of a cluster as 'a concentration of interdependent firms within the same or adjacent industrial sectors in a small geographic area' (Isaksen and Hauge 2002: 14). This means that clusters and RISs may co-exist in the same territory but that an RIS may contain several (or no) clusters. However, depending on the particular sets of relationships involved, a cluster is not necessarily a part of an RIS (Asheim and Coenen 2004). However, it should be noted that Porter's use of the cluster concept tends to conflate cluster and RIS: 'A geographic concentration of interconnected companies, specialized suppliers and service providers, firms in related industries and associated institutions (e.g. universities, standard agencies and trade associations) in particular fields that compete but also cooperate' (Porter 2000b: 253).

Although there are several ways in which the elements of an RIS can be categorized, for present purposes three features of regional and local innovation systems are particularly significant:

(1) The collectivity that encompasses and defines a region in its entirety. This includes all the firms of the main industrial clusters of the region as well as individual firms, including their support industries located within the region. They constitute various kinds of networks, both within the region and externally (supplier/client, cooperation, and information/knowledge networks) through which relevant information flows and interactions are enacted. These will be complemented by industrial associations and other organizations, and by public bodies that aim to support business and organizational networks that aim to lower innovation barriers. Financial institutions are also significant because of potential obstacles to innovation posed by lack of access to capital. R&D organizations, laboratories and universities act as potential knowledge suppliers. However, they only become effective elements of the innovation system if they interact with firms in the region and effect knowledge transfers. The characteristics of the labour force, that is of human capital, is another component of the innovation system and this is linked to the activities of education and training organizations. The existence of pools of skilled and knowledgeable, often mobile, workers can contribute to the creation of knowledge communities, and to positive knowledge spillovers. The overall net effect of the various networks is to reduce the transaction costs of innovation, including the associated levels of risk.

(2) The emphasis put on the 'soft' aspects of economic activity. This includes governance and learning capacities, and social and intellectual

capital, that promote certain historical trajectories of technology and innovation that are based upon localized 'sticky' knowledge as well as the attraction of appropriate 'ubiquitous' knowledge (Asheim and Isaksen 2002). Place specific, contextual knowledge of both tacit and codified nature is, in combination, rather geographically immobile and therefore may represent a significant 'soft' resource for innovation and competitiveness. In addition it also includes some of the intrinsic characteristics of place with respect to its attraction as an environment to live and work in, such as housing, amenities, social diversity and tolerance, and the natural environment. This 'soft' dimension of economic activity has been integral to the contentious notion of a creative economy (Florida 2002) and the design of liveable cities and regions (see Chapter 3). Significantly, the soft aspects of economic activity tend to be substantially place bound and relatively immobile. The significance of such soft dimensions is conveyed by the following statement from the Communauté Métropolitaine de Montréal (CMM) in their economic development plan (see Box 6.1):

> Quality of life – access to housing, education, employment, health care, culture, recreational green space, safety, etc. – is a variable with a tremendous effect on competitiveness. Quality of life also includes tolerance and cultural diversity. Although the Montreal metropolitan area is known for its excellent quality of life, it must still do more to protect and enhance its natural spaces, preserve and improve the quality of its built heritage, increase the diversity of its neighbourhoods, safeguard and optimize the use of its agriculture zone and enhance the free flow of people and goods.
>
> (CMM 2005: 6)

Box 6.1 An international future? A competitive Montreal region

> In today's global economy, the world's major metropolitan areas are essentially competing against one another. As a result, the Communauté Métropolitaine de Montréal (CMM) must do two things: fully understand economic globalization and prepare a bold economic development strategy to meet the challenges of international competitiveness. The very future of Quebec's metropolis is at stake.
>
> (CMM 2005: 3)

In 2003 the CMM adopted a strategic vision for the economic, social and environmental development of Montreal. Entitled *Charting Our International Future: Building a Competitive, Attractive, Interdependent and Responsible Community*, the vision outlined what the CMM could become by the year 2025:

A *competitive community*, because, if Montreal is to regain its position as one of the world's leading metropolitan regions, we must strive to be the best.

An *attractive community*, because we must optimize our assets, fulfill the expectations of our citizens and attract more people to the metropolitan region.

An *interdependent community*, because we must fight social exclusion, reduce the school dropout rate, and increase the number of immigrants contributing to our development.

A *responsible community*, because we intend to provide continuous information and an 'online government' to ensure that our citizens are involved in decision-making.

The economic development strategy is fourfold: the Montreal metropolitan community must become and remain: (1) a learning region; (2) competitive and prosperous; (3) attractive; and (4) world-class. The key issues that the region faces include:

- *An ageing population*. The Montreal population is ageing faster than the populations of other North American metropolitan areas.
- *Insufficient immigration*. Particularly of educated, highly skilled immigrants and business people.
- *An economy that has undergone radical restructuring and has a changing industrial base*. Since 1997, the region's job rate has climbed faster than the rate in any other metropolitan area in North America – the gap between Montreal's rate and the North American average fell to 0.9 points in 2002, compared to 6 points in 1993–7.
- *Issues of human capital*. The Montreal region has the lowest GDP per capita of the 26 largest urban areas in North America and is ranked 44th out of the 65 OECD metropolitan areas with populations over two million. In 2001, 20 per cent of the population held university degrees, compared to nearly 38 per cent in the most productive regions in North America.
- *Insufficient investment*. FDI has jumped since the late 1990s and, as of 2002, accounted for over half of all private sector spending in the metropolitan area. Although venture capital is perceived as being relatively accessible, most of it comes from public sector organizations rather than private foreign investors and returns are often unsatisfactory.
- *Demands of globalization*. Globalization has accentuated the need to transform Montreal's economy into a knowledge-based economy. By stimulating the production of manufactured goods and specialized services, globalization is regarded as increasing the demand for educated workers and reducing the demand for unskilled labour.

- *Quality of life.* Is regarded by CMM as a 'a variable with a tremendous effect on competitiveness' (2005: 6).
- *More efficient infrastructure.* The cost of rebuilding the metropolitan area's municipal infrastructure is estimated at nearly CDN$600 million annually. The transportation system also requires attention because it influences the location decisions of firms and their competitiveness.
- *Diversified revenue sources.* Like all Quebec municipalities, Montreal municipalities depend on property taxes as their prime source of revenue. From 1996 to 2002, municipal revenues rose only 12.5 per cent, compared to a 41.4 per cent increase in provincial revenues.
- *A cosmopolitan, Francophone culture.* Montreal is unique in large North American cities for its Francophone character:

  > According to the Bohemian Index – defined as the percentage of the population employed in creative and artistic occupations – Montreal ranks 10th among the 43 North American urban centres with populations of over 1 million, behind Toronto (4th), but ahead of Boston (12th). The Mosaic Index – the percentage of a city's population that is foreign-born – puts Montreal 7th within the same group of urban centres. In the highly competitive world of major metropolitan areas, Montreal must focus on its distinctive culture and diversity to attract investors and immigrants' (CMM 2005: 6).

- *A concern for social cohesion.* The Montreal metropolitan area has higher levels of poverty and unemployment than its two main Canadian competitors, Toronto and Vancouver. It also has a relatively low level of social housing in comparison with other North American urban centres.
- *Principles of sustainable development.* Sustainable development goals need to be drawn up to incorporate economic and land use planning, and transport management.
- *Coordinated action.* In a review of Montreal, the OECD emphasized that the metropolitan area needs to encourage maximum participation in its development by creating, for example, partnerships among the public sector, the private sector and civil society.

When defining the context of its economic development strategy, the CMM identified five global trends that particularly affected the region and to which it would need to respond in order to achieve its goal of increasing economic growth:

1   metropolitan regions as the engine of prosperity;
2   knowledge as the focus of the new economy;

3   industrial clusters as a stimulating, winning strategy;
4   the metropolis as a key to innovation;
5   creativity as a dynamic growth factor.

Given this context and the global challenges that are regarded as being pertinent to the city, the CMM identified four key strategies to make the Montreal area: (1) a learning region; (2) competitive and prosperous; (3) attractive; and (4) world-class; moreover, these would contribute to the region exceeding its projected growth rate of 2 per cent per annum up to 2025. These strategies are tied in with the goal of 'catching up' the top five North American cities in terms of GDP per capita: Boston, San Francisco, Denver, New York and Washington. Significantly, tourism is specifically identified as a component of the region's strategy within the context of the competitiveness strategy, which is founded on developing industrial clusters and encouraging synergistic collaboration among the actors in the region's production and innovation system.

In 2003, the CMM launched a project to identify and define metropolitan industrial clusters. This move was the first phase of a large-scale project aimed not only at developing, but also implementing an integrated innovation and economic development strategy for the entire region by September 2005. The CMM identified 15 different clusters in the metropolitan area, representing nearly 80 per cent of employment in the region. The large number of clusters partly reflects the area's diversified economy. Table 6.1 illustrates the characteristics of the four major types of clusters in the Montreal region as well as the role of the CMM as a key regional institution.

In order to assist the development of cluster initiatives and strategies, a number of additional actions will be taken including:

- Creating a competitiveness fund financed by the Canadian and Quebec governments, the CMM and firms to support major projects stemming from cluster development strategies.
- Giving a non-profit organization the mandate of providing the Montreal metropolitan region with an innovation strategy for area businesses.
- Drafting an international strategy for the Montreal metropolitan region that includes market position, branding and an approach for attracting foreign investment.

The role of tourism as a part of the 'visibility clusters' category suggested that it is not necessarily seen as innovative in its own right but is regarded as important to supporting the overall RIS:

> These clusters help market the metropolitan area by providing invaluable support to development efforts. These strategic clusters

Table 6.1 Characteristics of clusters in the Montreal metropolitan region

Type	Description	Contributing industries	Criteria	Role of CMM
Competitive clusters	Competing clusters that bring together internationally competitive segments	• aerospace • life sciences • IT • textiles and clothing	• world leader • role as economic engine • national importance • strong externalities	• planning and goal definition • coordination and monitoring
Visibility clusters	Strategic sectors for a city region's socio-economic development and branding	• culture • tourism • services	• obvious presence • multiple activities • importance for innovation	• support for production of the region's social and creative capital
Emerging technology clusters	Cross sectoral technologies with high, long-term growth potential	• nanotechnologies • advanced materials • environmental technologies	• sustained, multifaceted R&D • importance for future development	• support for technological and sector-based innovation
Manufacturing clusters	Clusters with growth potential that are based on the use of natural resources	• energy • bio-food • petrochemicals and plastics • metallurgy • paper and wood products	• diversified segments • geographically dispersed businesses • major industries	• support for local, regional and sectoral planning

Source: CMM (2005).

are essential to ensuring the overall quality of life that nurtures the dynamics of innovation. They all help make the metropolitan area more attractive.

(CMM 2005: 11)

This strategy, and the role it allocates to tourism, strongly echoes Florida's ideas about creative regions (Chapter 3). It also reinforces the need for a holistic understanding of RISs.

Sources: After CMM (2005); OECD (2007).

The importance of quality of life factors in regional economic development and innovation provides a significant cross-over into tourism that is acknowledged in the tourism literature, but not recognized as 'tourism' in the innovation literature. For example, books on tourism planning highlight the

importance of the adoption of community planning strategies and appropriate design so as to ensure a positive quality of life for local residents and
positive experience for visitors (for example, Hall 2008a). In addition, the
provision of positive place specific externalities is regarded as an important
element of the imaging of a destination, including the development of particular place brands (Page and Hall 2003; Shaw and Williams 2004). The
recognition of such factors is indicated by the OECD:

> A first consideration for regions is the actions that they can take to
> support the regional environment generally, in terms of physical, human
> capital and . . . other innovation assets. Many of the overall regional
> strategies focus generally on the attractiveness of the region for residents
> and the business community. The common denominator in current think-
> ing about territorial policy – including in relation to knowledge and
> innovation – is an emphasis on place-specific externalities based on
> exploiting unused potential. Policy instruments now tend to focus on
> providing collective goods that improve what has been termed the enabl-
> ing environment or the quality of place – the attractiveness and function-
> ing of the region as a whole.
>
> (OECD 2007: 71)

In this perspective, tourism and tourism, hospitality and leisure-related firms
and organizations therefore have an important *enabling* function for the RIS
as a whole, as well as assisting in its *visibility* in national and international
markets, not only for products but also in attracting people, firms and capital.

Unique attributes of regions, such as their environment, culture and social
networks, cannot easily be imitated, and firms can use this to secure competitive advantage, which is particularly prized given difficulties in establishing
property rights over knowledge in this area (see Box 6.2).

(3) Extralocal connections. These include the transport, finance, scientific,
technological, information and communication accessibility of the region to
other actors in national and international innovation systems, as well as markets. This accords with Bathelt *et al.*'s (2004) notion of there being 'global
pipelines' through which knowledge flows and learning are realized. For
example, transnational tourism firms, such as hotel chains, travel companies
and airlines, are actors who transfer technologies or other innovations through
international flows, realized via FDI, strategic alliances, transnational labour
mobility, and communities of practice (see Chapters 3 and 8). Furthermore,
some areas of innovation, particularly with respect to technology, are characterized by significant coordinated sectoral innovation in multiple regions. In
the case of some European projects, such as aviation, this may have been
integral to policy design and rooted in government support (Frenken 2000).
Extralocal connections are important because the learning processes that are
central to innovation occur at multiple scales, with both local and distanci-
ated networks usually being implicated in successful innovation projects: 'In

Box 6.2 The intellectual property of place

Firms draw on characteristics unique to their particular location, including the natural environment, labour force, physical infrastructure, local institutional relationships and linkages, and use these to secure competitive advantage. However, firms associated with products from specific regions may also gain a competitive advantage by associating with the place name or brand. Therefore, the intellectual property associated with regional and/or country names has become a significant area of intellectual capital that places and governments seek to protect. One of the key concepts is that place names are geographical indications that 'possess qualities or a reputation that are due to that place of origin' (WIPO 2006). The reputation of the region adds value (that is, place brand value) to products from the region and therefore they have intellectual property (cultural capital) that can be legally protected. A number of international treaties administered by the World Intellectual Property Organization (WIPO) and the WTO exist to protect intellectual property rights including geographical indications. These are particularly important for food and wine products, for example Champagne, as indications of quality, as well as other specific place associations with products. Tourism is also a beneficiary of place name protection as it can assist with place brand positioning and awareness in the marketplace, as well as in the attractiveness of a number of industrial tourism products such as food and wine tourism.

particular for projects of innovation and product development when it is usually necessary to combine both local and non-local skills and competences in order to go beyond the limits of the region' (Asheim and Coenen 2004: 8). Similar comments are observed by the UK Ministry of Trade and Industry:

> Geographical proximity between players will typically enhance [knowledge spillover] effects, and may contribute to the development of so called clusters. However, too much of a focus on local relations may come at the expense of national and international relations, and may result in a community blocking out external impulses. Consequently, international contact for purposes of tapping into new knowledge is of importance to the ability of a region, an industry, or a country to innovate. Innovation itself is often multidisciplinary, and successful innovations depend on product-specific competency being supplemented by other skills.
>
> (2003: 10)

Infrastructure provision is of crucial importance for urban and regional economic growth. The growth of agglomerations is limited by the capacity and quality of their infrastructures. For this reason, successful regional policy always requires a complementary transportation infrastructure policy. Tourism plays a significant role in enhancing extralocal connections via the availability of transport infrastructure. Although business travel or tourism is usually not explicitly recognized as significant in the innovation literature, the importance of accessibility infrastructure (telecommunications and transport) is. For example, the OECD review of regional innovation with respect to globalization and regional economies identified infrastructure concerns as a key issue in many of its case study regions. For example, while the Netherlands constitutes a transport and logistics gateway in Europe, around the Randstad area (which includes Amsterdam and Rotterdam), the IT clusters in the Eindhoven region are not as well served by the different transport networks. Similarly, in Ottawa, the lack of direct flights to Europe (other than to London) and northern California was viewed as a problem for the IT cluster. This represents a significant weakness, given that Silicon Valley is Ottawa's largest business partner and largest source of foreign venture capital (Box 6.3).

In contrast to Ottawa, the main metropolitan regions tend to be more concerned with accessibility within the urban region as they usually already have in place good international and national transport connectivity (OECD 2007). For example, in Stockholm the IT cluster is predominantly located in a science/industrial park on an axis between the main airport and the city

Box 6.3 Flight from Ottawa to Silicon Valley: discussion page

Discussions	Flight from Ottawa to Silicon Valley
01.59 pm 31/01/2007	It was great to see the article on a direct flight from Ottawa to San Francisco or San Jose.
	I travel to SJ every 2nd or 3rd week. The extra hop through Chicago, Toronto or Montreal has been a real hassle in terms of delays, extra time, . . .
	Because Ottawa is difficult to get to; my VP's who are based in SJ are somewhat reluctant to travel here. WE NEED A DIRECT FLIGHT. . . .
Comments	
Anonymous 09.03 pm 01/02/2007	Direct Flight In the good old days of the tech boom, we did have a direct route but that disappeared along with other things in the subsequent tech bust.
	The direct route was good for JDSU as they had the dual head-office situation (Ottawa, San Jose) and they even had their own plane for the big-wigs during the company's glory days.

Anonymous 08.19 am 02/04/2007	Re: Direct Flight Ottawa is somewhat at a disadvantage due to its close proximity to Toronto & Montreal in getting better air service to certain markets in the USA or overseas. Air Canada would rather cut costs by making the passengers connect on a short 'puddle jump' via those cities than offer direct service. Same applies with AIR FRANCE & KLM . . . they offer bus service from Ottawa or codeshare certain flights with Air Canada thus forcing the passenger into connecting.
Anonymous 10.32 pm 02/06/2007	Re: Re: Direct KLM Flight to Amsterdam via Montreal At least the Ottawa Montreal bus for Amsterdam is faster than the next-best KLM interlined with NW Air connection which is via Detroit. This requires pre-clearance in Ottawa, a 90 minute flight to Detroit, and a three hour wait in the terminal. The flight to AMS is then an hour and a half longer than it would have been direct from Ottawa or Montreal. You also have US border taxes etc in your ticket. Unfortunately the only way to book this is via a travel agent. Going to the KLM site sends Canadians to the NW site and they do not recognize the existence of the Ottawa bus – why?
04/05/07	**Ottawa International Airport Authority sponsored article**
[Not part of discussion thread but same publication]	Most travelers prefer to fly non-stop to their destination. Ottawa International Airport facilitates that with scheduled and charter flights to over 30 destinations. Even when traveling to a city without a non-stop flight, the good news for Ottawa business travelers is that no matter where you're going, you can get there from Ottawa. Ottawa is connected to several of the world's most important hub airports . . . The majority of business travel, which represents the bulk of Ottawa's 3.8 million air passengers, and the majority of flights from Ottawa are within Canada. Is Ottawa well connected? Yes. Is there demand for more air service from Ottawa? Definitely yes. The Ottawa International Airport Authority continually markets the airport and the National Capital Region to airlines, building the case that certain new routes will be supported by the community. Support in every form helps our case, including business travelers who fly directly from Ottawa, rather than using a competing airport. Flying Ottawa first helps build the data needed to strengthen the business case for new flights from Ottawa and makes the region an attractive market for new or enhanced services.

Sources: Ottawa International Airport Authority (2007); Ottawa Business Journal (2007).

centre. However, the high-speed airport access from Arlanda airport to the city does not stop there – adding significantly to the firms' transaction costs.

Although accessibility is regarded as significant (e.g. OECD 2007), Oinas and Malecki (2002) argue that the role of extralocal connections for the RIS has not received due attention in the literature (see also Lagendijk and Oinas 2005). They also propose that the concept of a spatial innovation system (SIS) is an appropriate way of conceiving of technological linkages in time and space that are located in and between RISs. SISs are the simultaneous and interdependent development of components of technological systems in two or more RISs, utilizing spatial divisions of labour, resources and intellectual capital, and possibly in more than one NIS. The connectivity between the RISs allows knowledge flows to occur in a co-evolutionary fashion.

> [N]o innovation system is located in one place only. This is why it is not enough to focus on particular RISs in trying to understand technological change. Instead, the development of a technological system takes place via the coterminous evolution of its various components in space and time. It is supported by an interlinked set of social relations in a number of RISs of different levels of socioeconomic development, (semi-) integrated by the requirements of a technological system, resulting in a distinct spatial division of labor in that system. Technological systems are not autonomous of the place-specific RISs where they originate or are transferred because local conditions may be decisive for sustaining creative interaction in making progress in specific technologies.
>
> (Oinas and Malecki 2004: 108–9)

The key elements are:

- the technological systems (the sets of technologies in use in specific inter-linked industries) or 'paths' themselves;
- the RISs that participate in creating the technologies or parts of them;
- the actors (firms and institutions) whose interaction locally and over space ultimately brings technologies about, as well as their (proximate or more distant) relations.

Tourism is implicated in the notion of SISs if only because of the notion of business tourism being one of the mechanisms that allows this interaction over space, and the maintenance and refreshing of distant relations. But the co-evolution of business and leisure tourism, and their joint generation and user of transport links, indicates that tourism also plays a significant indirect role in SISs.

A typology of RISs

The identification of the different technological systems that regions are connected to, and which are scaled in different ways, provides a means of distinguishing between different types of RIS. 'Such distinctions are important, as SISs consist of various kinds of activities with different levels of sophistication organized in space (within and between different RISs) according to a division of labour that is specific to each SIS' (Oinas and Malecki 2004: 111). Industrial diversity is regarded as significant as research indicates that diverse regions are more effective in promoting innovative firm behaviour than specialized industrial regions. Kelley and Helper (1999), for example, found that regional industrial diversity was especially significant for the innovation capacities of small firms because they necessarily lacked such diversity internally. Oinas and Malecki (2004) argue that the SIS becomes significant for the RIS, and relationships between actors, because of the insights it provides into relationships between firms: in contrast, diversity itself does not reveal the basis of inter-firm relations and, therefore, levels of engagement in innovative interaction. Therefore, attention to SISs draws attention not only to intra-regional relations between firms but also those that occur externally between RISs, or between firms, either as part of particular sector innovation systems, or in terms of accessing specialized knowledge.

A typology of RISs can therefore be established out of an assessment of the relative technological trajectories of regions and their relative industrial diversity. Oinas and Malecki (1999, 2004) identify three types of RIS with respect to their ability to bring about innovation:

- *Genuine innovators*: These are regions in which genuinely novel combinations take place and best practice occurs. All stages of innovation cycles may exist within them as they host actors able to exploit mature innovations as well as actors seeking radical innovations. These regions also maintain competitive and collaborative relations with other leading RISs.
- *Adaptors:* These regions mostly engage in innovations by incremental innovations, potentially leading to higher quality. The RIS in such locations is able to adopt new innovations from external sources early in the innovation cycle and improve on them.
- *Adopters*: These are RISs in which innovations diffuse relatively slowly. Learning is undertaken by imitative strategies that produce mature products that are not significant improvements on the original innovation but which still have a market due to being part of more routine production systems. In the case of services such as tourism, an approach of serial reproduction may be innovative in regional markets but may not prove competitive on a larger geographical scale.

The interweaving of industrial diversity and relative maturity at the regional scale is outlined in Table 6.2. The labeling of the various categories used by Oinas and Malecki (2004) have been retained for reasons of consistency rather than scale. As the table suggests, the trajectory of each RIS does not mean that it is not possible to move from one category to another. This is particularly the case in the tourism sector where some locations, which were initially specialized tourism destinations, have diversified over time, perhaps as a result of having a desirable living environment that generated the in-migration of people and capital over time. In the cases of the Gold Coast and Sunshine Coast (SE Queensland, Australia), and Las Vegas (Nevada, US), municipal and regional governments have been extremely active in trying to diversify the sectoral base so that local economies are not over-dependent on tourism even though it is still seen as a key element of the economy. Such an approach could be contrasted with that of some Mediterranean coastal regions where there has been little attempt to diversify from tourism and related sectors.

Table 6.2 A typology of RISs

Characterization of region	Regional competitiveness strategies	Sectoral diversity	Sectoral specialization
Genuine innovators (best practice regions)	HIGH ROAD – network enhancing • Enhancing internal and external (non-regional) networks • Benchmarking assessments • Investing in superstructure and infrastructure • Scanning globally for new knowledge • Development of information and communication networks • Development of external transport links, especially airline and airfreight links, and good intra-regional links • Tourism as enabler	STARS Location of leading-edge innovations. The RIS is maintained by the multiple relations among diverse industries. Close links are also maintained with other stars. i.e. Silicon Valley, Stockholm.	SHOOTING STARS Survive as long as they are able to on the strength of an innovation or a set of inter-related sectoral specific innovations. In production terms an example would be Detroit. In tourism terms historical examples would be Atlantic City (casinos), Las Vegas (casinos and entertainment) or Margate (seabathing). Contemporary examples include Queenstown, New Zealand (adventure tourism) and the Napa Valley (wine and food tourism).

| Adapters (regions of relatively high levels of diverse competences) | MIDDLE PATH – growth enhancing <ul><li>State funded programmes for training and fostering entrepreneurs intellectual property</li><li>Structures to help and mentor new firms and entrepreneurs in the form of business advice and the reduction of uncertainty</li><li>Local state as coordinator and an investor in infrastructure</li><li>Tourism as enabler and to give visibility to region</li></ul> | LIVING ROOM LAMPS/RISING STARS Host actors maintain close links with non-local sources of innovation as well as local connections so as to improve local production conditions, for example, Hong Kong, or Manchester. These regions may also be rising stars, particularly with the input of government assistance, that may lead to genuine innovation, for example, Singapore. | SPOTLIGHTS Engage in mainly incremental innovation through strong external connections. Able to respond to relatively advanced R&D-related improvements. In tourism terms an example would be Macau (casinos and heritage tourism) which has strong connections to Las Vegas and Portugal. In some cases sectoral innovation systems may provide sufficient non-tradable environmental assets to attract other industries and increase sectoral diversity. Las Vegas in the US or the Gold Coast in Australia provide examples of sectoral diversification while still retaining a strong tourism focus. |
| Adopters (regions with production-oriented competences) | LOW ROAD – zero sum and imitative <ul><li>Place marketing and promotion. High emphasis on visibility</li><li>Focus on capturing mobile investment, firms and capital</li><li>Focus on tourism (visitors) on the basis of numbers</li></ul> | CHANDELIERS Regions where many sectors are co-located but are not strongly linked with each other. They are, in effect, islands of isolated industrial activity. Such co-location may even have been supported by government funds | CANDLES Survive as long as their relatively simple production-oriented competences are supported, in production terms, by externally-based customers or corporate structures, or in service terms, a |

(Continued overleaf)

Table 6.2 Continued

Characterization of region	Regional competitiveness strategies	Sectoral diversity	Sectoral specialization
	• Subsidised investment and means of production, e.g. sites and premises	as well as improvements to the innovative milieu with respect to education, finance and infrastructure, that is, Auckland, New Zealand; Bangkok, Thailand.	regional market that has no consumption alternative.

Source: Derived from Cheshire and Gordon (1998); Oinas and Malecki (1999, 2004); Malecki (2004); Hall (2007, 2008a).

Destinations whose attraction is based on natural resources do not fit easily into sectoral categorizations, although even here the construction of demand around particular fashions changes over time, and innovations may be required to sustain growth. Examples of such destinations include the Niagara region of Canada which, although originally based on the Falls, has since diversified to include cultural attractions, wine and food tourism and casinos, as part of the development of a more complex destination product with appeal to a wider market, or enhanced capacity to generate return visits.

Low roads or high roads for tourism?

The specific trajectories of different RISs potentially display some similarities to the life cycle of tourism destinations (Butler 1980), a model that also considers the potential of innovations to 'rejuvenate' mature destinations. Significant in such an assessment is the role of SISs that provide connectivity, not only to other sources of knowledge but also improved access to markets in the case of transport innovations. The significance of access has been highlighted in reviews of the tourism area life cycle concept (Coles 2006; Hall 2006) and was also noted as important in Butler's seminal article, but subsequent critiques of the subject have usually failed to recognize the importance of changes in spatial connectivity (access) as a driver of changes in visitor numbers to destinations. Market access aside, the extension of the life cycle of a destination via rejuvenation strategies is also typically connected with the import of innovations from other locations. Examples of such imports include theme parks, casinos, mega-shopping malls and ferris wheels (such as the 'London Eye'), as well as entire redevelopment strategies, particularly with respect to former industrial waterfront areas that include hybrid retail/leisure/tourism complexes, and those that focus on the branding of cultural or heritage districts.

Many such 'local' innovations have been realized through access to transnational firms that develop the local innovation, with possible minor modifications to different cultural and institutional settings, from a template that has been established in a 'home' RIS (see Chapter 3 on the transfer of knowledge by transnational companies). This particular model is especially evident with respect to large-scale casino development that is dominated by the investment, management and/or consultancy services of a relatively small number of companies. For example, in 2005 Harrah's Entertainment, the world's largest gaming group, announced agreements to develop Caesars-branded gaming resorts at Ciudad Real in Spain, the Caribbean's largest single phase resort in the Bahamas; and a resort in Slovenia as part of a joint venture with Hit Group, Slovenia's largest casino operator. Previously Harrah's had developed casinos in Australia (subsequently sold off) but, as of 2007, it owned or managed land-based, dockside, riverboat and Indian casino facilities in most US casino jurisdictions, and owned or managed properties in Canada, the UK, South Africa, Egypt and Uruguay (Harrah's Entertainment 2007). Similarly, MGM Mirage had taken a shareholding in a casino development in Macau, and had been unsuccessful in bidding for a casino in Singapore (see Chapter 7).

As with NISs, RISs have significant contributions from the local and, sometimes, national-state. This arises out of innovation policies as well as part of broader goals of place competitiveness. Such perspectives are exemplified by Kotler *et al.*'s (1993) statement that we are living in a time of 'place wars' in which places are competing for their economic survival against other places and regions not only in their own country but also throughout the world:

> All places are in trouble now, or will be in the near future. The globalization of the world's economy and the accelerating pace of technological changes are two forces that require all places to learn how to compete. Places must learn how to think more like businesses, developing products, markets, and customers.
>
> (Kotler *et al.* 1993: 346)

There are both benefits and problems inherent in place competition, within which tourism is clearly embedded. As this and previous chapters have indicated we can identify in alternative approaches to innovation and regional development, a contrast between what might be termed 'low-road' and 'high-road' policies (see Table 6.2). Within the general literature on innovation and regional development, tourism is primarily seen as part of an imitative 'low-road' policy in contrast to an innovative 'high-road' knowledge-based strategy (Table 6.2). Malecki has noted:

The disadvantages of competition mainly concern the perils that low-road strategies build so that no strengths can prevail over the long term, which presents particular difficulties for regions trying to catch up in the context of territorial competition based on knowledge.

(2004: 1103)

Boxes 6.4 and 6.5 provide illustrations of these strategies in Singapore and Dunedin (New Zealand).

Low-road strategies focus on 'traditional' location factors such as land, labour, capital, infrastructure and locational advantage with respect to

---

Box 6.4 Tourism development and innovation in Singapore

Singapore has sought to create a more diversified economy and to reduce its dependence on electronic exports. Consequently, it aims to increase the amount of international visitor arrivals and is focusing on developing casinos and other entertainment attractions to grow tourism's contribution to GDP, which was about 5 per cent in 2007. The government wants to double the number of visitors to 17 million a year by 2015, while nearly trebling tourism receipts to US$30 billion. Casinos would also help Singapore recover much of the US$180 million a year it is estimated that Singaporeans spend each year in neighbouring Malaysian casinos (BBC 2005). Focusing on newly affluent Chinese, Indians and other Asians who increasingly travel internationally, Singapore had begun work in 2007 on several new attractions, including two big casinos, a Universal Studios theme park, and a ferris wheel. It had also won rights to host Formula One racing, which was expected to raise its profile abroad and generate US$150–200 million a year.

In a bid to generate more entertainment 'buzz', it has opened clubs such as Ministry of Sound and is pitching to be a film location for Bollywood blockbusters such as *Krrish*, which Singapore hopes will attract more Indian tourists. A number of developments, even though imitative, are designed to compete with other regional attractions, particularly Macau (casinos) and Hong Kong. Although the casino developments have been controversial within Singapore, it was regarded by government and key business stakeholders as integral to the strategy for doubling visitors. Two casino contracts were awarded. The first was awarded to gaming firm Las Vegas Sands for more than US$3 billion. Sands runs the Venetian in Las Vegas and a casino in Macau. The Singapore government has stated that it wants the waterfront site to become an icon for the city-state (BBC 2006a). The second, also for US$3 billion, was awarded to Malaysian firm Genting International, which already runs a casino in Malaysia, and includes a Universal Studios theme park (BBC 2006b).

The question of legalizing casinos had sparked an unprecedented public debate in Singapore, with almost 30,000 people signing a petition against the idea. But Prime Minister Lee Hsien Loong said the casinos were necessary to help Singapore attract more tourists: 'We want Singapore to have the x-factor – that buzz that you get in London, Paris or New York, he said, saying that his country was in danger of becoming a "backwater" ' (BBC 2005).

Box 6.5 Dunedin and the low road to development

Dunedin, in the South Island of New Zealand, exemplifies some of the economic development issues faced by smaller urban centres. Previously, one of the manufacturing and industrial centres of New Zealand, the city has been affected by successive waves of restructuring since the late 1960s, as a result of changes in the New Zealand and global economy, leading to substantial changes in employment structure, closures and relocations of firms, and reduced population growth.

In Dunedin, as with many other cities, the low-road approach has been adopted, as illustrated by Dundein City Council (DCC) measures such as rates relief for businesses as well as market support programmes, youth wage subsidies, and the construction and lease back of premises. Although these represent a 'low-road' approach that can be easily replicated by other regions, they were embraced by Dunedin in 2006 as an integral component of its 'economic renaissance' (One News 2006). The city also embarked on an attempt to increase direct airline links with Australia through a NZ$21.5 million redevelopment of Dunedin International Airport, as part of what was known as 'Project Gateway'. However, two of these trans-Tasman connections have since ceased.

More recently, the fusion of urban entrepreneurialism with neo-liberalism has provided the ideological justification for place competitive re-imaging strategies, including hosting mega-events. This has affected a number of smaller urban centres in New Zealand, including Dunedin, with respect to hosting the 2011 Rugby World Cup, whereby local policy coalitions are arguing for the development or upgrading of sports stadia for a one-off event, even though such stadia will remain under-utilized subsequent to such events. This is a significant local economic policy debate as such developments are being primarily paid for out of public funds rather than those of sports associations or the event itself. There are therefore high opportunity costs in relation to other strategies to enhance the RIS. In Dunedin, a new covered 25,000-seat stadium on land adjoining the University of Otago has been proposed by the Carisbrook Stadium Trust as the best of option it for securing the future of the existing Carisbrook stadium (Burdon 2007). The stadium, costing an estimated NZ$188 million, would – according to the Carisbrook Stadium Trust chairman, Malcolm Farry – 'revolutionise our city and create a new vibrancy to our region' (cited in Page 2006). The website of the Our Stadium Visionaries Club (OSVC), a group supportive of the stadium proposal, stated under the heading of 'New heart of the region will pump':

> This will become a new heart for the region. And like Westpac Stadium in Wellington or the Telstra Dome in Melbourne, the stadium will lead a change of land use and is predicted to kick start significant investment in North Dunedin.
>
> International and national events attract extensive media coverage and each year television would beam the Otago brand into the living rooms of millions of homes worldwide. Without this exposure, Otago would become a forgotten territory, adding an incentive to the northward drift of its businesses and allowing other centres to capture the imaginations of thousands . . .
>
> (OSVC 2007a)

The OSVC chairman, Sir Clifford Skeggs, prominent local businessperson and former mayor, is quoted on the home page: 'Big projects often get captured by a noisy minority who claim to speak for everybody. They don't. Our job is to unite the positive people in the region and their voices will make the local authorities decision to say YES a much easier task' (OSVC 2007b).

The new facility would be New Zealand's only rugby stadium with the capacity to close its roof. At the time of writing, it was proposed that funding for the stadium would come mainly from DCC (NZ$65 million), Otago Regional Council (NZ$30 million) and Otago University (NZ$10 million, with an additional NZ$30 million to NZ$40 million to fit out its facilities in the stadium). The Carisbrook Stadium Trust chairman, Malcolm Farry, said that cheaper options had been looked at but they did not have the support of the university, which would provide financial backing and oversee the day-to-day usage of the stadium. According to Farry, this was preferable to incremental changes to the existing Carisbrook stadium, which would never generate sufficient revenue to meet operating costs. He also added that the new stadium could attract 400–500 more students to the university, which would generate, via multiplier effects, an additional NZ$25 million– NZ$60 million in the region (Burdon 2007).

A (necessarily selective) reader response poll conducted by the Otago Daily Times (2007) showed that 82 per cent of respondents were in favour of the new stadium proposal. However, many of the respondents clearly echoed concerns over place competitiveness:

I see it as a vital requirement for this city if it is to promote itself into the future with pride and self respect. To fail to provide this visionary facility will mean that we, today's citizens, will be letting our future generations down in a very big way . . . This stadium will be a focal point in Dunedin for at least the next 100 years, and it is my belief that the people of tomorrow will be saying something like we say now of our railway station. What a wonderful building it is, imagine Dunedin without it.

(Bill Thompson cited in Otago Daily Times 2007)

We must not drop off the list of important places in New Zealand . . . It is unthinkable that important events are held no further south than Christchurch.

(Vic Isbister cited in Otago Daily Times 2007)

Yet the sustainability of such serial place competitive strategies, let alone their real benefits, are increasingly questionable. In the case of Dunedin, funds invested in a new stadium are unavailable for investing elsewhere, while developing a new stadium in Dunedin or even just redeveloping Carisbrook only serves to match recent stadia developments or redevelopments in other New Zealand cities: Auckland, Christchurch, Hamilton, Tauranga and Wellington. All these cities have larger market catchment areas than Dunedin. The extent to which a new stadium would revolutionize the city in terms of economic development is therefore questionable. Yet critics of the hosting of sporting events in New Zealand as an economic and social development mechanism are doubly hampered by the image of regeneration via the visibility of stadium development, as well as the mythology of the social benefits of sport (Hall 2005). Many large-scale sport infrastructure and event projects continue to be publicly funded because they provide opportunities not only for furthering sport and the real-estate interests of growth coalitions, but also for local politicians to be seen to be 'doing something' in the face of global place competition.

Dunedin also supports high-road strategies such as improved education, health and communications, and a diversified job creation strategy that are more likely to have significant longer-term benefits for regional economic and social well-being. For example, DCC has fostered close relationships with the activities of educational and research institutions, such as the University of Otago, including direct funding of entrepreneurship-related positions, as well as support for new colleges of residence. Moreover, the DCC places emphasis on quality of life factors. As Dunedin Mayor Peter Chin commented: 'You get a sense of belonging, that you're part of something. Dunedin has a sense of community that makes everybody feel good' (cited in Aynsley 2006: 20). Indeed, as Malecki (2004: 1109) observes, in smaller urban centres that cannot really afford the highly visible development projects of larger cities, even though they may try, it is the 'soft' cultural and social variables that 'matter most for regional development: institutions, leadership, culture and community'. Nevertheless, it is important to recognize that many such high-road strategies are not as immediately tangible and visible to ratepayers as compared with, for example, the construction of a new building or stadium.

Source: Hall (2007).

markets or key elements of production, as well as direct state subsidies to retain firms: more intangible factors, such as intellectual capital and institutional capacity, are secondary. Low-road strategies are generally regarded as being tied into property-oriented growth strategies linked to the packaging of the place product, re-imaging strategies and securing media attention. For example, investment in infrastructure such as meeting and convention facilities, sports stadia, event facilities, entertainment and shopping malls is often imitated from city to city because they are aiming at the same visitor markets, with few places being able to 'forgo competition in each of these sectors' (Judd 2003: 14). Such low-road strategies can lead to the serial replication of homogeneity of the waterfront marketplace, heritage precinct, art gallery, museum, casino, marina and shopping centre. This process was described by Harvey (1989: 12) as being a part of 'urban entrepreneurialism' whereby 'many of the innovations and investments designed to make particular locations more attractive as cultural and consumer centers have quickly been imitated elsewhere, thus rendering a competitive advantage within a system of cities ephemeral'. More recently, the fusion of urban entrepreneurialism with neo-liberalism has provided the ideological justification for place competitive re-imaging strategies including the hosting of mega-events (Peck and Tickell 2002).

Arguably, popular media presentation of what it takes 'to win' in regional competition also influences the entrepreneurial strategies employed by some, or even many, places (for example, see Aynsley 2006 on New Zealand's major cities). The established serial reproductive strategies are now being added to by concern about the 'people climate' (Malecki 2004), including amenities and culture and the attraction of the 'creative classes' as an element in competitiveness (Florida 2002). The focus on amenity and creativity as elements in the stickiness of places, as well as being essential to innovation and learning, has been long recognized. However, there is often insufficient attention given to how development strategies actually serve to differentiate one place from another with a standardized 'check-list' for becoming a 'creative city' or 'competitive', being transferred from one region to another in imitative policy making or rote learning. Such a view has developed even though the discourse of place competitiveness 'is based on relatively thinly developed and narrow conceptions of how regions compete, prosper and grow in economic terms' (Bristow 2005: 291). For example, with reference to the key determinants of place competitiveness, Deas and Giordano (2001) argue that the literature tends to offer a 'one size fits all' approach to identifying the drivers of competitiveness, even though there has been inadequate empirical research to ground this.

In contrast to the low-road approach, Malecki (2004) argues that a high-road approach of genuine innovation through the development of learning regions is possible although it is a more difficult path to follow. RISs that utilize agglomeration economies, institutional learning, associative governance, proximity capital and interactive innovation (Cooke 2001, 2002) may become the rising stars of regional development. Regional infrastructure, both hard (communications, transport, finance) and soft (knowledge, intellectual capital, trustful labour relations, mentoring, worker–welfare orientation, quality of life), is required to encourage (disruptive) innovation rather than adaptation (see Box 6.6 for the example of Manchester).

Box 6.6 Manchester: cultural capital and the high road to development

The writer Bill Bryson once described Manchester as 'a perennial blank – an airport with a city attached'. The picture is very different now. Over the past 20 years, the city has staged a dramatic turnaround and is now so successful it is snapping at Birmingham's heels to become England's second city.

(Bawden 2007)

Culture is the City's 'fingerprint' – the unique characteristics that make it different from any other city. Everyone has something to contribute to the cultural development of our City. It is the diversity, skills and ideas of our community that make Manchester a creative city where people choose to live, work and visit.

(MCC 2007)

In 1995 Manchester's economy was valued at £25.6 billion, but it increased 58 per cent in the subsequent 10 years to £40.4 billion in 2004. The city has also hosted the Commonwealth Games and become recognized as a major creative centre. Describing itself as a 'cultural capital', there are 10.5 million visits to key cultural attractions in the city each year. Much of this success can be put down to the city's dynamic and stable leadership. A policy double act for more than a decade, Sir Richard Leese, the leader of Manchester City Council (MCC), and the chief executive, Sir Howard Bernstein, have been instrumental in transforming the city's fortunes. Bernstein says the political leadership of Manchester has been outstanding and argues that the winning formula mostly stems from the priority placed on regeneration and genuine commitment to the city:

> Manchester's enjoyed a renaissance over the last 20 years . . . We started from a low position. Now we are approaching the threshold where, if we can get it right, we can make lasting change. Success needs passion, drive for the place and the ability to roll one's sleeves up and work their socks off . . . Regeneration is not for the short haul. You have to be very resilient, passionate and have focus.
>
> (Cited in Bawden 2007)

The MCC's strong ties with neighbouring local authorities is a significant contribution to Manchester's success. Only 430,000 people live within the municipal boundaries – but more than two million live in the Greater Manchester area. The conurbation has a long history of collaboration. The Association of Greater Manchester Authorities (AGMA) was set up in 1986, after the abolition of the Greater Manchester Council. The ten local authorities in the conurbation – Bolton, Bury, Manchester, Oldham, Rochdale, Salford, Stockport, Tameside, Trafford and Wigan – cooperate across a wide range of services. Blackburn with Darwen, Blackpool and Warrington councils are associate members. As well as leaders of the ten councils, the executive also includes the chairs of the fire, police, waste disposal and passenger transport authorities. Such is the degree of cooperation that, in 2006, AGMA put forward proposals to formalize its partnerships by creating a city region. The city region would be led by an executive board, with greater levels of autonomy over planning, skills, transport and economic policy.

Manchester Enterprises, the Chamber of Commerce and Midas (Greater Manchester's inward investment agency) have also drawn praise for their role in the region's booming economy. One of the main reasons for success in attracting new businesses is being able to develop a significant level of trust to enable the area to operate a single economic development agency, investment agency and chamber of commerce across Greater Manchester. Finance and professional services are a focus, with the hope that more US banks will follow the Bank of New York in establishing operations in the city. Creative and digital industries, building on Salford's success in luring the BBC there, as well as biotechnology and life sciences, are also being supported. Over 22,000 people are employed in cultural businesses in the city and £395 million has been invested in sports facilities, museums, art galleries, theatres, parks and squares. However, development of the northern part of the city has been less successful although there are plans to increase new residential housing and employment in the area. Manchester's cultural strategy, which uses the tag-line, 'our creative city' aims to secure 'recognition and support for the City's regeneration as a vibrant cultural capital [and] to encourage greater participation of local residents in cultural activities' (MCC 2007). Tourism is, of course, inextricably linked with the cultural industries, and tourists constitute a critical component of demand for these activities.

Sources: Derived from Bawden (2007) and MCC (2007).

Conclusions

Although regarded as integral to the development of innovative strategies, the soft infrastructure of learning, knowledge and interaction is difficult to plan, manage and measure. The cognitive aspects of an RIS are also difficult to change quickly, particularly when faced with a long history of 'ways-of-doing', or routinized behaviour and institutions, in business that shape perceptions of competition, cooperation and innovation (Maillat 1995). As Malecki (2004: 1108) noted: 'The objectives are less sporadic or ephemeral than permanent, incremental and focused on long-term development.' This therefore raises political problems for politicians and growth coalitions who are often geared towards demonstrating competitive success in relation to election cycles. Yet, the higher road with its focus on the construction of territorially rooted immobile assets (Amin and Thrift 1995; Brenner 1998; Asheim 2002) inherent in RIS and learning regions, takes considerably longer to achieve than the periodicity of local and national election cycles. Indeed, it is often much easier to build a science or industrial park or a stadium with university faculty attached as symbols of local innovation than it is to create an intense bundle of interaction between firms and institutions. Therefore, those places that are perceived by political, business and public stake-holders as not having potential to generate returns quickly from investing in the high-road path to competitiveness are in danger of shifting back to low-road imitative learning strategies of urban entrepreneurialism (Leitner and Sheppard 2002):

> [O]nly a very small number of regions can attain the characteristics needed to be a 21st-century economy. A large number of the necessary ingredients (i.e. in particular, those that are not ubiquitous) cannot simply be imposed from the top down, but grow out of the region or community, and this can take a long time.
>
> (Malecki 2004: 1114)

As noted above, this is not to suggest that although often conceived as part of a low-road strategy of territorial competition (Cheshire and Malecki 2004), tourism does not have a part to play in the development of RISs. On the contrary, high-road strategies emphasize connectivity, through transport and aviation as well as communication linkages, and high levels of amenity that may attract visitors as well as being important for residents. In addition, high-road approaches tend to place value on cultural diversity. However, from a regional innovation perspective, tourism development in the high-road context is an enabler of human mobility and networks that support RISs rather than being a goal in its own right, although tourism can be a significant contributor as part of a range of interrelated sectors. In the vast majority of locations, tourism can most effectively contribute to regional innovation and development over the long-term through establishing linkages with other sectors. Indeed, as Doel and Hubbard (2002: 263) argue, policy makers need to 'replace their place-based way of thinking with a focus on connectivity, performance and flow'.

7 Firm organization
and innovation

Introduction

Sectors and firms are as integral to the notion of innovation systems as they are to the study of innovation as a whole. This chapter looks at the notion of a tourism sector system of innovation, as well as firm innovation. As Malerba (2005a: 9) observed: 'Innovation takes place in quite different sectoral environments, in terms of sources, actors and institutions. These differences are striking.' In particular, we seek to identify some of the elements of innovation that may be particular to tourism innovation systems and/ or tourism firms.

The chapter is divided into three main sections. The first discusses the tourism sector innovation system. The second examines tourism firm innovation and presents a model of the tourism firm that highlights the key innovation aspects. Finally, the chapter discusses issues of firm survivability and innovation.

The tourism sectoral innovation system

The previous chapter examined tourism within the context of RISs. Tourism was identified as being a significant enabling factor for all innovation systems and was also regarded as being important for the visibility of the 'rising stars' (outstanding exemplars) of regional innovation. However, it was also noted that there was a danger of tourism being used in a highly imitative learning form that was likely to produce little real innovation, except in a highly localized context, and is perhaps better understood in context of territorial competition. In addition, issues were raised with respect to the extent that places would be better positioned economically by having a specialized or diverse economic base.

The question of whether industrial specialization or diversification promotes more consistent, higher rates of, or more innovative, economic growth has received considerable attention in the regional science and innovation literature (for example, Glaeser 2000; Cheshire and Malecki 2004). In the US, Drennan (2002) found that specialization was preferable for optimizing innovation, and found no evidence of spillovers from R&D into other sectors, while employment effects appeared concentrated in the same sector, thereby reinforcing specialization. In contrast, Quigley (1998) suggested that diversity improved regional economic performance, while a number of studies also found that diversity contributed to increased innovation (for example, Kelley and Helper 1999; Duranton and Puga 2000). As Cheshire and Malecki (2004: 257) comment, 'the answer lies in which question is being asked. If spillovers of knowledge are the focus, diversity may well be advantageous. If employment impacts are the issue, specialisation in the "right" sectors of the moment may be best.' This is an observation that has implications for broader policy objectives with respect to innovation and industrial development as well as for tourism. In addition, we can note that the answer to this critical but consistently puzzling question is also affected by how it is asked, with different methods and theories being called into play, as well as different scales of, differently inter-layered scales of, analysis. Furthermore, any response to this question is temporally specific: the time period under examination is critical, so that the effects of 'wildcard events' (or external shocks), such as economic or political crises, are not unduly factored into any time series analysis of growth and innovation. The key to unravelling the issues around this question, as Duranton and Puga (2000) suggest in an urban situation, is that there is likely to be a need for both diversified and specialized industrial approaches, depending on the local and national contexts for innovation, and how these are inter-related. The most critical aspect is that whatever a region's developmental trajectory, it must avoid being 'locked-in' to an industrial base that will prevent it from adapting to changing conditions, by stemming the flows of creativity, knowledge and new technologies.

With these comments in mind, let us now turn to a definition of a sectoral innovation system. A sectoral system of innovation and production (SSIP) is defined by Malerba (2001: 4–5) as

> a set of new and established products for specific uses and the set of agents carrying out market and non-market interactions for the creation, production and sale of those products. A sectoral system has a knowledge base, technologies, inputs and a demand, which may be existing, emerging or potential. The agents composing the sectoral system are organizations and individuals (e.g. consumers, entrepreneurs, scientists). Organizations may be firms (e.g. users, producers and input suppliers) and non-firm organizations (e.g. universities, financial institutions, government agencies, trade-unions, or technical associations), including sub-units of larger organizations (e.g. R-D or production departments) and groups of organizations (e.g. industry associations). Agents are characterized by specific learning processes, competences, beliefs, objectives, organizational structures and behaviours. They interact through processes of communication, exchange, cooperation, competition and command, and their interactions are shaped by institutions (rules and regulations). Over

time a sectoral system undergoes processes of change and transformation through the coevolution of its various elements.

Malerba's (2001, 2002, 2005a) concept of an SSIP is notable as it departs from the traditional concept of a sector that is used in industrial economics. Instead, a sectoral system is a collective emergent outcome of the interaction and co-evolution of various constituent elements. The concept of SSIP examines non-firm agents as well as firms, it places substantial emphasis on non-market and market interactions, and focuses on the processes and dynamics of system transformation over time. Furthermore, it does not consider sectoral boundaries as given and static. Such an approach has significant resonance with the analysis of tourism where there has long been a debate about the definition of the tourism industry or sector. On the one hand, there is a sectoral conceptualization drawn from industrial economics, such as a tourism satellite account approach that identifies tourism as a sector of tourism-related industries and industry groups. On the other hand, this contrasts with a tourism systems approach, that is a broad system of market and non-market relationships between people voluntarily away from their home environment, the services and products they consume, the environments they consume in, the institutional arrangements that enable consumption and production, and the externalities that are produced (Hall 2005).

As with the analysis of tourism, the aggregation of system components in an SSIP approach may be undertaken in a number of different ways and may refer to sectors and sub-sectors, agents or functions (Malerba 2001, 2002, 2005a, 2005b). Sectoral systems may be examined in a narrow sense in terms of a small set of product families, or in a broad way. For example, whether the focus is on tourism in general or a narrower category such as medical tourism, ecotourism or nature-based tourism. In addition to firms (producers and suppliers) and non-firm organizations (state tourism bodies, financial institutions), agents at lower (individuals or firm sub-units) and higher (i.e. public–private consortia) levels of aggregation may be the key actors in a sectoral system. Similarly, Malerba (2001) proposes that, for analytical purposes, one could examine separately a sectoral innovation system, a sectoral production system and a sectoral distribution-market system, which in turn could be related more or less closely.

Some of the key elements of an SSIP according to Malerba (2001, 2002, 2005a, 2005b) are:

Products – What the system produces.

Boundaries and demand – Technologies and demand constitute major constraints on the full potential range of diversity of firm behaviour and organization in a sectoral system. These constraints differ from sector to sector and, together with the links and complementarities amongst sectoral artefacts and activities, consequently affect the nature, boundaries and organizations of sectors as well as being a source of sectoral transformation and growth. A given level, composition and elasticity of demand and/or a specific technological environment therefore defines the nature of the problems that firms have to address in their innovative and production activities, the resources available for this, and the types of incentives and constraints to particular behaviour and organizations. However, within these constraints, there is persistent and substantial heterogeneity in firms' innovative and productive behaviour and organization. 'Interdependencies and complementarities define the real boundaries of a sectoral system. They may be at the input, technology or demand level and may concern innovation, production and scale' (Malerba 2002: 250–1).

Knowledge and learning processes – Knowledge is central to innovation and production. Knowledge differs across sectors in terms of particular domains, that is, a scientific and technological field of knowledge can be distinguished from knowledge with respect to product demand. Furthermore, knowledge also differs in terms of accessibility (both internal or external to firms), opportunity (capacity to actually utilize knowledge), cumulativeness (the degree by which the generation of new knowledge builds upon previous knowledge), and appropriation (the possibility of protecting an innovation from imitation) with respect to the technological and learning regime of each sector (Malerba and Orsenigo 1996, 1997, 2000; see also Chapter 3). Box 7.1 illustrates some of the knowledge sourcing experiences of firms in Australia.

Box 7.1 Knowledge-intensive service activities in the Australian tourism industry

Martinez-Fernandez *et al.* (2005) examined the role of knowledge-intensive service activities (KISAs) in the Australian tourism industry. For the purposes of their study, KISAs were defined as the production and integration of service activities (technical and non-technical) undertaken by firms in the tourism sector, in combination with manufactured outputs or as stand-alone services. KISAs can be provided by private enterprises or public sector organizations. For example, R&D services, business consulting, IT services and legal services. Knowledge-intensive services depend on the active transmission of specialist knowledge and experience of applications to clients, and between sectors, regions and states. Their role in the innovation system in terms of the creation and distribution of tacit and codified knowledge is important in helping to overcome the limitations of local networks. This is a much wider process than that associated simply with adoption of new IT:

> The role of knowledge-intensive services in national and regional innovation systems is closely tied to the 'products' these services supply to the market. Specialised expert knowledge, research and development ability, and problem-solving know-how are the real

---

products of knowledge-intensive services. Given increasing differentiation and the accelerating growth of knowledge and information, indirect effects, like the early recognition of problems and more rapid adjustment to current economic and structural change, can be expected when firms succeed in utilising this external knowledge.

(Strambach 1997: 35 cited in Lundvall and Borrás 1997: 120)

A survey of 44 tourism firms found that they were relatively innovative in terms of implementing product, process and organizational changes, with innovation being mostly incremental:

- 39 of the 44 firms (89 per cent) made some changes involving a new product, process or other change.
- 64 per cent of firms introduced a new product.
- 52 per cent implemented a new process.
- 50 per cent identified a new way of doing something, for example, a new or substantially changed accounting system or human resource management system.

The most commonly used services were:

- R&D (essentially market analysis and product development);
- marketing and promotion;
- accounting and financial services; and
- IT services.

KISA-related services were used differently when mapped against the business life cycle. Start-up businesses did not use any service very often. Mature businesses used services regularly, especially IT services. Expanding businesses used all services but especially marketing and IT. Firms considered that they were most likely to access services intermittently (that is, once or twice a year).

The most important source of KISA-related services was in-house delivery, which provided 32 per cent of all KISA inputs. The next most significant source was the private sector, with 20 per cent, followed by industry associations (14 per cent). The least significant sources were universities (2 per cent), federal government (3 per cent) and local government (5 per cent), demonstrating a strong preference for the private over the public sectors. Thirty per cent of external sources were local and 25 per cent were from within the state. Eight of 44 firms (18 per cent) received government grants and these funds were used for marketing and promotion, and training.

Source: Derived from Martinez-Fernandez *et al.* (2005).

Agents – Several agents are actors in an SSIP, including firms, their users (including consumer demand as an end-user of service products, or inter-mediate business users) and suppliers. In contrast to an industrial economics approach, in an SSIP approach demand is not seen as an aggregate set of similar buyers, but is composed of heterogeneous agents with specific attrib-utes, knowledge and competences who interact in various ways with produ-cers (Malerba 2001). Similarly, firms are also regarded as heterogeneous with respect to a wide range of attributes including values, behaviour, experience, organization, learning processes, trajectories, innovative capacities, and rela-tions to consumers (demand). Non-firm agents are also elements in an SSIP and may include a full range of government and non-government organiza-tions that support firm innovation, diffusion and production. These also dif-fer greatly across sectors, in the same way that has already been discussed with respect to policy initiatives in NISs and RISs. For example, there is substantial variance in national sectoral systems with respect to the role of government in encouraging knowledge transfer in tourism. In Australia the government has supported a cooperative research centre for tourism knowledge transfer from universities to tourism firms (see Chapter 4) whereas no such support exists for tourism in Canada, even though there is a similar federal system of government, economic framework and significance of tourism in many regional economies. As noted above, the unit of analysis in sectoral systems can range from individuals through firm sub-units, firms themselves and on to firm networks or consortia.

Networks and mechanisms of interaction – Within SSIPs heterogeneous agents are connected through market and non-market relationships. The types and structures of such interactions and networks among heterogeneous agents will differ between and within sectors as a result of different knowledge bases, beliefs, values, competences (including learning), technologies, inputs, demand characteristics and behaviours (including the creation of linkages and complementarities) (see also Edquist 1997).

Institutions – As noted in the three previous chapters, institutional arrange-ments are critical to innovation systems and the combination of generic and sector specific institutions will determine how these intersect with national and regional innovation systems.

Processes of variety generation and selection – Processes of variety gener-ation refers to products, technologies, firms, institutions as well as strategies and behaviour and are related to entry, R&D, innovation and exit mechan-isms that interact and contribute to creating variety and to agent hetero-geneity at various levels. For example, there may be significant differences between sectors and countries as to the entry and survival of new firms in different sectors (see discussion on firm survivability and innovation on pp. 32–34). In contrast, processes of selection reduce heterogeneity and refer not only to the crucial role of the market but also the effects of non-market selection processes, for example, government support for some firms, regions and sectors but not others.

Service SSIPs such as tourism are clearly different from manufacturing systems. However, as noted in the introduction, and underlined by Tether and Metcalfe (2005: 287): 'The great diversity of service activities is not reflected in a comparable depth in the understanding of innovation in services, which has been neglected in favor of studies of manufacturing.' According to Malerba (2001; see also Tether and Metcalfe 2005) the key features of service systems include:

- Products are closely related to processes.
- Considerable emphasis is given to knowledge embodied in equipment and in people. In particular, studies of services highlight the significance of knowledge forms other than, or complementary to, technological knowledge and R&D, particularly market and procedural knowledge.
- R&D appears less relevant for services, apart from specific sectors such as IT.
- Interaction is especially important in services, with the innovation process in new services often being the result of interaction (co-production and co-creation) between service providers and users, as well as between providers and equipment suppliers.
- Institutions play a major role both in terms of procedures, regulations, and standards.
- Services are produced locally, although internationalization is increasing as a result of technological innovation.
- Services and service system boundaries show continuous change and transformation over time.
- Service SSIPs often develop around identifiable problems or opportunities that are framed by a number of regulatory, cultural and technological contingencies.

Malerba (2005b) provides an useful comparative assessment of a number of European sectors, including various service sectors. There is clearly a need for such studies:

> Services are a heterogeneous set of activities. Some service firms are small, labour-intensive and use only primitive technologies, while others are capital-intensive, knowledge-intensive and major users of information and communication technologies. Some operate in local environments where there is little competition, while others, such as telecommunication and financial services, have become international and have experienced a radical increase in the intensity of competition. The role of innovation in these different sectors is very different and we need to map more closely what is going on in terms of process and product innovation in the different kinds of services, including publicly procured services, and establish indicators.
>
> (Lundvall and Borrás 1997: 117)

Unfortunately, there is a lack of research on SSIPs for the tourism sector, or which at least include – some aspects of – tourism (for example, see Holbrook and Hughes 1999). However, Larsen (2004) provides insights into some features of the SSIP for food and tourism in Sweden, but we still lack a comprehensive study for tourism (see Box 7.2).

Box 7.2 Systems of innovation in the tourism and food sectors:
        Dalarna, Sweden

Based on a series of interviews with firms and supporting organizations in Dalarna, Larsen (2004) investigated the modes and nodes of innovation in the tourism and food sectors. The region has significant ski resorts as well as water-based and cultural activities. The region is relatively peripheral in the European and Swedish national economic space and most of the visitors (over 80 per cent) are Swedish, and only about 1 per cent are from outside Europe.

The spatial system of innovation extends outside the region and suppliers and customers (visitors) were especially important, although the local and national market is also significant. Most of the innovation activities identified in the interviewed firms in tourism and food sectors in Dalarna were incremental, and innovation activities were seen as integral to the strategy for firm development and survival (Table 7.1).

Table 7.1 Modes of innovation in the tourism sector in Dalarna, Sweden

Type of innovation	Level of introduction	Extent of change	Drivers of change
Product and process Product: concept travel, artificial snow Process: new ways of branding and marketing	Firm level	Incremental	Lifestyle entrepreneurs Reach new markets abroad Production efficiency, particularly prolonging tourist season outside of winter
Inter-organizational	Intra and inter-sectoral	Incremental and radical	Explore synergies within and between sectors
Policy programme	Policy programmes (regional, national and EU level)	Incremental	Policy-learning

Source: Derived from Larsen (2004)

In terms of institutional aspects of innovation, there appeared to be a significant implementation gap between the policies and institutional arrangements for innovation and the perceptions and needs in firms. SMEs in peripheral regions in Sweden are the main targets for several EU, national and regional government regional development policy programmes. The explicit goals of these programmes is renewal and knowledge driven growth of the industrial structure. Measures include:

- investment support in national regional industrial policy;
- support for environmentally friendly agricultural farm practices in the Common Agricultural Policy;
- network building between the public and private sector in the EU structural fund policy; and
- innovative actions, an EU initiative.

The managers and owners of SMEs have limited confidence in, or even awareness of the range of measures, which are supposed to address their needs. Instead, managers and owners of SMEs in peripheral regions are highly dependent on personal skills and professional networks as their main source of competitive strength, although the incentives to growth are often limited. Process and product innovations are of more or less daily concern in firms in all sectors. However, the needs of the interviewees were more often for basic rather than sophisticated public services, and were expressed in terms of demand for skilled and motivated labour, professional business services and a more business-friendly climate at the national scale (with Swedish tax and labour regulations being mentioned most frequently as the major barriers to growth and renewal of SMEs in Dalarna).

However, several firms, in the food and tourism sector, have participated in and have benefited from the innovation policy framework although entrepreneurs in SMEs in Dalarna are faced by a 'virtual jungle' of supporting agents at regional, national and EU level (Larsen 2004: 20). The innovation policy framework in peripheral Sweden encompasses a wide range of projects, generally lasting for 2–3 years although often prolonged under a different name – and managed by various actors and facilitators. Programmes sometimes overlap, and coordination between projects as well as between programmes is rather loose. Furthermore, there are numerous facilitators and stakeholders in this 'project economy': ALMI, Företagarna, Hushållnings-sällskapet, Region Dalarna, County Administration, the muncipalities, Teknikdalen, the University College and private consultants. Consequently, 'it is difficult – or impossible – for the SME entrepreneur to get an overview of which facilities and services are supplied for his/her needs' (Larsen 2004: 21). As a result, for example, although financial capital for investments is generally available and supported by quasi-public agencies in Dalarna, tourism firms stressed the lack of investment capital in their line of business.

The most important driving force in the region is the managers' and entrepreneurs' own experiences, motivations, contacts and networks, in the business start-up, in daily or incremental innovations, and in recruiting key personnel. The formal education of both employers and employees in most SMEs in Dalarna plays only a limited role in facilitating innovations, or none at all. Although a wide variety of product and process innovations was being pursued in the firms interviewed, 'innovating by doing' was regarded as an appropriate descriptor for this strategy. In most cases, the role of customers and suppliers inside, as well as outside, the region was crucial for innovation as a result of adjustment to customers' changing demands and the offering of new material and technology by suppliers.

Managers and entrepreneurs in SMEs claimed that university contacts were of minor importance to most firms. However, some larger firms did interact with the regional university in specific competence areas, for example, design, zoology, tourism, education and business management. As a result of the poor labour supply in parts of Dalarna, there was a widespread lack of confidence in the school system among many SME entrepreneurs and it is regarded as poorly adapted to the needs of the small business sector that finds it difficult to attract young workers with what is considered to be a relevant education. In response to this situation, entrepreneurship and tourism education programmes have been initiated in the region. The labour supply situation was regarded as being further exasperated by the perceived low attractiveness of Dalarna for immigrants.

In many ways the innovation issues faced by Dalarna reflect those of many other peripheral locations. The combination of poor communication infrastructure and the small and insular labour markets in some parts of the region limit efficient firm networking and knowledge exchanges. Nevertheless, even in the face of these constraints, innovation has been occurring.

The Dalarna experience indicates that there is a challenge for innovation policy makers to learn from the experiences of innovating firms in order to respond to future needs for new core competences and innovation networks and to cope with changing conditions between and within sectors. One of the major problems in focusing innovation policy more on tourism is that innovation policy in general does not deal with service innovations very effectively outside of IT. This is despite the fact that value-added statistics indicate the substantial value-added creation in the service industries.

In a Finnish review of best practices in innovation policies, Kotilainen (2005) recommended that in the case of services innovation instruments should be designed with non-technological innovations, business models or infrastructure improvements in mind. 'Because innovation in the service sector differs greatly from innovation in manufacturing, a different support system could be devised' (2005: 81). For example, this could include implementation of a tax credit system to boost the service sector and its interest in R&D, or a specific service sector development fund could be created. Moreover, it was also noted that service innovation research often has a different knowledge base than other sectors, with multidisciplinary social research, that is an understanding of processes of knowledge transfer and innovation in SSIPs being important for the service sector rather than just technical knowledge.

Source: After Larsen (2004).

A central difficulty in conducting an aggregate assessment of tourism firm innovations is that tourism cuts across different categories of services. Figure 7.1 illustrates the four different categories of international trade in services recognized under GATS (Hall and Coles 2008; Hall 2008b). Although tourism firms are often identified within GATS Mode 2 'consumption abroad' where services are inseparable, tourism firm activities occur in all the other three modes. This is particularly the case with passenger aviation which, although excluded from GATS, fits into Mode 1, as well as other forms of passenger transport and bookings.

One of the few comparative studies at the national level is of service innovation in Norway, a country in which 'the service sector represents three out of four working hours' (ECON Analysis 2006: 4), with close to 50 per cent of total employment being within the private service sectors (for example, retail trade, transport, finance, IT, tourism, entertainment, business consulting, domestic services). In order to compare innovation within the different sectors, a new typology of service groups has been created. Table 7.2 indicates the typology along with its characteristics, examples, relative employment contribution and innovative characteristics. Although tourism is generally acknowledged as a form of leisure service, this category primarily described firms and organizations '*in situ*' at a destination. Passenger transport is categorized under distributive services, while electronic booking and ticketing fits under digital distributive services. Similarly, contracted back-stage operations in the hospitality sector would be classified as an assisting service.

The 'problem-solving' group represents the largest group of service employment in Norway and has more that doubled the number of employees since 1980. Producers of distributing services have faced decreasing or stagnating employment but have demonstrated high productivity growth with the highest rate, as may be expected, among digital service providers. There are also significant differences in firm size. Assisting service producers and digital distributive service producers are characterized by some of the largest firms

USUAL UNIT OF ANALYSIS	MODE 1 CROSS-BORDER SUPPLY	MODE 3 COMMERCIAL PRESENCE
FIRMS	Service delivered to the territory of country X, from the territory of country Y *Importance:* • professional services • computer services • reservation services • telecommunications • transport, courier and postal services • consultancies *Measures affecting trade:* • commercial presence requirements • residency requirements • citizenship requirements • authorization and/or licensing requirements • limitations and restrictions on insurance	Service delivered within the territory of country X, through the commercial presence of the supplier from country Y *Importance:* • telecommunications • hospitality services • finance and investment • marketing • environmental services *Measures affecting trade:* Restrictions on: • type of legal entity • number of suppliers • participation of foreign capital • discriminatory taxation
	MODE 2 CONSUMPTION ABROAD	**MODE 4 PRESENCE OF NATURAL PERSON**
PERSONS	Service delivered outside the territory of country X, in the territory of country Y, to a consumer from country X *Importance:* • tourism consumption and travel abroad *Measures affecting trade:* • commercial presence requirements • residency requirements • citizenship requirements • authorization and/or licensing requirements • limitations and restrictions on insurance • discriminatory taxation	Service delivered within the territory of country X, with supplier from country Y present as a natural person *Importance:* • management, marketing and other professional services • consultancies • construction services • hospitality labour *Measures affecting trade:* • visa and work permit processing delays • quotas and/or restricted entry for some professions • economic needs and market tests • licensing and/or certification requirements • spousal employment or entry conditions • residency and nationality requirements • training, educational and qualification requirements
	Service supplier **not present** within the territory of the GATS member (country X)	Service supplier **present** within the territory of the GATS member (country X)

SUPPLIER PRESENCE

Figure 7.1 GATS modes of supply and their significance for tourism.

Source: Hall (2008b).

Table 7.2 Comparison of the innovative characteristics of service sectors in Norway

Category	Characteristics	Examples	Employment contribution, 2004*	Innovative focus	Share of firms with product innovation (approx.)	Share of firms with process innovation (approx.)	Share of turnover due to new services in innovators only (approx.)
Problem solvers	Create value by solving specific and unique problems for their customers. There is a low degree of standardization among these services. To a large degree such suppliers provide services that the clients are not able to produce themselves	Law firms, medical doctors, engineers, architects, and researchers	227,000 (22.5%)	Innovation as core activity. Strong focus on customer adaptation and tailor made solutions. Relatively large share of innovative activity invested in product innovations as opposed to process innovations. Focus on new solutions, diagnostic tools, analytical concepts and differentiating brands. Strong presence of organizational innovations, where firms to a large extent are concerned with skill development and optimal incentive schemes.	40%	24%	34%

(Continued overleaf)

Table 7.2 Continued

Category	Characteristics	Examples	Employment contribution, 2004*	Innovative focus	Share of firms with product innovation (approx.)	Share of firms with process innovation (approx.)	Share of turnover due to new services in innovators only (approx.)
Assisting services	Generate customer value by taking over time-consuming activities for firms and households that are easy to standardize.	Cleaning, security services	107,000 (10.6%)	Innovations aimed towards process improvements. Much in common with traditional commodity production, but have been able to improve processes through digitalization and industrial processing. Process innovations are often linked to improved worker efficiency through standardization, quality control and scale effects.	14%	13%	12%
Manual distributive services	Generate value through the facilitation of interaction between customers, for instance by selling goods and transporting commodities, passengers and information.	Passenger transport and freight distribution	508,000 (50.4%)	Innovation is substantially a question of how to reduce transaction costs between customers. This is done through process innovations as well as new services, including automation and more efficient producer user interface. Integration of logistic systems is a typical example of important process innovations among transporters.	17%	14%	20%

Digital distributive services	A large sub-group of the above that distributes services primarily by digital means	Telecom services, financial services	61,000 (60.5%)	As above but with focus on digitalization. When distributive services are attached with network externalities (the value of a service increases with the number using it), customer segmentation represents an important form of organizational innovation.	45%	40%	15%
Leisure services	Generate values by stimulating the emotions, perceptions and spiritual experience of customers. Leisure services are highly heterogenous.	Arts, museum, entertainment, restaurant and media services	105,000 (10.4%)	New experiences are regarded as the most important product innovations in this group. New technology enables firms to multiply their services, improve their storage capacity and simplify distribution. Tourism services tend to focus on organizational innovations that link several providers together in a network.	10%	5%	24%

Source: Derived from ECON Analysis (2006).

Note: * Represents percentage of service-related employment not total employment.

in the country, this is likely due to advantages of scale. In contrast 'the presence of strong heterogeneity among problem solvers and leisure service suppliers curbs their scale advantages. Thus a smaller proportion of these firms become really large' (ECON Analysis 2006: 11). Overall, Norwegian research suggests that, at an aggregate level, service firms invested less in innovation than the manufacturing sector. Approximately 28 per cent of service firms displayed product innovation and 20 per cent process innovation compared with the manufacturing sector's 35 per cent and 30 per cent respectively. However, the aggregate figure fails to reveal the substantial differences among the five different service groups (Table 7.2). Reasons for the differences relate to a number of factors and are not 'necessarily only driven by the way they contribute to value for their customers. Political regulations and the competitive pressure can also shape the incentives to innovate' (ECON Analysis 2006: 11).

The Doblin consulting group from 1988–2000 undertook a series of studies that has sought to distinguish the innovation profile of different tourism and tourism-related industry sectors. Doblin Inc. (2007) examined some of the innovation features of firms in a number of manufacturing and service industries, and tracked trends over time. According to Doblin, passenger airlines are regarded as being moderately innovative but have primarily concentrated in innovation with respect to networks, business enabling processes, service and channels, with relatively little attention to brand and product performance. Lodging is similar to passenger airlines with innovations centring on business networks, enabling processes, services and channels with little innovation elsewhere in business processes. The restaurant sector shares broadly similar features. The Doblin profile of different sectors emphasizes that different elements of firm activity may be subject to innovation, and the next section examines this in more detail.

Tourism firm innovation

The logics of value creation in the service sector are linked to how different service producers create customer value. Value creation can occur in different areas of firm activity (Kim and Mauborgne 1999; see also Chapter 2). Ideally, these elements are mapped by firms in the development of service designs or blueprints for particular products, with the different elements then becoming part of a service-profit chain (SPC), which is a framework for linking service operations, employee assessments and customer assessments to a firm's profitability (Heskett *et al.* 1994). An SPC provides an integrative framework for understanding how a firm's innovations and investments in service operations are related to customer perceptions and behaviour, and how these translate into profits and revenue growth (Kamakura *et al.* 2002; Coviello *et al.* 2006). A number of variants of SPCs have been produced that emphasize particular dimensions such as service satisfaction or environmental management practices (Kassinis and Soterlou 2003), or have reconceptualized such frameworks as a form of value chain (for example, Parasuraman and Grewal 2000; Heskett *et al.* 2003).

Although the value chain approach is increasingly being conceptualized as a form of network or grid (for example, Pil and Holweg 2006), it can still be a useful means for identifying some key areas of innovation both internal and external to the firm. Indeed, its components are often recognized as elements of a business model in their own right. A business model is a conceptual tool that contains a set of elements and their relationships that allows the expression of the business logic of a specific firm:

> It is a description of the value a company offers to one or several segments of customers and of the architecture of the firm and its network of partners for creating, marketing, and delivering this value and relationship capital, to generate profitable and sustainable revenue' streams.
>
> (Osterwalder *et al.* 2005: 17–18)

In their review of the business model literature, Osterwalder *et al.* (2005) demonstrated that the most cited papers on the conceptual dimensions of business models covered nine 'building blocks' that relate to four different dimensions of business models. The dimensions are product/service; customer interface; infrastructure management; and financial aspects. The building blocks are the value proposition; target customer; distribution channel; customer relationship; value configuration; capability; partnership; cost structure; and finally, revenue model (Osterwalder *et al.* 2005). Several of these elements have been incorporated into Figure 7.2, which presents a service business model of the innovation value creation points in the tourism firm. The main idea of creating a reference model is that it identified the domains, concepts and relationships shared among a specific community of practice. In the case of tourism the elements of a tourism firm or organization have not been formally identified, in part because of the wide range of trade contexts in which tourism occurs. Nevertheless, the service aspects of tourism allow for the consideration of a number of common points. Eleven points are identified: business model (referring to the overall approach); networks and alliances; enabling process; service design and development; service value; distribution; brand; servicescape; customer service experience; customer satisfaction; and customer loyalty. However, it should be noted that the elements of the model are not causally related. In other words, an element such as 'enabling process', which includes human resource management, does not imply that employee satisfaction will cause customer satisfaction, although it does suggest that firms that exhibit high levels of success on elements of the model will be more successful than those that do not.

Reflecting the characteristics of services, as discussed earlier, tourism firms tend to cluster into two groups with distinctly different innovation strategies:

1   When services are inseparable and difficult to standardize, there exists a

INNOVATION POINTS IN VALUE CHAIN	Business model	Networks and alliances	Enabling process	Service design and development	Service value	Distribution	Brand	Servicescape	Customer service experience	Customer satisfaction	Customer loyalty
INTELLECTUAL CAPITAL	How the firm makes its money and how it is accordingly structured	Economic and knowledge relationships with other firms and actors	Support of the firm's core processes and employees	Service development architecture and systems. Matching of service to market segments	Provision of value to customers and consumers with respect to products	How the product offerings reach the market	The symbolic embodiment of all the information connected to the product, and associated, values and expectations	The physical evidence of service and physical manifestation of brand. Managing demand and capacity	The experiences that customers have at point of co-creation/co-production	Levels of customer satisfaction with experience over time	Long-term relationships with customers
INNOVATIVE CAPACITIES AND POTENTIAL	New business models, including ownership structure, payment and cash flow system, and location	New sets of relations with actors create new flows of economic and intellectual capital. New sets of supply chains will also affect product offerings	Improving employee satisfaction, retention and productivity	New service design, development and testing, including development of service blueprints, assessment of internal service quality and processes, and market segmentation	New services and means of adding value for customers	Utilization of new channels, combinations of channels and intermediaries	Utilization of new ways to communicate offerings and create brand value	Development and design of new servicescapes, including in the virtual world	Providing new experiences	Tracking customer satisfaction	Customer relationship management strategies

INCREASING EXTERNAL FOCUS

INCREASING INTERNAL FOCUS

Figure 7.2 Innovation value creation points in the tourism firm.

fundamental problem of information asymmetry. In such situations, customers will have difficulties, or not be able, to evaluate the quality of a potential service supplier beforehand, since alternative offerings are hard to compare. Innovation among firms in this group often tends to focus on building reputation through customer solutions that reduces the risk for clients (ECON Analysis 2006). Examples of this type of operation include events, museums, art galleries and tours. This type of firm or organization has a strong external focus (see Boxes 7.3, 7.4, 7.5).

2   When services are characterized by a stronger degree of separation and standardization, innovations are more geared towards process improvements (ECON Analysis 2006). Examples include airline and transport operations or, in some situations, forms of accommodation that are very similar (note the case of Accor's Formule 1 noted in Chapter 2). This type of firm or organization has a strong external focus (see Boxes 7.5, 7.6, 7.7).

However, each of the value creation points has innovation potential, as we see below.

Business model – The specification of a set of business model elements, as well as their relationships to one another, 'is like giving a business model designer a box of Lego blocks' (Osterwalder *et al.* 2005: 24). Different components of the model can be combined in different ways to create new ways of doing business thereby potentially creating new sources of competitive advantage (Mitchell and Coles 2003). E-business, for example, has created new business models for tourism paving the way for new sets of customer relations and economic transactions, while other advances in communication technology will likely have future impacts for how consumers and businesses are brought together. Amit and Zott (2001) explicitly perceive business models as a locus of innovation and value creation not only for the firm but also its suppliers, partners and customers (Box 7.3).

Hitters and Richards (2002) examined two cultural clusters in the Netherlands, the Westergasfabriek (WGF) in Amsterdam and the Witte de Withstraat (WdW) in Rotterdam, and evaluated their contrasting creative management strategies. At the time of the study the WGF had been fairly successful in creating an attractive mix of different cultural activities, based on the creative potential of the buildings on the site, its image as a cultural centre and the general atmosphere of creativity. The more 'top-down' approach of the local authority owned but commercially managed WFG was regarded as having injected new commercial skills and investment into the cluster, and created the conditions for innovation through managing the mix of creative functions. In contrast, the WdW took a more 'bottom-up' approach to the problems of cultural management, and at the time of the study the participants had resisted the imposition of formal management. Hitters and Richard's (2002) noted that while this may have allowed cultural and commercial functions to co-exist there appeared to be less evidence of innovation.

Box 7.3 The business model of space tourism: the 'next big thing'?

In the 1990s the idea of private investment in space tourism seemed like science fiction. Interest in space tourism expanded after the 2004 X-Prize winning flight of Burt Rutan's SpaceShipOne, which was the first privately funded rocket to reach space (Hall 2005). Rutan's company, Scaled Composites, is building a larger SpaceShipTwo for Richard Branson's company Virgin Galactic to accommodate tourists for brief sub-orbital flights. According to Nussbaum (2005):

> When SpaceShipOne was being built, there wasn't a business model that made much sense. Yet Rutan and Branson went ahead with the daring deed, hoping, assuming that a business model would evolve and present itself. It now has. That's how breakthrough innovation tends to work. It requires a leap of faith that most managers can do.

Although high profile entrepreneurs such as Branson and Microsoft's Paul Allen have supported space tourism development, attracting a wider range of investors has proven difficult. However, the business model for space tourism appears to be changing. In July 2007 Northrop Grumman, a US$30 billion defence and technology company, agreed to increase its stake in Scaled Composites from 40 to 100 per cent. At the other end of the corporate scale, in June 2007 the infant space tourism industry received a boost when US investment group Boston Harbour Angels backed a private rocket company, XCOR Aerospace, in developing a spaceship that will take off and land like an aeroplane.

> 'This is our first angel group investment,' said XCOR CEO Jeff Greason. 'We hope other angel groups and possibly institutional investors will follow the Boston Harbor Angels example.'
> 'XCOR Aerospace has a team that understands the value of staying focused,' said Boston Harbor Angels investor Andrew Nelson. 'The company has presented a strategy to align all activities toward a specific, attainable, and profitable set of commercial products and services with a strong portfolio of intellectual property.'
> Boston Harbor Angels is a group of 36 angel investors – successful entrepreneurs, corporate leaders, and venture capitalists – looking for personal investment opportunities in high-growth early stage companies. Members make their own investment decisions but collaborate on due diligence and rely on each others' expertise when making these decisions. Since 2004 members have invested in 25 companies.

(XCOR Aerospace 2007)

The deal is believed to be the first investment by a group of angel investors in a commercial space tourism company. (An angel investor is an affluent individual, often a retiree, who provides capital for a business start-up, usually in exchange for ownership equity, a scenario made famous in some parts of the world by the 'Dragons' Den' television series.) To help assist the process, a Space Angels Network has been established to try and bring investors into space-related ventures. The organization has the tag-line, 'where visionary capital meets visionary ideas'.

Sources: XCOR Aerospace: http://www.xcor.com; Boston Harbour Angels: http://www.bostonharborangels.com; Space Angels Network: http://www.spaceangelsnetwork.com; Virgin Galactic: *http://www.virgingalactic.com/*; Scaled Composites: http://www.scaled.com/.

Networks and alliances – The development of networks and alliances and associated areas of actor cooperation and trust has been a significant theme in tourism research since the early 1990s (Hall 2008a). The creation of networks allows for the development of mutual learning and knowledge spill-overs among actors as well as for more pragmatic actions with respect to cost sharing and cooperative action with respect to marketing, lobbying and strategy (Tracey and Clark 2003). The development of new sets of relations over time and the maintenance of valued existing relationships can provide a means of innovation on an individual and shared level (Medina *et al.* 2005). For example, networks can share the cost of new technologies which otherwise may have been prohibitive to members at an individual level. Advanced marketing networks can also share resources to undertake innovative market segmentation and product matching exercises. In a broader sense the network concept can also be expanded to included members of the destination community and customers who can also have a role in assisting in the innovation process if lines of communication and appropriate incentives are developed.

Enabling process – The enabling process refers to the way in which organizations give support to core business processes and the maintenance and enhancement of human capital via appropriate human resource management strategies. In some tourism firms one of the most basic means of innovation is for managers to listen to feedback from customer service staff so as to be able to respond to information and issues. However, in order to enable this to happen there needs to be an appropriate culture in place in which service staff are highly valued and respected – which is not the case in all service organizations.

Service design and development – This refers to the process by which new services are developed, designed and introduced to the market. A meta-analysis of new product studies by Henard and Szymanski (2001) indicated that the most reliable predictors of success for new introductions were product characteristics (meeting customer needs, advantage over competitors), strategy characteristics (dedicated R&D and human resources to support initiative), process characteristics (pre-development, marketing, technological and launch proficiencies), and market characteristics (market potential). An important innovation in new service design has been the increasing focus on customers as a source of learning for new service development, with customers often being regarded as more innovative than professional service developers (Matthing *et al.* 2004) (Box 7.4).

Service value – Service value refers to the value that customers gain from products both with respect to the basic product as well as value-added services, which is where innovations tend to be made as well as via the customer value chain.

Box 7.4 Boeing's lighter, 'greener' airliner of the future

In 2007 Boeing unveiled its much-hyped new 'green' passenger jet, the 787 Dreamliner, which boasts a series of fuel-efficient design features that have become more attractive to users as a result of increased fuel prices. According to Boeing, '[t]he airplane will use 20 per cent less fuel for comparable missions than today's similarly sized airplane' (Quemener 2007). Boeing's first new model since 1994, the Dreamliner takes advantage of big advances made in aviation technology in the past decade, and was designed using high tech plastic composites instead of aluminium. Up to 50 per cent of the primary structure of the plane – including the fuselage and wing – are made of composites such as carbon-fibre, which reduce the weight of the planes.

Boeing aims to build 2,000 Dreamliners by 2030 and, as of July 2007, had received 677 orders from 47 companies for the plane, which has an asking price of between US$146 million to US$200 million. The plane is scheduled to commence commercial service with All Nippon Airways in May 2008.

The Dreamliner comes in three models for both medium- and long-haul flights and has a seating capacity of between 210 and 330 places, depending on seating and class configuration. It is able to fly up to 15,750 km without refuelling and can manage a flight between New York and Manila, or Moscow and Sao Paulo, routes so far only open to bigger planes such as Boeing's 777 or 747. Boeing hopes the Dreamliner will be used to open up profitable flights between cities that so far have no direct links. The Dreamliner's other innovations include potentially greater levels of comfort for passengers, with bigger windows, higher cabin humidity levels so as to reduce passenger dehydration, and a new anti-turbulence system (Quemener 2007).

Distribution – This is the means by which product offerings get to the market and the customer. Often the innovation focus is on the distribution channel, the chain of intermediaries between the producer and the final consumers. For most tourism businesses this aspect refers to flows of marketing information as well as booking, as final consumption will be co-produced. However, for some large tourism firms distribution can also refer to the selection of a range of locations at which co-production of experiences can occur (Box 7.5). E-business, for example, has meant the development of significant innovations in the flow of product information and capacity to purchase that have bypassed traditional distribution channels such as the travel agent

---

Box 7.5 Harrah's distribution, marketing and innovation

Harrah's Entertainment, one of the world's largest gaming, entertainment and hospitality companies has developed a distributed system of casino entertainment facilities providing capacity for what Harrah's (2007) terms 'cross-market' play, or the ability to generate play by customers when they travel to locations at which Harrah's have a presence. This has been combined with Harrah's customer loyalty programme, Total Rewards, and has allowed the company 'to capture a growing share of our customers' gaming budget and generate increasing same-store sales' (Harrah's Entertainment 2007: 6).

> Our Total Rewards customers are able to earn Reward Credits and redeem those Reward Credits at most of our U.S. casino entertainment facilities. . . . Total Rewards is structured in tiers, providing customers an incentive to consolidate their play at our casinos. Depending on their level of play with us in a calendar year, customers may be designated as either Gold, Platinum, Diamond, or Seven Stars customers. Customers who do not participate in Total Rewards are encouraged to join, and those with a Total Rewards card are encouraged to consolidate their play through targeted promotional offers and rewards.

Harrah's has developed a database containing information from their customers including aspects of their casino gaming play. This information is used for promotions, including direct mail campaigns, electronic mail and the company's web site. Harrah's were issued five US patents covering some of the technology associated with the Total Rewards programme, one of which has subsequently withdrawn (Table 7.3). Although these innovations centre on codified knowledge, as always it requires tacit knowledge to maximize their innovation potential (see Chapter 3).

Table 7.3 Harrah's patents for its casino entertainment distribution system

US patent number	Issued	Expires	Covers
5,613,912	25 March 1997	5 April 2015	Real time bet tracking system for betting activity at gaming tables (subject to a licensing agreement with Mikohn Gaming Corporation)
5,716,647	2 June 1998	24 May 2016	Subsequently withdrawn
5,809,482	15 September 1998	15 September 2015	A system automatically tracks player gambling transactions in a casino. The system includes a casino database, the store's betting summary records for each of a plurality players, where each betting summary record is associated with a player identification code, and includes the player's betting rating
6,003,013	14 December 1999	24 May 2016	A system and method for differentiating customers according to their worth to the casino. Customer information is accumulated at each affiliated casino through one or more local area network-based management systems, updated to a central patron database (CPDB) that is coupled to each casino LAN through a wide area network, and made available to each affiliated casino property as needed
6,183,362	6 February 2001	24 May 2016	A system and method for implementing a customer tracking and recognition programme that encompasses customers' gaming and non-gaming activity alike at a plurality of affiliated casino properties

Source: US patents, various.

(Buhalis 2006), and therefore potentially allow for direct sales to customers. However, in some cases innovative 'alternative' distribution strategies may actually signal a return to traditional distribution channels. For example, many small agricultural producers may sell their products directly to visitors at the farm gate, farm store or at a market, thereby often serving visitors, rather than through mainstream retail channels.

Brand – Brands are the symbolic embodiment of all information connected to a product and are evidenced via names, slogans, logos, symbols, designs, sounds, smells and colours. However, 'brand assets are difficult and expensive to develop, maintain, and adapt. The supply-side environment is cluttered, confused, and complex in part because of the proliferation of products, brands and sib-brands' (Aaker 2004: 6). Brand innovation can refer to new ways of reinforcing existing brands, the development of new ones and new means to protect the values and designs of existing brands (Box 7.6). Significantly, innovation can itself contribute to the value of a firm's brand as a reputation for innovation is often regarded as enhancing company credibility (Aaker 2004).

Box 7.6 Marketing the French wine experience

In October 2006 the French wine industry launched one of the biggest rebranding exercise in its long history with a new focus on mass marketing and wine 'experiences'. The new focus was a result of increasing competition from Australian and other new world wines in the UK and international markets (Hall and Mitchell 2008). According to Florence Rhydderch of Sopexa, the marketing agency masterminding France's representation at the Wine Show:

> This year we are trying to create a short cut to French wines. They are often criticised for being too complicated and not easy to understand, so we are testing a new way of communicating to consumers in a more modern and accessible way. It's not a typical French exhibition: normally, you have to go from region to region, but not everyone is familiar with what they are and probably don't care.
>
> For a while, France thought it was just a setback, but then came the realisation that we have to do some things differently and communicate differently. Often you have to lose your leadership before you can rise to a challenge. Some of the regions are pulling their socks up to meet the competition. I'm optimistic that we'll become number one again, but we want to do it through innovation and quality, not price promotions.
>
> (Cited in Smith 2006)

In 2005 when the Wine Show, a trade event targeted at consumers in London, was held for the first time, the French had only a single stand. In 2006 they commanded a quarter of the floorspace under a new branding, 'The French Wines Experience', which promised 'a series of fun lifestyle zones' in which consumers could sample a wide array of wines. These included 'nights in', 'nights out', 'dinner parties', 'celebrations', 'outdoor living' and 'Christmas'.

Matt Skinner, an Australian who works for Jamie Oliver's Fifteen restaurant (a British restaurant made famous by a television programme), said that a coordinated French approach was welcome:

> They're having to become experts in marketing. For the first time in their wine-producing history, they're facing the challenge from Australia, South Africa and others. You go to these countries and you're met at the gate with open arms by the owner, encouraging wine tourism. In France, you usually need a prior appointment or to know the owner, so it's not welcoming for consumers.
>
> (Cited in Smith 2006)

Servicescape – A servicescape is the physical evidence of a service and refers to physical environment dimensions such as ambient conditions, space/function and signs, symbols and artefacts such as customer perceptions of the servicescape (Bitner 1992). The concept is closely related to branding as the servicescape can be used to reinforce brand identity via common design features, as in many hotel chains and airlines. Innovation can occur in many different ways but substantial attention is being given to how the servicescape contributes to atmosphere and experience (Pine and Gilmore 1999). Servicescape innovations are one of the most common areas of innovation in tourism given the relative ease of changing physical surroundings, that is, new displays in museums, galleries or heritage attractions or adding new experiential dimensions, such as adding smell or sound or making experiences more interactive.

Customer service experience – This refers to innovation with respect to the experience the customer has with a particular organization as well as that organization's understanding of the experience. A primary focus of innovation in the area is therefore with respect to providing new innovative experiences through both tangible and intangible means. An example of a technological innovation in customer service is the development of self-service technology for ticketing, hospitality and even attractions.

Customer satisfaction – This refers to the satisfaction a customer has with a service encounter as well as a tourist firm or destination overall. In addition, customer satisfaction is also a focus for innovation with respect to tracking satisfaction over time.

Customer loyalty – Customer loyalty refers to the maintenance of customer relationships over time so they continue to purchase company product as well as tracking these relationships (Box 7.7).

Maintaining and innovating along the various points of the service business will potentially bring greater returns to the firm and therefore enhance the likelihood that the firm will survive and/or expand. However, as the next section discusses there is actually relatively little research on the survivability of tourism firms in relation to their innovative behaviour.

Box 7.7 Loyaltybuild: supplier-led tourism innovation

Loyaltybuild is an international loyalty marketing company, head-quartered in Ennis, Co. Clare, Ireland. Loyaltybuild programmes work to build customer loyalty for businesses and brands using unique, what the company terms, 'brilliant-value' 'one price' travel and leisure offers. User firms do no incur any direct costs associated with Loyaltybuild setting up and managing the programme from creative concept through to client branded web sites and call centre supports. Instead, Loyalty-build receives a return on its investment of time, and knowledge, through income generation related to customer bookings. Since the company's launch in 1999, Loyaltybuild programmes are claimed to have gener-ated over d1.5 billion in revenue for its clients. The essence of Loyalty-build's programmes are custom designed web and database 'solutions', which allow clients to offer their customers literally thousands of 'one price' leisure breaks in domestic or overseas destinations. Every client campaign is supported by a web site and call centre, branded according to their preferences, and to their brand guidelines. It is claimed that technologies are adaptable and can support Loyaltybuild programmes in any industry sector, market or language.

This is a classic example of bought-in tourism innovation, in the form of a mixture of tacit and codified knowledge imported from suppliers.

Source: Loyaltybuild, http://www.loyaltybuild.com/.

Firm survivability and innovation

As noted in Chapter 1, it is a basic tenet of Schumpetarian notion that innovation plays a major role in the survival of firms. Schumpeter (1942: 84) argued that innovation 'strikes not at the margins of the profits and the outputs of the existing firms but at their foundations and their very lives'. Similarly, Baumol (2002: 1) noted that innovative activity is 'mandatory, a life-and-death matter for the firm and innovation has replaced price as the name of the game in a number of important industries'. Firm survival has long been recognized as being influenced by age and size, both of which are related to innovation, although the direction of growth matters more than the initial size (Freeman *et al.* 1983). Research also suggests that small firms, which are more likely to operate below the minimum efficient scale, are more exposed to the risk of exit, than larger firms (Caves 1998).

It is also well recognized that new firms have extremely high mortality rates and relatively few survive the start-up period. However, there is substantial debate over the extent to which the post-entry performance of firms can be generalized across sectors and markets. For example, Sutton (1995: 4) observes 'the fact that a wide range of different patterns occur across different markets, [means] that it is difficult to make any generalisations'. Start-up and post-entry performance may instead potentially be shaped by characteristics specific to the firm, industry, region or the location, *including innovation* (Audretsch 1995a, 1995b; Tödtling and Wanzenböck 2003).

One of the very few tourism specific studies of firm survival and mortality was undertaken by Santarelli (1998) in Italy, with respect to the survival of hotels, restaurants and catering firms between 1989 and 1994. Examining new firm survival rates, defined as the share of new firms starting in 1989 that were still in existence at the end of each subsequent year, it was observed that one year after start up 68 per cent of firms still operated, dropping to 45 per cent by the sixth year. This was significantly lower than the 59 per cent survival rate identified for Italian manufacturing firms during approximately the same period, but similar to that identified for American manufacturing firms (Audretsch 1995a, 1995b). The survival rates for tourism firms showed considerable variation amongst Italian regions, ranging from a 33 per cent six-year survival rate in Piemonte, in northern Italy, to 62 per cent in Campania, in southern Italy (Santarelli 1998). In general, survival rates were higher in northern than in southern Italy.

In examining regional variations in survival rates, Santarelli (1998) observed that in those areas where the barriers to entry (measured in terms of such factors as advertising and capital-raising requirements, shortage of bank credit, lack of modern infrastructures in the surrounding area) are lower, the entry process is less selective and a larger share of entry attempts are more likely to fail or have a short life expectancy. In addition, the duration of firm life appeared to be affected by the dynamics of industry evolution within particular regions. It may therefore be easier for new firms to survive in those regions in which the tourist industry was growing at higher rates: since their entry into the industry is less likely to inflict market share losses on their rivals, the likelihood of retaliation by incumbents will be lower. In addition, Santarelli (1998: 162) identified in the Italian data that

> the mean start-up size (in employment terms) of firms found to be still operating at the end of the relevant period is higher than that of all firms entering the market in 1989, for the large majority (eighteen [out of twenty]) of regions, and for the country as a whole.

This reinforces the notion that firm size is conducive to new-firm survival. According to Santarelli (1998: 162), this can be

> explained by the fact that larger firms survive longer because they are in general more efficient, employ more capital intensive methods, achieve more easily economies of scale, have a larger availability of internal finance besides benefiting from easier access to external finance.

Moreover, when the opportunity cost of staying in the market increases, larger firms may decrease in size before they exit whereas under the same circumstance their smaller counterparts will be the first to leave the market.

Although such factors have been recognized as important in other studies of tourism firms (for example, Ateljevic and Doorne 2004; Zapalska and Brozik 2004), there is nevertheless a shortage of empirical analysis as to the extent to which innovation is intrinsic to new-firm survival.

In the New Zealand case the accommodation, cafés and restaurant industrial category has the highest proportion of businesses with tourism-related sales (74 per cent), with the next largest being the transport and storage category at approximately 35 per cent (Statistics New Zealand 2006). The sector's innovation rate of 50 per cent of businesses engaged in innovative activity is just below the overall innovation rate of New Zealand businesses (52 per cent). However, the sector had the lowest continuation rates for enter prises over the period 2001–6 with only 33.1 per cent of firms surviving to 2006 (Ministry of Economic Development 2007).

Technology and R&D activities have been recognized as important for shaping the conditions for firm survival, as technology intensive sectors, like science-based and specialized suppliers appear more favourable to firm survival (Christensen *et al.* 1998) (but it is also the case that most research has focused on the high tech sectors). Although technology has been recognized as an important aspect of innovation in tourism (see Chapter 3), there has been no longitudinal assessment of the relationship to business survival specifically with respect to tourism. In general, the attempts to link firm survival to their technological capabilities have tended to focus selectively on inputs into the innovation process (for example, R&D or technology use) or inventions (for example, patents), tending to neglect some of the more intangible tacit knowledge forms, and there have also been few attempts to link survival with the innovative output or the ability of the firm to commercialize new innovations successfully (Choonwoo *et al.* 2001; Cefis and Marsili 2005).

As noted in Chapter 1, the product life cycle theory suggests that in the early stages of an industry, new firms enter on the basis of product innovation (Utterback 1994). As the industry matures, process innovation then becomes dominant. In these later stages, there tends to be a high rate of exit. This suggests that early in the life cycle industry product innovation should be associated with survival, while in later stages of an industry's development, process innovation should be associated with survival. However, there is little empirical evidence about the contribution of either type of innovation to firm survival. In organization theory, the focus tends to be on the firm-ageing process and the environmental features of survival, while in industrial economics the focus is on firm-specific determinants of survival, tending to focus on structural characteristics such as firm age and size. Neither field says much about innovation. As Sorensen and Stuart (2000) argue, the link between innovation and firm survival is a 'largely undocumented' and 'unresolved' issue of empirical enquiry.

Cefis and Marsili (2005) analysed the relationship between innovation and firm survival using microeconomic databases in the Netherlands. They implemented a survival analysis based on both non-parametric and parametric analyses. Their results were in line with previous findings, confirming that age and size positively affect firm survival (with decreasing returns to firm size in terms of survival probability) and that the firm growth rate appears to play a major role in survival. A univariate analysis of the survival functions of firms demonstrated a marked difference between innovators and non-innovators, regardless of the type of innovation. In a multivariate analysis, when the effects of age, size, growth and nature of technology were controlled, the role of innovation remained positive and well defined. In addition, they were also able to detect a distinctive difference between product and process innovators. Firms that introduced new products did not have higher chances of survival than non-innovators. However, in contrast, firms that implemented process innovations did have a higher likelihood of survival. Overall, innovation was identified as increasing the survival probability of firms by 11 per cent. According to Cefis and Marsili (2005) the scale of the effect is comparable to that of firm age, which traditionally has been considered a key determinant of firm survival. Their results suggest that there is an 'innovation premium' than can help balance the liabilities of being a new firm, and support the notion that innovation does matter for the very existence of a firm not only because of the nature of innovations, such as technology, that can affect the general conditions for firm survival in the market (Agarwal and Audretsch 2001), but also because of the firm specific capacity to deal with external change.

Conclusions

This chapter has discussed the relationship between innovation and tourism firms in the context of a tourism sector system of innovation, as well as with respect to the business model of the tourist firm. As with earlier chapters we have noted how firms are embedded within a system of innovation in which institutions and a variety of other agents and contingencies play important roles. Equally importantly, it was also emphasized that different sub-sectors of the tourism industry will have different innovation characteristics as a result of the different ways within which services are traded.

The nature of the services offered was also identified as significant with respect to innovation within firms. A business model of 'innovation points' within tourism firms highlighted the different internal and external orientations of some of these dimensions that reflected the relative extent to which services were separable. A number of cases was used to illustrate innovation in this context. Finally, the chapter discussed issues of firm survivability and innovation and noted that, although the empirical evidence was limited, innovation is a factor in increasing the probability of survival. Yet the survival of firms and the relative importance of innovation is, in itself, partly dependent on their start-up and the entrepreneurial characteristics of their founders, and it is to these issues that the next chapter will turn.

8 Entrepreneurship and innovation

The inseparability of innovation and entrepreneurship

Following on from the focus on the firm in the previous chapter, here we consider the role of the individual and in particular of the entrepreneur. The two concepts of innovation and entrepreneurship overlap in key ways, not least because many definitions of the latter implicate, explicitly or implicitly, notions of innovation. It is also impossible to conceive of innovation occurring without the participation of individual entrepreneurs. Typical of this perspective is Blake *et al.*'s (2006: 1104) comment that '[e]ntrepreneurial ability is an important source of competitiveness, as entrepreneurs who start up new businesses introduce innovative practices and new technology that challenge incumbents' performance'. They also note that there is evidence of above average growth in firms, after a change of ownership, implying an input of fresh entrepreneurialism. Similarly, and writing specifically about tourism entrepreneurship, Ateljevic and Doorne (2000: 280) conclude that '[k]ey descriptors of the entrepreneur have come to include: risk-taking, innovation, creativity, alertness and insight'. Although entrepreneurialism is usually understood as being a characteristic of individuals, it can also be understood – as argued later in this section – that it also represents a form of collective behaviour, whether of the entrepreneurial state or the entrepreneurial company.

The origins of much modern thinking about entrepreneurship lie in Schumpeter's (1934) work that suggested that the entrepreneur's role was to disturb economic equilibrium, which itself can be understood as the balance between supply and demand for a particular good or set of related goods (and, indeed, tourism services), as well as the stability of prices. Entrepreneurs create a disturbance through innovation. By changes in the process of production, or by introducing new products, the entrepreneur disturbs the balance between demand and production, leading to existing relationships being supplanted by new ones.

There is however some ambiguity in how Schumpeter conceived the role of the entrepreneur, whether as a bearer of change and disturbance, or as someone who instigates this. In other words, there is uncertainty as to the driver of innovation. As Te Velde (2004: 104) writes, Schumpeter seems caught between 'describing the entrepreneur as an active external agent of change, a generator of novelty de novo, or merely as a passive bearer of the mechanisms of change'. There is real tension here between seeing the entrepreneur as originating new ideas and implementing them, and seeing the entrepreneur as the bearer of the mechanism of change, and moreover of changes 'generated by the evolution of the socio-economic system [that] would have occurred anyway but they have to be effectuated by an acting individual: the entrepreneur' (Te Velde 2004: 111). The former sees the entrepreneur as a heroic figure changing the landscape of the economy, and the latter sees the entrepreneur as a necessary figure in creating disturbances, but not as significantly shaping the innovation.

However, it is important not to belittle the role of entrepreneurs as a group of actors, for according to Schumpeter they make a number of key contributions to innovation (Te Velde 2004 123):

- identifying emergent social trends at an early stage and, critically, in advance of others;
- connecting these trends to new combinations in how goods and services are produced and the types of products;
- spinning a social network around the innovation that links together the right kind of people (investors, workers, intermediaries etc.) and the right kind of non-human actors (investment, the assembly of equipment and inputs etc.);
- enhancing the productivity of this social network through creating a protected niche in which the entrepreneur serves as a gatekeeper in the outside world;
- taking responsibility for 'upscaling' the niche as the disturbance effects are maximized.

The entrepreneur, therefore, can be seen as a perceptive and resourceful coordinator, and also as a focal point where trust is built amongst the different agents who contribute to innovation. This accords with a growing consensus in the research literature that entrepreneurship is a process whereby individuals first discover, and then exploit, new business openings by creating new business ventures either within existing companies, or by establishing new ones (Davidsson and Wiklund 2001). They therefore provide the essential link between invention and innovation (Burgelman and Sayles 1986), although – as noted above – the nature of that link remains contentious. Another way to approach this is to understand entrepreneurialism not so much as a dichotomy between active and passive roles in innovation, but as a position along a continuum ranging from conservative to entrepreneurial. At one extreme, conservative firms have strategic postures that are risk averse, non-innovative, and reactive. At the other extreme, entrepreneurial firms are associated with strategic postures that are risk taking, innovative and proactive (Jogaratnum and Tse 2004: 250).

In a sense, this parallels Schumpeter's distinction between incremental and radical innovations, while emphasizing a range of possibilities within a continuum. In practice however, it remains difficult to measure entrepreneurialism and, like knowledge and innovation, it remains a rather nebulous term. Moreover, while entrepreneurialism is a necessary condition for innovation, there is still relatively little understanding of how different forms of entrepreneurial behaviour and orientation relate to innovation and to firm performance.

Considering the characteristics of business owners provides another perspective. Chell's (2001: 83) typology is useful, identifying four types of business owners:

- entrepreneur;
- quasi-entrepreneur;
- administrator;
- caretaker.

This makes the point that not all owners are entrepreneurs – rather their collective role has been to recognize the potential of innovations and to facilitate this through the provision of capital. If they are also the innovator then they may be considered entrepreneurs, or at least quasi-entrepreneurs depending on how active they have been in the innovation process. But other owners of businesses may see themselves as administrators or caretakers (for future generations or other shareholders) and may have a far more conservative orientation. Jogaratnam and Tse (2004) provide one of the few examples of an attempt to explore this in tourism studies, through their case study of hotels in Asia (Box 8.1).

While most of the literature focuses on the role of individuals as entrepreneurs within firms, there is also a burgeoning literature, especially with human geography, on the role of the state and the local state as agents of change (see also Chapters 5 and 6). Probably the most influential contribution to this was David Harvey's (1989) argument that there has been a shift in the late twentieth century from managerialism to entrepreneurialism in the local state, often locked into a game of 'leap-frogging innovations':

> Many of the innovations and investments designed to make particular cities more attractive as cultural and consumer centers have quickly been imitated elsewhere, thus rendering any competitive advantage within a system of cities ephemeral. . . . Local coalitions have no option, given the coercive laws of competition, except to keep ahead of the game thus engendering leap-frogging innovations in life styles, cultural forms, products and service mixes, even institutional and political forms if they are to survive.
>
> (Harvey 1989: 12)

Box 8.1 Entrepreneurship in Asian hotels

This case study of 4- and 5-star hotels in China, Hong Kong, Malaysia and Singapore analyses entrepreneurialism in terms of three main dimensions:

- *Proactive:* These hotels constantly seek new opportunities, experiment with new ideas, anticipate emerging trends and seek to preempt innovations from their main competitors in particular arenas.
- *Innovative:* These hotels consistently commit resources to promoting new ideas, whether in terms of products, services or technology.
- *Risk-taking:* These hotels are less risk averse than the others, and are willing to make 'bold resource commitments' to particular innovations, which offer considerable rewards but also a relatively high risk of failure and loss.

The study found that – unsurprisingly – an entrepreneurial stance is a key ingredient to successful hotel performance. The high performing hotels generally had a more proactive strategic orientation to entrepreneurialism than low performing establishments. A proactive firm was characterized by a competitive strategy that involved a continuous search to identify and exploit new products and services, as well as market prospects. There was also a capacity for, and commitment to, forward thinking about markets and inputs, and an attempt to anticipate future trends. Such firms were characteristically first movers, whether in terms of products or processes. In short, these companies actively seek to shape their future trajectories, rather than reacting to events as they unfold in the external environment. They continuously scan their external environment for opportunities, and their behaviour is likely to disrupt that environment, compared to low performing hotels. The latter were more risk averse, and more reactive. They also tended to prefer the status quo, rather than engage in rapid changes that were considered relatively risky.

High performing hotels were also more innovative in their strategic orientation compared with low performing establishments. Their tactics included identifying marketing opportunities, anticipating opportunities and problems, utilizing new technologies ahead of their rivals, and generally investing in higher risk initiatives. In contrast, managers in low performing hotels tended to favour the status quo and failed to keep abreast of, let alone ahead of, the competition. They were more likely to imitate than to innovate in a disruptive manner.

Source: After Jogaratnam and Tse (2004).

Drawing particularly on Baltimore, Harvey identified three distinguishing characteristics of 'urban entrepreneurialism'. First, that public–private partnerships are often central, with traditional strategies to boost economic growth being reinforced with the (limited, but significant) powers of the local state to attract external investment and funds. Second, that the risks associated with the activities of the partnerships are unevenly distributed, with the local state rather than the private sector being the main underwriter. And, third, that the benefits of urban entrepreneurial projects, such as waterfront redevelopment, are also unevenly distributed, with tourists and visitors benefiting more than local residents, and mobile capital more than local, immobile capital. Subsequently, Jessop (1998) has reworked the notion of the entrepreneurial city, defining entrepreneurialism more in terms of innovation than risk. For him this involves 'new combinations' – whether in economic, political or social terms – that can enhance urban competitive advantages. In practice, and in relation to tourism, this might involve securing new funds (from international agencies, from the national state, or from commercial sources) to fund new uses of urban spaces for tourism, or to reinvigorate existing tourism facilities and services. As discussed in Chapter 6, this is illustrated by a wide range of examples, including much of the wave of waterfront development in urban centres in the developed world.

Harvey (1989) regarded such urban strategies as entrepreneurial because they were speculative, whereas Lovering (1999) argued that such serial reproduction of similar forms of development represented commodification, as the notion of entrepreneurship implies a product is new or innovative rather than just replicated. Indeed, Harvey also acknowledged that the 'search to procure investment capital confines innovation to a very narrow path' (1989: 11). Nevertheless, despite the zero sum or negative sum prospects of speculation and place serialization, particularly given the inability to predict success in attracting mobile production and consumption flows into a particular space for a period of time (Malecki 2004), this still dominates the strategies of many local states with respect to tourism's role in regional competitiveness (see Chapter 6).

Tourism entrepreneurs: heroes in the evolution of tourism

The entrepreneur is one of the most intriguing of characters in what is often the rather abstract and dehumanized territory of economic theory. As stated earlier, the entrepreneur is not an inventor (although some are), but rather is someone who implements an idea. Some individuals are serial entrepreneurs, implementing a sequence of ideas, whereas others may be once in a lifetime entrepreneurs (Rosa and Scott 1999). In any case, they are key figures in bringing about change in economic systems. As Baumol (2002: 58) writes:

> The entrepreneur is at once one of the most intriguing and one of the most elusive in the cast of characters that constitutes the subject of

economic analysis. In the writings of the classical economist the appearance of this important figure was frequent but shadowy, without clearly defined form and function.

And he also observes that '[o]ne can even offer the plausible conjecture that most of the really revolutionary new ideas have been, and are likely to continue to be, provided preponderantly by independent innovators' (Baumol 2002: 56).

Schumpeter, we have noted, formulated two different views of the role of the entrepreneur. Here, we are concerned with the first of these, the notion of the individual as a 'heroic' entrepreneur, standing astride and shaping the process of innovation. This was also Galbraith's (1969: 75) observation that 'the entrepreneur – individualistic, restless, with vision, guile and courage – has been the economist's only hero'. The contrast with Schumpeter's later notion of the entrepreneur as a mechanism in the implementation of changes, driven by shifts in the wider socio-economic environment, is partly an issue about approaches to conceptualization but also reflects that he was writing in the first half of the twentieth century, at a time when R&D had become less routinized in R&D departments and agencies than it would become subsequently.

Despite these reservations, the entrepreneur is key figure in economic change in modern economies. There is however a debate as to whether he or she is a heroic or a 'deviant figure' (Kets de Vries 1977); the latter is based on the argument that the capacity to innovate originates from the responses of individuals to social marginality, which informs both motivation and capacity to think outside the box. Bunnell and Coe (2001: 581) give a further twist to this argument: '[W]hether as hero or deviant, work on entrepreneurship perhaps overplays the role of the individual as site of innovation.' Rather they contend that there is a need to understand the innovation in more relational (to other individuals, agencies and objects) terms, and 'as sites for the creation, storage and dissemination of knowledge for broader innovative processes' (see also Howells and Roberts 2000, and see Chapter 7 with respect to the sectoral system of innovation).

Not surprisingly, there has been considerable debate, and some research, as to how to identify entrepreneurs, or how to define their key characteristics. Chell *et al.* (1991: 76; cited in Chell 2001) provide the following summary of the characteristics of a prototypical entrepreneur:

- alert to business opportunities;
- pursues opportunities regardless of the resources currently controlled;
- adventurous;
- an ideas person;
- restless/easily bored;
- high profile image maker;
- proactive;
- innovative;

- thrives on change;
- adopts a broad financial strategy.

Kanter (1983) provides a rather different perspective on a group of individuals that he terms '*change masters*' (a selectively gendered category) who have the following key skills:

- kaleidoscopic thinking: ability to look at situations from different angles, and to challenge accepted wisdom;
- ability to communicate a vision;
- persistence in the face of obstacles;
- coalition building to effect changes;
- ability to working through teams, that is to engage in participative management;
- willingness to share the credit with others, which can be understood as essential to building trust.

Chell and Kanter provide contrasting view, in part because they focus on characteristics and skills, which are not necessarily the same. In any case, we can see their descriptions echoing the writings of Schumpeter and others with regard to being risk taking, providing a focal point for trust and networks, and having an ability to challenge the status quo.

How do these notions apply to tourism? Whatever theoretical lens we adopt, there is no doubt that the history of tourism bears the imprint of the heroic entrepreneur. This may be as a heroic or as a deviant figure, and it may be as the leader of or as the mechanism of innovation, but in any case we agree with McKercher (1999: 427) that 'the defining moment in most tourism destinations can be attributed to the actions of rogues who actualised its tourism potential'. There are a number of influential figures who are change masters, or heroic innovators such as Thomas Cook, Freddie Laker (budget airline carrier founder), Michael O'Leary (founder of Ryanair), Kirk Kerkorian (one of the most important figures in the development of Las Vegas and, with architect Martin Stern Jr, regarded as the father of megaresorts), Gérard Blitz and Gilbert Trigano (founders of Club Med) and Walt Disney (Disney World). Some of the key innovators have in fact been unintentional innovators, notably celebrities whose holiday preferences have influenced the activities of others. Butler and Russel (2005), for example, write about the influential role of royal personalities in popularizing particular modes of behaviour (such as George II of Britain's preference for spas) or destinations. They illustrate this argument through reference to the role of Queen Victoria and her consort, Prince Albert, in popularizing the Scottish Highlands as a tourist destination. At an earlier date, Walter Scott, the famous Scottish novelist, was an influential figure – an innovator – in managing the visit of King George IV to Edinburgh in the 1820s. The front-stage reception that he organized created and recreated Scottish 'traditions' which boosted a particular view of Scotland and Scottish culture, enriched with tartan-clad clansmen, that still resonates with the marketing of present-day Scottish tourism. Indeed, the recreation of tradition is often integral to innovative event strategies in present-day tourism.

There was no greater heroic figure in the evolution of modern tourism, especially of package tourism, than Thomas Cook and if there is one single key date in the origination of package tourism, then it is 1841 when Cook organized his first excursion by rail. Although an essentially local trip in the British Midlands, it was to foreshadow a form of tourism organization that came to dominate mass tourism in the next century. Soon he was offering not only discounted travel costs but also accommodation and guiding services. As Laws (1997: 4) writes:

> An advertisement at the time exactly defined Thomas Cook's view of the tour agent: 'The main object of the conducted tour apart from being able to calculate the exact costs before starting is to enhance the enjoyment by relieving the traveller of all the petty troubles and annoyances from a journey.'

By 1855 he had internationalized his fledgling tour operator business, offering trips to the European mainland. Many of these trips were largely based on his own interpretations of leading guidebooks of the day, such as Baedeker's.

Perhaps the most distinctive feature of Cook's tours was the provision of a comprehensive range of services to the tourists: travel, hotels, meals, entrance fees and guides. But he also noted that tourists sometimes lacked access to banks while on holidays abroad. Therefore, he introduced a 'Circular Note', or a form or letter of credit, which most of the hotels he had contracted services with agreed to accept in lieu of payment. This was to evolve into the modern traveller's cheque system. Taking advantage of industrial advances with respect to communications (the advent of the telegraph), time regulation (international agreements on time zones were reached that enabled transport schedules to be developed), and transport (railway and steamship), Cook organized his first around the world tour in 1872. His innovative package tour business model, when combined with changes in leisure, income and preferences in society, also led to social innovations with respect to enabling women to travel as well as lower income socio-economic groups.

Over time, the company established by Thomas Cook was caught up, and often surpassed by its rivals, but for a long time it was at the cutting edge of innovation in package tourism. And as late as 1953 it produced what effectively became the forerunner of the modern tour brochure, 'Holidaymaking' (Laws 1997: 5). Although based on the existing design approaches of women's magazines, this was a major innovation in tourism, offering romantic impressions of a range of destinations in a format that was significantly different from that of earlier brochures.

Box 8.2 The birth of the British air inclusive holiday package

Vladimir Raitz, the founder of Horizon Holidays, is often credited with being the originator of the air inclusive holiday. This was sparked almost by accident, when he was invited in 1949 to holiday with friends in Corsica. As he later wrote, a friend propositioned him while on holiday:

> Listen Vova . . . My father, the old Baron, and Tao Khan have excellent connections with the Calvi Mayor and the Municipal Council, and can get a concession on a large piece of land right on the beach between the Club and the town. We'll get some tents and equipment, and you can get us some British clients to supplement the French.

His first question was whether there was an airport and the answer was not entirely reassuring. He was told:

> Not exactly an airport, but there's a runway built by the American Seabees . . . . Mind you there are no airport buildings – not even a shack. I'm sure the Municipality could provide something, though. Why don't you just charter some planes when you get back to London. We'll be opening the Club in May next year, and you can have sole rights for the UK.

He had the capacity to recognize an opportunity which was in tune with the changing social climate in post-Second World War Britain, but he now had to turn this invention into an innovation. After returning to the UK he discovered that it would be quite easy to secure the service of the required aircraft when he visited the Instone Air Transport company. Converted DC3s – Dakotas with 32 seats – were available for hire. However, he also learned that he would need to obtain a licence from the Ministry of Transport to operate such a service, and that this was unlikely – underlining the importance of institutions. He was initially despondent but '[s]till, I was 27 years old, full of optimism, and determined to see this matter through to the end'.

Displaying a classic willingness to accept risk, and persistence in the face of difficulties, he employed a secretary but: 'I still had no office, no company, no name and licence to fly. What I did have was some money. My grandmother had left me just under £3000, and I decided to risk it all on this venture.'

For the name he decided on Horizon Holidays. Meanwhile, he spotted an office while travelling on a London bus and promptly rented it. Then he bought some second-hand furniture, and a typewriter, and 'the day after that, the office was open'. At first his risk looked foolhardy and it remained so until, after five months, he was finally given permission for his flights by the Ministry of Civil Aviation, but only for carrying students and teachers, using a special ruling covering educational tours. Although a much smaller market than he had originally anticipated, he was not deterred and placed advertisements in three specialist newspapers, emphasizing there would be plentiful food and wine, and beds under canvas, all for £32.05.

The first flight took off in May 1950. Although it was only one-third full of paying clients, the other seats were filled with friends on a return flight only, who were given two hours to look at the facilities; in other words, an invaluable promotion opportunity. The first season was a modest success but he only secured 300 of the 350 passengers required to break even and provide funds for launching another season. He duly borrowed £2,000 from a local bank – again demonstrating a risk taking capacity – and the following summer season flew 420 passengers. The modern air inclusive holiday had been successfully implemented, and it was soon to prove a disruptive innovation that fundamentally changed existing holiday behaviour in the developed world.

Source: After Bray and Raitz (2001).

Cook is therefore undoubtedly a heroic entrepreneur, who created and developed a model of guided touring holidays that dominated mass tourism until late in the twentieth century. Of course, he also relied on other agents – the railway and shipping companies, or hoteliers being willing to innovate – as well as institutions relating to inter-governmental relations, and in this sense his role has to be seen as relational. But his vision, commitment and ability to act as a focal point of trust for other agents marks him out as truly heroic. Vladimir Raitz is another heroic entrepreneurial figures (Box 8.2). Based on a casual proposal, with few resources and little experience, but with a capacity to read social trends, a willingness to take risks, and persistence, he established Horizon Holidays in the UK in 1949 and implemented the first air inclusive package holiday. Persistence – but also the politics of monopoly capital – is also one of the lessons to be drawn from the experiences of Ballston Spa and Saratoga Springs in New England (US), and explains why one succeeded and one failed to develop into a major spa resort (Box 8.3).

SMEs and tourism entrepreneurship

SMEs have featured prominently in discussions about economic policy, whether in generic terms or specifically in relation to tourism. Tether (1999), writing about the former, argues that this is hardly surprising when there is

Box 8.3 A tale of two entrepreneurs: the development of Ballston Spa
and Saratoga Springs, New England

Nicholas Low was the entrepreneur who dominated the development of
Ballston Spa for three decades, and was largely responsible for its initial
success although he also contributed unwittingly to its eventual decline.
His interest in the resort was first manifested in 1803 when he planned
to build a hotel there. However, he was an absentee owner, who with
hindsight did not give sufficient time to confronting the severe obstacles
to developing the resort: a short season, a lack of appropriate local
labour, a failure to build up a loyal client base, and erratic spring
weather than often deterred guests. The problem was that: 'Low was a
superb businessman but was not the right kind of entrepreneur for a
resort' (Corbett 2001: 38–9). Moreover, his monopolistic landlordism
was also an obstacle to other investors and entrepreneurs engaging with
the resort's development.

Saratoga Springs had a contrasting history of development. Here the
responsibility for the development of the resort lay in the hands of
several entrepreneurial individuals, such as Walton and Clarke who
were familiar with English spas and sought to translate these ideas to a
'New World' setting: 'Walton and Clarke derived the ideas for pleasure
parks from their experience with the picturesque gardens that had been
introduced on English estates in the 1720s' (Corbett 2001: 74). They
adopted elements of the design of these pleasure gardens, as well as
proven popular novelties such as a circular railway and rustic cottages.
Comparing the resorts, Corbett concludes that:

> Saratoga Springs succeeded because it had several public-spirited
> entrepreneurs who were willing to invest their resources in projects
> without immediate return . . . the diverse leadership of Saratoga
> Springs succeeded, while the solitary landlord-developer was only
> as effective as his interest in the community – and this involvement
> was often fleeting or misguided
>
> (2001: 82)

Source: After Corbett (2001).

such a contrast between, on the one hand, the way many large companies
have downsized while, on the other hand, there have been spectacular
examples of meteoric growth in particular companies, especially in the production of IT hardware and software. Whereas Apple, for example, had only
12 employees in 1976, this number had increased to over 5,000 just six years
later. He concludes: 'The cliché of the little acorn becoming a great oak appears

to have some validity, at least on the other side of the [Atlantic] Pond' (Tether 1999: 2).

The root of these spectacular growth stories lies in the innovation lead established by these small companies and, indeed, several studies were published in the 1980s and early 1990s which contended that small firms were disproportionately innovative, accounting for more innovations than, for example, would be expected on the basis of their share of total employment (Tether 1999: 3). These empirical findings led to assertions that smaller firms were more effective innovators than larger ones. However, more recent empirical evidence – at least at the aggregate level – suggests that larger service firms generally have a higher propensity to innovate than smaller ones (Tether *et al.* 2002: i) and that the development of new products and processes was associated with larger firms. The differences between these two apparently contradictory interpretations centre on how the impact of innovations is measured. It may be true that smaller firms generate disproportionately more innovations, but the value of these innovations tends to increase with the size of the firm.

As usual, there is scant information about how entrepreneurship and innovation vary according to firm size in tourism, but we can draw on three case studies that provide partial insights.

First, in a study of Spanish hotel companies operating in the Balearic Islands (Spain), Mexico and the Dominican Republic (Jacob *et al.* 2004), there is a consistent and direct relationship between size (measured by number of hotel bedrooms) and the number of innovations introduced in that establishment. For example, there was a mean of 13 innovations per hotel in hotels with less than 100 rooms, compared to 14.7 in hotels with more than 500 rooms.

Second, in another Spanish study, Orfila-Sintes *et al.* (2005: 862–3) demonstrate that hotels with only 1 and 2 stars – an approximate indicator of small scale – lag significantly behind 3-, 4- and 5-star establishments in terms of numbers of innovations. In part this is due to resources, of course, especially the human capital at their disposal. But it also relates to being better able to differentiate their product, and being able to respond more rapidly to the opportunities for innovation.

Third, in the US Siguaw *et al.* (2000) examined different types of innovation in the lodgings sector. They found very different strategic approaches. In general, the main focus of lodging firms was on innovations that contributed to improvements in the productivity of their employees, followed by revenue enhancement and the implementation of guest-service technologies. When they considered scale factors, they found that the highest rates of innovation were recorded by the larger, as well as the upmarket, hotels, particularly those that specialized in conferences or provided other dedicated facilities such as a casino, rather than only providing standardized accommodation in motel formats. Independent hotels innovated less than those that belonged to large hotel chains.

In summary, larger hotels do appear to innovate more than smaller establishments. However, none of these studies has been able to trace the impact of the innovations. This is particularly important because, as Tether (1999) notes in his generic comments on the service sector, small firms can make a very specific and substantial contribution to innovation in particular ways, especially through the provision of specialized equipment and services. Not only can they be innovative in these niche areas, but the innovations may enhance production and innovation in larger firms as well. This accords with Rothwell's (1983) view that small and large firms are not necessarily alternative vehicles of innovation but, rather, may be complementary.

This is a view that applies particularly well to tourism where not only is innovation essential to the survival of small firms, but small firms also play a key role in innovation. The first contention about survival echoes our discussion in Chapter 2 about the need 'to innovate or die' in the increasingly competitive environment within which most firms operate. In particular, the return to innovation is critical for those firms that are at greatest risk from failure (Cefis and Marsili 2006: 627). These are disproportionately small firms, and especially those in resorts stocked with large numbers of relatively similar businesses that face strong external competition. Yet there is no convincing evidence that these are the types of firms that have greater innovation potential. Indeed, our earlier discussion suggests that they are less innovative in general than larger establishments.

This leads us to our second contention, that SMEs can be significant sources of innovation under those conditions that favour experimentation in niche markets, or where markets are relatively small scale (see Chapter 3 and see also Shaw and Williams 2004). Moreover, there is an argument that structural economic shifts make small firms even more important as sources of innovation, as Bunnel and Coe (2001: 579) contend in a generic context, drawing on Piore and Sabel (1984) amongst others:

> During the 1980s, in the context of an apparently dramatic restructuring of the Fordist regime of mass production, there was a resurgence of interest in small firms as sources of innovation in developed economies. A number of scholars suggested that small firms were perhaps more flexible, and thus better adapted to fostering and adopting innovations, than large vertically integrated firms

They also present the alternative view (drawing on Harrison 1994; Lazonick 1991) that large, vertically integrated firms are more innovative because they have access to economies of scale. Here, however, we focus on the former argument. Christensen and Overdorf (2001: 103–4) have expanded on this, stressing that large companies can lack flexibility in their responses to new opportunities compared to smaller one. They emphasize not so much resources, as changes in organizational values:

As a company grows, what it can and cannot do becomes more sharply defined in certain predictable ways. . . . When a company is young, its resources – its people, equipment, technologies, cash, brands, suppliers and the like – define what it can and cannot do. As it becomes more mature, its abilities stem more from its processes-product development, manufacturing, budgeting for example. In the largest companies, values – particularly those that determine what are its acceptable gross margins and how big an opportunity has to be before it becomes interesting – define what the company can and cannot do. Because resources are more adaptable to change than processes or values, smaller companies tend to respond to major market shifts better than larger ones.

Of course, this is not to argue that most, let alone all small firms are highly innovative. Rather there may be specific conditions under which they are more innovative than larger firms. Those conditions are particularly evident at different stages in the evolution of a firm (see Chapter 7). But they are also to do with the inbuilt stasis in large companies, which means that they focus more on incremental than on disruptive or radical innovations. Large companies are reasonably effective in responding to evolutionary changes that demand small scale or incremental innovations. In contrast, disruptive innovations are likely to challenge the careful equilibrium that has been constructed in a large company over time. In short, 'disruptive innovations occur so intermittently that no company has a routine process for handling them' (Christensen and Overdorf 2001: 114). And it is precisely under these conditions that small firms, however, selectively, may become innovation leaders.

This is particularly evident in relation to the debates about lifestyle innovation, which we consider below in context of the barriers to innovation in SMEs.

Innovation barriers faced by entrepreneurs in tourism SMEs

There are three main types of barriers faced by entrepreneurs in tourism SMEs relating to capital, human resources, and a complex of lifestyle-related motivations and behaviour. First, there are obstacles related to access to capital. There is a strong reliance on individual or family sources of capital, and on informal as opposed to formal channels such as banks (Williams *et al.* 1989; Thomas 1998). In part this is due to preferences (although these may be shaped by imperfect knowledge of financial institutions), but it is also because '[c]redit market imperfections mean that lenders may not obtain accurate assessments of the viability of investment projects proposed by small businesses' (Blake *et al.* 2006: 1102).

Second, there is a strong tendency in the tourism SME sector, especially in hospitality, for owners to lack formal training or working experience specific to the industry (Williams *et al.* 1989). They may have sufficient informal capital to be able to open up a restaurant or a hotel, but lack the knowledge of networking, coordination and human resources to oversee successful innovation. Moreover, this is compounded because their own lack of formal training may overflow into their approach to training their staff. And employees may also not value training, which may further reduce the scope for innovation: 'The absence of a traditional career ladder in tourism leads some employees to think that training is not worthwhile, while employers are concerned that once employees are trained, they may be poached by rival businesses' (Blake *et al.* 2006: 1102). The lack of human resource skills may be especially critical in the tourism industry because of the significance of service quality. For example, it is not enough to introduce new technology into the firm: there is also a need to train workers in its use, and adjust organizational practices to incorporate it effectively (Jacob *et al.* 2003).

Third, there are particularities of tourism entrepreneurship relating to the way that business and 'tourist' motivations are often interwoven, particularly in those locations where there are highly valued non-urban tourism attractions (beaches, mountains) and high rates of entrepreneurial in-migration and return migration. This can lead to acceptance of sub-optimal profits, and exacerbate the challenge of firm survival. Shaw and Williams (1998: 251) consider there is a substantial presence of such 'non-entrepreneurs' in British coastal resorts, often retired or semi-retired persons, who move into the area, using their personal savings to start a small tourism business: '[W]hen such motives combine with a lack of experience and an aging owner, there tends to be a very limited level of entrepreneurial activity'. However, they do not ascribe all such laggard or passive entrepreneurship to motivations, for they also identify a second group that they term 'constrained entrepreneurs', who are likely to be younger, more economically motivated, but to be constrained by their low levels of business skills and difficulties of accessing capital, for the institutional reasons indicated by Blake *et al.* (2006).

There is considerable evidence for the existence of this lifestyle factor, although most of the case studies come from a few, mostly English speaking, countries such as the UK, US, New Zealand and Australia. This leads Ioannides and Petersen (2003: 411) to contend that:

> A key question remains – to what extent are the operators of SMTEs in a particular destination innovators or 'leaders,' and to what extent are they, as some authors suggest, 'passive entrepreneurs' or 'laggards' (Morrison *et al.* 1999)? Laggards perceive tourism to be an industry with low entry barriers and an opportunity for them to supplement their income during the tourist season, but can hardly be described as professionals (that is people intending to make a long-term career in the tourist industry).

In many cases successful innovation is measured as much by lifestyle values as it is by profit for many tourism SMEs. Evidence for this is drawn from a number of countries, but especially the United Kingdom and New Zealand. There are several variants on this thesis of non-economic entrepreneurship in tourism. For example, in rural New Zealand, Ateljevic and Doorne (2000: 379) found that quality of life and a more individualistic approach were characteristic of many businesses that had constrained business growth (although there are also examples in urban settings – see Box 8.4). However, their goals were expressed not so much in terms of balancing work and leisure in their own lifestyles, as in terms of a broader commitment to a 'lifestyle entrepreneurship which adheres to values embracing a broader ideological context of sustainability'. Whatever the precise motivation, it contributes to what they term 'staying within the fence', understood as an explicit rejection of the commodification demands of capitalist markets, and the pursuit instead of alternative values.

Box 8.4 Urban and rural tourism SMEs and alternative lifestyles: Black Water Rafting and Wellington backpacker accommodation

Tourists to New Zealand from some countries, notably Australia, North America and Europe have demonstrated an increasing propensity for independent travel, and for the pursuit of 'alternative' tourism experiences. For example, an important motivation for Australians was a change in their own lifestyles, whereby they had begun to feel they had little control over their life trajectories, and the intensity at which these unfolded. These contrasted with other lifestyle alternatives, some of which emphasized socio-environmental values. These were particularly important for German visitors who constituted 'environmental evangelists'.

The New Zealand tourism industry has both shaped this demand, as well as been shaped by it. Its small scale structure has both made it attractive to these more individual, and alternative lifestyle seeking tourists, and been influenced by the particularities of tourism interests and willingness to pay for particular experiences.

Some two-thirds of New Zealand's tourism businesses employed less than ten people in the 1990s, according to official statistics, but in reality most are micro businesses (Table 8.1).

Above all, New Zealand demonstrates a highly complementary dovetailing of the interests and values of tourism businesses and tourists in particular sectors: 'The environmentally conscious values around which certain visitor markets are segmented . . . cannot be separated from a corresponding set of values motivating entrepreneurial activity' (Ateljevic and Doorne 2000: 384). These values and entrepreneurial orientations are evident in both urban and rural businesses, although the latter are probably relatively more significant. For example, the innovative entrepreneurs who established Black Water Rafting, were a group of individuals in search of lifestyle opportunities in highly valued

Table 8.1 Structure of New Zealand tourism industry, 1996

Number of employees	Number of businesses	Percentage
>100	70	1.5
50–100	100	2.1
10–49	1,500	31.4
6–9	1,800	37.7
<6	1,300	27.3
Total	4,770	100.0

Source: Based on NZ Statistics, Annual Enterprise Survey, 1996.

environments and landscaped regions. They were classic innovation leaders, and other businesses soon imitated their product which was based on 'guiding rides through underground rivers whilst floating on rubber rings'.

Another example is provided by the provision of specialized accommodation for backpackers in Wellington. These businesses commonly embraced collaboration with like-minded entrepreneurs, that is on trust-based networks within the community. Over time, 'the innovation of these entrepreneurs was . . . (re)produced, with successful elements of the products subject to imitation by businesses displaying high levels of cross-sectoral integration and product packaging' (Ateljevic and Doorne 2000: 388).

Both examples demonstrate the scope for SMEs as sources of disruptive innovation

> given the subsequent reproduction of the products created and the stimulation of regional economic development, the innovative and creative attributes of these individuals closely resemble Schumpeter's observation of entrepreneurs as dynamic elements in the economy, despite their efforts to limit the growth of their own businesses (Ateljevic and Doorne 2000: 389).

Source: After Ateljevic and Doorne (2000).

However, such small lifestyle businesses are not necessarily characterized by non-entrepreneurship or passive entrepreneurship. A national survey of bed and breakfast operators in New Zealand (Hall and Rusher 2004) found that, for slightly more than a third of all respondents, earning income was not a significant necessity. This might be seen to support the notion that such operations are developed only for lifestyle considerations and are therefore not well managed according to business principles. Yet the vast majority of respondents saw profit as being extremely significant and there was also a strong desire to keep the business growing although this was also matched by enthusiasm for lifestyle gains and job satisfaction. As Hall and Rusher (2004) noted, such a combination of goals may cause tensions with the business model but it does not mean that operations were any less well managed or customer oriented than in the 'formal' tourism sector. Indeed, the social motivations of running a bed and breakfast operation clearly indicate the potential for stronger customer service orientations and – under some conditions – innovations.

Taking up the earlier arguments by Christensen and Overdorf (2001), some small businesses – in contrast to larger firms – can be innovation leaders, precisely because they are not constrained by internal routines that are predisposed to maintaining rather than challenging the equilibrium. Ateljevic and Doorne (2000: 378) found evidence of this in New Zealand. Many of these small businesses were based on the pursuit of individualistic lifestyles, and a passion for particular interests, notably outdoor activities, whether horse riding, trekking or kayaking. But at the same time they were highly innovative: 'The ability to position products in a highly segmented marketplace is dependant [*sic*] on the creative and innovative capacity of individual entrepreneurs to identify and to colonise new, "green niche" markets.' The rejection of an explicit profit-driven orientation did not place them on a road to inevitable financial ruin, because their businesses represented disruptive innovations that positioned them favourably in expanding niche markets. Moreover, they provided a positive innovation demonstration effect, which has contributed to the phenomenal growth of entrepreneurship in such sustainable and outdoor tourism activities in New Zealand, and – although to a lesser extent, in relative terms – in other countries. Ateljevic and Doorne (2000: 389) express this in Schumpeterian terms:

> Paradoxically, the search to distance themselves from a 'suffocating' market environment has provided a niche opportunity to simultaneously engage with that market on their own terms and to sustain their businesses in socioeconomic terms. Furthermore, given the subsequent reproduction of the products created and the stimulation of regional economic development, the innovative and creative attributes of these individuals closely resembles Schumpeter's observation of entrepreneurs as dynamic elements in the economy, despite their efforts to limit the growth of their own businesses.

In summary, entrepreneurs in tourism SMEs are not necessarily passive and neither are they necessarily innovation leaders. Rather there is a need to recognize that such entrepreneurs, owners and managers lie on a double continuum, defined by both their commitment to commercial versus noncommercial goals, and passive versus active innovation. Figure 8.1 presents four idealized positions within this double continuum, reflecting whether the businesses are leaders (active – in incremental or disruptive innovation), or

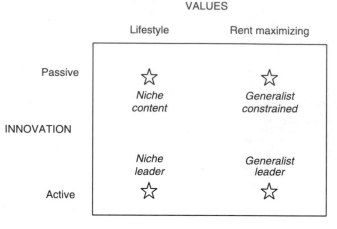

Figure 8.1 Entrepreneurship: a double continuum.

contented/constrained (passive), and in either niche (lifestyle driven) or generalist (rent maximizing) markets. Where individual businesses are located on this double continuum is in part dependent on the previous life trajectories of the individual entrepreneurs, and their motivations, but it also depends on the particular environments in which they are operating, and especially on the existence of niche and, one could add, creative or innovative consumers (see Chapter 3). However, some words of caution are required here. Other positions are possible within this double continuum, and moreover individual businesses may relocate over time, reflecting changes in the internal and external environment of the firm, including product and sector life cycle shifts. Individual lifestyle entrepreneurs may well be leaders of innovation, but even in the New Zealand case many later entrepreneurs were in effect imitating the innovations of the early leaders. They were essential as mechanisms for further developing these niche tourism markets, but could not be considered to be instigators of disruptive innovation. Ioannides and Petersen (2003: 412) in their study in Denmark similarly found a high level of repetitive business practices which, at best, contributed to incremental innovations. It is difficult to argue with their conclusion that we need to replace generalization about entrepreneurship in SMEs with greater recognition of historical and geographical contingencies.

Families and entrepreneurship

Entrepreneurship, despite the ideology that attaches this to individualism, is always relational and this has been recognized in terms of research on the networks within which entrepreneurship occurs. The family also provides context for entrepreneurship, either as a passive agent impacted on by the activities of one individual, or as active partners, in varying ways, in the process itself. This remains surprisingly under-researched in most contexts, let alone tourism:

> During the past two decades, the notion that entrepreneurs are embedded in social relationships has become almost axiomatic in the entrepreneurship literature. . . . Rather ironically, however, the embeddedness approach has virtually neglected the one social institution in which all entrepreneurs are embedded – the family.
>
> (Aldrich and Clift 2003: 589)

The family is particularly important in understanding entrepreneurship in tourism, given the nature of some sub-sector activities – for example, small guesthouses or pensions, restaurants or farm accommodation, where home and workplace overlap to a considerable extent. To some extent this may be constrained, as when a farm has to diversify into tourism activities to survive, but there are also several positive reasons for active family engagement.

First, as Morrison *et al.* (1999) note, many small tourism businesses are initially stimulated by motivations linked to preferred lifestyles, involving a different balance between income, way-of-life and the family. This is probably epitomized by two individuals who decide to stop pursuing high pressure careers as employees, and seek an alternative lifestyle based around the family and shared activity in a small tourism enterprise. In practice, they may have idealized the working and living conditions associated with such ventures, but this does not deny the importance of the motivation.

Second, individuals may be driven by obligations to provide for their kin, friends or members of particular tribes or other groups. For example, parents may decide to develop farm tourism, involving all the family, so that they can guarantee to pass on the farm and the land to the succeeding generation. This can be understood as a form of altruism that is articulated through the notion of 'stewardship' of the land and enterprise (Zahra 2003). The kinship expectations relating to entrepreneurs are even stronger in many less developed countries. For example, Hitchcock (2000: 205–6) writing about Indonesia contends: 'Entrepreneurs, however, are not driven solely by profit since the desire for prestige and the constraints and obligations of membership of a particular group (e.g. kinship group) may also influence behaviour.'

Third, the family also represents a resource that can be utilized in support of setting up or expanding an enterprise (Chrisman *et al.* 2003). Family members may be more or less equal partner, or – as is often the case – relationships can be highly gendered. Hitchcock (2000: 220) again provides interesting insights, in context of Indonesia. He argues that the unpredictable behaviour of governments, and poor regulatory regimes create a high risk operating environment for entrepreneurs. One way to minimize such risks – and to some extent this applies to any operating environment – is to call on networks of kin and other related persons, so that at least the staffing of the enterprise can be founded on trust-based relationships. And moreover, 'not only do goods and services travel along networks, but so do knowledge and skills' (Hitchcock 2000: 221). But although there is a theoretical basis for anticipating that effective use of family and other kin can increase the competitiveness of enterprises, the empirical evidence for this is still limited (Chrisman *et al.* 2003).

Fourth, and an extension to the general argument about the family providing resources to support entrepreneurship, it is likely to be particularly important in the start-up stages of business development (Aldrich and Clift 2003: 577). The family is of course a source of capital but also of labour (Williams *et al.* 1989). Moreover, this labour is highly flexible – family members can be called upon to provide variable amounts of labour, according to demand fluctuations, and can be 'un-employed' without the constraints of contracts and obligations that are usual for non-family workers.

There are, however, limitations to the role of family in entrepreneurship and innovation, in that it can become a constraint. Succession and stewardship pay scant regard to issues of capacity for management, let alone for innovation in response to the logic of 'innovate or die'. The original founder of the business may have been highly creative and a disruptive innovator, but his/her successors may be unable to look beyond incremental innovation. Family businesses can respond to this by putting aside primogeniture and other succession rules, and instead, seek to appoint the individual – family or otherwise – who is best able to provide effective leadership of an enterprise (Tan and Fock 2001). But in reality, social expectations, and well-embedded social routines relating to succession, may inhibit this approach.

However, the changing nature of the family unit in western society raises significant questions as to family business innovation and succession. For example, in their survey of bed and breakfast accommodation in New Zealand noted above, Hall and Rusher (2004) reported that less than 10 per cent of respondents indicated that their children or other family members were moderately to fully involved in running the business. Yet the majority of respondents described themselves as a family business. Such a situation raises fundamental questions about the notion of family businesses particularly as there was only limited support (just under 30 per cent) for the statement that the business was an important means of keeping a property in the family.

Although it is clearly debatable as to who or what constitute a family unit, it would seem likely – at least in more developed countries – that the role of couples as entrepreneurs may be far more important than the notion of a family business as being operated on an inter-generational basis. Therefore, the idea of co-preneurship (Marshack 1994) would seem to be an useful avenue with which to investigate such businesses, and others like them in the tourism industry, as part of a life-course approach to examining business development and entrepreneurial behaviour.

The determinants of innovation-related entrepreneurship

In this final section of the chapter we return to the question of whether entrepreneurship is to be understood as a heroic and creative means of disruptive innovation, or – and rather more prosaically – as a mechanism for innovation. Baumol (2002: 59–60) argues for the latter, in that he sees entrepreneurship being driven by external conditions:

> [The] overall determinants of levels of entrepreneurship are the level of returns available in a sector, or indeed in an economy over time. They move between sectors in response to their reading of market signals. As such they make major contribution to the dynamism of the economy.

However, even in this largely mechanistic view of entrepreneurship, it is evident that some entrepreneurs are more innovative than others, and some external environments are more conducive than others to fostering innovation, of whatever kind. Here we consider the key determinants of the emergence and application of talent, enterprise and creativity in particularly settings. These can be seen to constitute layers of inter-related scales.

Structural conditions. These are shaped at both the national and regional level as illustrated by our earlier discussions of what may be termed national and local innovation systems (Chapters 5 and 6). Essentially, some environments – for reasons related to how markets are constructed and their institutions – are more favourable than others to innovation. The particular reasons are necessarily complex and centre on capital markets, the specific roles of state intervention, the existence of inter-agency relationships and trust, and the existence of a cosmopolitan social environment that is not only tolerant of, but also encourages and rewards, difference and dissent

Hitchcock (2000: 218) considers that Bali is exceptionally favourable to entrepreneurship, and acts as a training ground 'for entrepreneurs who eventually open businesses on other islands; small-scale traders often refer to Kuta Beach as the *Universitas Pantai*, the university of the beach'. They are multilingual and this gives them a pivotal role in how tourists negotiate and experience some aspects of the Bali tourism experience. This is largely unplanned, emphasizing the difficulties faced by policy-led, top-down innovation strategies. The Tamaki family in New Zealand provide a different example of indigenous entrepreneurs drawing on particular cultural and material resources for tourism innovation (Box 8.5).

Not only is place and space important, but so also is the *temporal dimension*. This is related to the notion of the product cycle with Dahmen (1988) contending that the introduction of a disruptive innovation is typically followed by relatively stable conditions, as demand matures for what are increasingly well-defined products. This is a period when barriers to entry are relatively low, and there is a considerable amount of imitative entrepreneurship as passive entrepreneurs 'fill the gap' arising from the rapid expansion

Box 8.5 Indigenous entrepreneurship: Tamaki Tours

The sale of a much-loved Harley-Davidson motorcycle is not the traditional source of funding used to start most entrepreneurial ventures. However, having been declined a bank loan, this is how Mike Tamaki convinced his brother Doug that they should initially fund their now multi-million dollar, award-winning tourist operation, Tamaki Tours Ltd (also known as Tamaki Heritage Experiences) which they own with their wives (Tamaki Heritage Experiences 2007). The way in which the company was first funded is now legendary (Tourism New Zealand 2007) and is an exemplar of Maori innovative business (Maori Innovation Summit 2007). Yet, as Timmons and Spinelli (2007: 132) comment, 'businesses that can be started with little or no capital are rare'.

While the case focuses on Mike Tamaki as a successful New Zealand entrepreneur, he cannot be singled out from his brother Doug and their wives, Karene and Kate, when considering the success of Tamaki Tours as the business was very much a family venture from the outset. While Mike identified the initial opportunity, the success and growth of the firm has been a team effort. This is evidenced by the company's own web site that credits 'the business' and not specifically Mike, as winning the Young Entrepreneur of the Year Award in 1998 (Tamaki Heritage Experiences 2007).

Mike Tamaki's initial concept for the business was 'sketched out on half an A4 page' (Smith and Liu 2002: 25). Although Mike himself admits this was far from being a substantial plan (Smith and Liu 2002), what he had identified was the opportunity for a unique New Zealand cultural tourism operation that focused on providing a more authentic experience of Maori culture. Initially this was based on tours, but now it is focused on a recreated Maori business and a tribal marketplace. Tamaki Tours benefited from the work backgrounds of the brothers. They had gained general confidence, as well as entertainment and hosting experience, by performing in bands, while Mike's previous employment as a tour coach driver gave him a 'good, general understanding of the New Zealand tourism industry infrastructure' and an intuitive sense 'for what tourists wanted' (Smith and Liu 2002: 25). However, one of the company's weaknesses was that nobody involved had any 'experience in administration, bookkeeping, or anything similar' (Smith and Liu 2002: 26). So Karene completed a government-subsidized course in general bookkeeping in order to take on this role for the company in its early years. Subsequently, the company has rapidly grown so outside expertise, as well as a more formal organization structure, are now required. However, the family remain 'the ones who are driving the process . . . We're the ones with the visions, the dreams, and we know exactly how it will work and why it will work' (cited in Smith and Liu 2002: 33).

The family business dimension is integral to many small tourism businesses. However, while the family aspect is important it also needs to be understood within a cultural context as it was culture that provided a point of creativity and innovation and hence differentiation over their competitors. '*Tamaki Tours* is, according to its owners and operators, a *Maori tourism business*' (Te Puni Kōkiri 2001: 116), referring not just to its product but its business model. However, Maori knowledge is non-cosmopolitan and culturally specific and provides a significantly different framework for innovation as compared to knowledge obtained via the connectivity of technological innovation systems, although it may be complementary in many circumstances.

The brothers' family background, born to a European mother and a Maori father has significantly influenced the firm. While their formal education did not necessarily value Maori knowledge highly, the brothers' focus on Maori culture evolved simultaneously with the formation and growth of the business. In creating a Maori company they have discovered and reinforced their own identity and been motivated to create an organization that gives emphasis to and protects Maori heritage. Mike Tamaki (cited in Hatton 1999) maintains that

> 'New Zealand Maori are in an excellent position to take a lead role in this kind of development as every other indigenous nation in the world acknowledged us as being leaders in adapting to a westernised society so well and so quickly, and yet maintaining our heritage and culture so intently.'

Indigenous entrepreneurship has often been overlooked in contemporary entrepreneurial research (Schaper and Volery 2004). Peredo *et al.* (2004: 3), go so far as to assert that while 'general motivations and strategies of entrepreneurs' are widely accepted in traditional entrepreneurial research, 'a question whether these generalisations are, in fact, applicable to indigenous peoples' entrepreneurial ventures remains'. Much indigenous knowledge is non-cosmopolitan and also highly localized, yet this may provide a significant point of differentiation and innovation in tourism terms as well as potentially supplying a dense network of social and economic relations within which indigenous firms are embedded. Indigenous entrepreneurship therefore reflects the importance of 'institutional proximity – that is, shared norms, conventions, values, expectations and routines arising from commonly experienced frameworks of institutions' (Gertler 2003: 91). The micro-level learning activities of firms such as the Tamaki Brothers can be understood as being shaped by macro-level societal institutions (Lam 2000). In the Maori context this is extremely important as there is great stress on the importance of family and *iwi* (tribe) not only as institutions but also as drivers of economic activity for transgenerational transmission (Te Puni Kōkiri 2001). Whether indigenous cultures should be regarded as separate innovation systems is debatable. Nevertheless the indigenous dimension does provide another avenue for understanding innovation and entrepreneurial drivers, as well as highlighting the role of cultural institutions in influencing the trajectories of innovation systems.

of demand (see Box 8.5). Eventually demand growth stagnates or declines, so that the barriers to entry for passive entrepreneurs become more substantial (Ioannides and Petersen 2003: 414): 'Gradually, as the destination matures and becomes saturated with similar tourism establishments catering to a narrow market niche (e.g. bed and breakfast facilities), competition increases, and business owners are forced to innovate their product to stay in business.'

Box 8.6 Tourism entrepreneurship, Bornholm, Denmark

The principal motivation for starting a tourist business on Bornholm was lifestyle choice rather than the pursuit of economic goals. This was underscored by a high rate of in-migration (half of the business owners were in-migrants). There was also a relatively stable economic structure, with some two-thirds of tourism businesses having been in existence for more than ten years. And, significantly, very few of the majority of businesses that had operated for more than ten years had experienced any noteworthy – that is more than small scale, incremental – product or process innovations. Not surprisingly, therefore, the leaders in innovation were new or younger rather than well-established businesses.

Many of the other features of the tourism businesses also accorded with the classic characteristics of non-entrepreneurs (Shaw and Williams 1998). The majority were aged over 45, most had very few employees, and they were reliant on informal funding sources. This contributed to relatively low levels of innovation in most arenas of the firms' activities.

IT could be expected to be one of the critical areas of innovation for such firms, especially given their relatively isolated locations. At first sight this appears to be the case: all but two of the firms in the survey owned computers and virtually every one of these used e-mail regularly. However, their use of IT was relatively limited, for only five of these companies had online reservation facilities, and none offered prepayment/credit card facilities to secure such online reservations. Similarly, most accommodation establishments only used e-mail as a means of obtaining reservations, and they still required customers to mail deposits to them. The authors conclude that despite the heavy usage of computers, the SMTEs in our study do not use information technologies with software specifically designed for the needs of their operation or in a manner that allows them to practice significant process innovation. Rather, it appears that these businesses are passive users of existing well-known information technologies, which they adopt in order to keep up with their competitors.

In other words, these are not innovation leaders, even in terms of IT where initially they seemed to perform favourably. The reasons for this are complex, but include a weak institutional set-up and the extreme peripherality of tourism in the islands, which limits the scope for realizing returns from high risk initiatives. Not only have such conditions limited the propensity to innovate amongst SMEs, but they have also discouraged external actors (such as hotel chains) from investing in innovations in the islands. The authors conclude that Bornholm's tourism industry is characterized by 'gap filling'.

There are some examples of innovative firms, including the Bülow glassworks, whose rapid growth has been driven by constant product and market innovation. Such leading innovators, whether nominally tourism businesses or not, have often test marketed their innovative products on tourists to the islands in the summer. However, the study is not able to address the critical question of why some individuals, but not others, have been leading innovators.

Source: After Ioannides and Petersen (2003).

At this point, there are likely to be relatively greater returns for those entrepreneurs who can pioneer radical innovations. This schema has close parallels with Butler's (1980) account of the tourism resort life cycle, although the latter also stresses the increased role of external entrepreneurs in the middle stages of the evolutionary cycle of destinations. In terms of innovation, of course, the critical change in the life cycle is in levels of competition, which in turn drives innovation.

Family–individual relationships. Not only is the family a partner in many entrepreneurial ventures, but the family system can determine the rate of entrepreneurship (Aldrich and Clift 2003: 591). In particular, establishing new enterprises seems to be associated with major family transitions; critical points in the trajectory of individual families – whether divorce or children leaving home, for example. There are also unanswered questions as to whether particular family norms, attitudes and values determine rates and types of entrepreneurship, some of which we have hinted to in relation to examples about family farm diversification.

Finally, there are key characteristics that determine why some *individuals* rather than others become entrepreneurs. These are only partly explained by accounts that focus on socio-economic characteristics, such as social marginalization, or ethnicity and blocked mobility opportunities in the workplace. Rather, there are also critical socio-economic characteristics related to individuals' approaches to risk, their social identification (Terry *et al.* 1999), and achievement versus affiliation motivation (McClelland 1985).

9   Conclusions

Although tourism is often regarded as 'an ill-defined sector' (Cheshire and Malecki 2004: 260), it is an area that is becoming increasingly recognized as a significant economic base of urban and regional development strategies, as well as a component of territorial competition. However, the innovative capacity of tourism along with that of other primarily consumer services has not been given the attention it deserves, whether at the territorial or firm level.

Tourism, territory and innovation

Concepts such as the 'learning firm' (Starbuck 1992), 'learning economy' (Lundvall and Johnson (1994), the 'learning region' (Maskell and Malmberg 1999), 'creative economies' (Florida 2002), 'knowledge economies' (Cooke 2002) and 'intelligent cities' (Komninos 2002) all convey the systemic nature of continual learning and effective knowledge transactions as the basis for innovation in the face of increasing competition. Tourism plays an important enabling role for macro or meso-based approaches to innovation, providing physical connectivity of places, enabling temporary clustering via the meetings and exhibitions sector, as well as contributing via the cultural, leisure sectors, to attractive place environments in which intellectual capital can be anchored or 'stuck' in context of societies increasingly hallmarked by mobility. Furthermore, tourism helps to image regions and develop place brands thereby assisting in the visibility of places in national and international markets, with the protection and maintenance of place brands becoming an area of knowledge-intensive services in its own right. Tourism is an important – and sometimes the leading – export sector or industry in many regional and national economies, and as important to welfare levels in those places as the electronics or financial services sectors are in iconic learning regions such as Silicon Valley or the City of London. Nevertheless, despite this undoubted significance, national and regional innovation policies usually fail to recognize tourism's role, and – even more surprisingly – most national tourism policies also fail to engage effectively with this.

The relative lack of recognition of tourism in innovation policy is unlikely to surprise those familiar with the innovation policy landscape. Innovation success is often measured by factors such as patents. With the exception of IT, and some transport technologies, the nature of what are usually described as service industries means that the intellectual property they generate is often difficult to protect, particularly with respect to (highly visible) service process and product innovations. The tourism innovation landscape in particular is characterized by public goods, free riding and weak barriers to imitation. Yet the difficulty of protecting innovations does not mean that they should not be encouraged. Indeed, the predilection of most innovation policy settings to focus on science and technology, and manufacturing, without due regard for the service dimensions of the economy, and especially consumer services, is increasingly recognized as a weakness in such policies. This is especially germane with respect to the transfer of innovation from concept to market and the dramatic macroeconomic shift from goods to services in the development world (for example, Ståhle 2007).

At the macro level (national and supranational), tourism is usually formally unacknowledged in national innovation policies. It is more likely to be acknowledged in national tourism policies but, even where this is the case, these primarily focus on product innovation or what is regarded as an innovative marketing strategy. There is, however, greater recognition of the role of tourism in innovation strategies at the regional level. In part this is simply a function of the increasing specialized nature of economies when viewed at this scale (with tourism more likely to be considered a significant economic sector) but it is also a reflection of the territorially competitive nature of many regional policies. Of course, the degree to which policies can actually 'create' innovative and learning regions or prolong the lives of such regions that have appeared 'organically' is an open question (Cheshire and Malecki 2004), with a number of regions utilizing an imitative as opposed to innovative approach to knowledge and learning. Nevertheless, it also apparent that the variable capacity of places to make themselves 'sticky' (in terms of knowledge, knowledgeable people, innovative companies etc.) is itself a product of their economic and cultural trajectories, lived-in experiences of innovation, and prior innovation system. The outcome is that tourism innovation policy resembles a patchy, sometimes threadbare, quilt, where 'the weavers' have combined elements imitated from other regions, with new ideas responding to the particular interests of their constituents and the regional or national institutions.

As Chapter 6 noted, many regions find it difficult to take a 'high road' to innovation because of the potential long time lag in realizing the benefits of this route. There is a growing consensus among researchers on the need to focus on long-term competence building in firms, and in society as a whole, with respect to supporting innovation processes (Lundvall *et al.* 2002). However, the political and financial institutional arrangements tend to be focused on short-term returns, because the electoral cycle shapes public policy just as much as shareholders dictate the actions of publicly quoted private companies. Although the concept of innovation systems is useful in helping to understand innovation and policy–action relationships it does not necessarily provide for early positive policy returns or 'solutions', especially in an age of mobility and competitiveness. Moreover, the concept of innovation systems, which highlights the role of connectedness, relationships and networks between actors and institution as well as more intangible concepts such as non-tradable externalities, does not sit easily in institutional frameworks that generally operate on bureaucratic, silo principles. For such concepts to work effectively, there needs to be connected innovation champions at the highest levels of government, industry and key institutions, such as universities, as well as a culture of innovation. This is much easier to write about than to develop.

The firm: innovate or die, or innovate and die?

The traditional mantra of 'innovate or die', has been eloquently expressed by Baumol (2002: 1): 'Under capitalism, innovative activity – which in other types of economy is fortuitous and optional – becomes mandatory, a life-and-death matter for the firm'. Similarly, Poon (1993: 267) was in no doubt that this applied to tourism:

> As a result of changes in today's tourism marketplace, industry players virtually have to be masters of innovation in order to survive. Industry players have to be innovative in order to stay ahead of the game. In a sea of change, where innovative sharks are gobbling up small and big fishes alike, players have to use their ingenuity to survive. Innovation is definitely the way to go.

Tourism firms have always innovated in the face of such competitive pressures, and in context of knowledge shifts, but tourism research has lagged behind in analysing this until recently. However, as this book has shown, a number of conclusions can be drawn with respect to innovation. First, the customer, whether end customer or intermediate (that is, business to business) is the reference point. In many areas of tourism the customer experience is regarded as the critical product output. This was recognized before Pine and Gilmore (1999) coined the idea of the 'experience economy' but the attention given to Pine and Gilmore's work has served to reinforce the importance of the tourist experience as a focal point of innovative tourism business activity. In addition, the focus on such intangibles as brand (whether company or destination) as part of the experience has also drawn attention to the issue of how firms can add value for customers as a point of competitive advantage, as well as enhanced productivity and returns.

Second, many innovations in tourism are increasingly grounded in service products that have shifted or blurred the boundary of the firm. There is increasing realization that the tourism firm is not a discrete entity, with clearly defined borders, but instead is embedded in formal and informal networks and relationships. This means that innovations can occur not so much 'within the walls' of the firm, but via the different tasks that actors perform in the value chain, for example the roles of customers and customer relationships as a source of innovation, as well as key role of IT and other suppliers in driving innovation. This has sometimes been recognized in terms of clustering or network concepts, which have become an increasingly important focus of tourism research activity (for example, Thomas 2004; Michael 2006; Hall 2008a).

Third, entrepreneurship is a core process in innovation at the firm level as well as with respect to the role of industry actors in innovation systems. It is not an 'add on' activity, but an essential activity in the survival or growth of the firm, over anything except the shortest of time spans, and outside anything but the most monopolistic of sub-markets. Entrepreneurship is a complex process, characterized by failure as well as success. By definition – particularly if it is disruptive – innovation involves risk, as well as the promise of greater competitiveness and new markets. The risk takes many forms – the opportunity costs of managers' time, market uncertainties for untested products or processes, and the capital invested in particular ventures. That is why it is not only a case of 'innovate or die' but equally – if unsuccessful – of 'innovate and die'.

Although innovation remains relatively neglected in tourism studies, there is an emerging corpus of research on entrepreneurship. Within this, the tourism literature has become particularly focused on the concepts of lifestyle entrepreneurship. Understanding the lifestyle motivations of many tourism entrepreneurs itself is potentially a major contribution to a broader conceptualization and understanding of entrepreneurship beyond narrow profit maximization perspectives. However, there are limited longitudinal studies of tourism firm innovation and survivability that limit our understanding of tourism entrepreneurship in comparison with other sectors. Such comparisons would emphasize that lifestyle entrepreneurship is not unique to tourism, but as in all sectors there is a continuum between rent maximizing and lifestyle goals. Individual entrepreneurship, and other economic activities, always involve compromises between these supposed poles, and moreover they shift through time.

Fourth, IT capabilities have become a critical focus of tourism service innovation because of their potential to commercialize or '"productize" (that is, make more repeatable) innovative service concepts. In many ways, IT is the production department of the services era in much the same way factories and machines were for the goods era' (Tekes 2007: n.p.). IT capabilities have also allowed the development of new service concepts, and have impacted on the value chain and value networks of products and firms, with the internet being central to these changes. Nevertheless, while the internet is a major technological focal point for all service sectors, in the case of tourism, changes in transport are also vital for the co-production and creation of tourist experiences.

Fifth, while the focus is often on the external drivers for innovation such as IT and networks there are numerous innovation points within the tourism firm that provide sources of value creation. These include such points as the business model, service design and development, customer relationships and support of the firm's core processes and employees. Although many of these points are hard to protect from imitative strategies of competitors, innovations can still provide first mover advantage while significant intellectual capital that may be difficult to replicate can also be kept within firms. At the heart of this lies tacit knowledge (Chapter 3), the most elusive but essential ingredient in innovation. This is easier to protect in tourism than many forms of codified knowledge, although there can be, and are, knowledge spillovers, for example via the mobility of individual workers and managers.

Taking forward the innovation agenda

The insights and conclusions provided above, as well as throughout this book, should be regarded as tentative, for the volume has been more exploratory in nature than an attempt to synthesize a largely non-existent literature. Tether and Metcalfe's (2005: 287) observation that 'more research needs to be done before we can claim a comprehensive understanding of the problems of innovation generation and diffusion' applies as much in relation to tourism as it does to the services field as a whole. The intrinsically multidisciplinary nature of service innovation also requires different research approaches compared to those that can be applied to many areas of manufacturing or product-oriented industries, which typically seek predictability and control in operations, as opposed to the variability that is part of many service offerings. The Finnish funding agency for technology and innovation, Tekes (2007), articulated this point:

> Unfortunately, the science of innovation is still a mystery. The innovation movement is where the quality movement was 25 years ago. The train has barely left the station, and service innovation is the caboose on that train. But the lessons of the quality movement tell us what to expect in the next few years:
>
> • Our knowledge of service innovation is incomplete
> • Some things that we believe to be true about service innovation will prove to be inaccurate
> • Deep research is needed to move toward a true science of innovation
> • Our operating models will need to change

All of these observations raise the fundamental question of 'why innovate?', particularly as the business outcomes of such innovations are unclear and sometimes highly risky. Indeed, this is a critical point as the reality is that many firms and destinations survive with minimal innovation for what the owners/managers consider an acceptable period of time. Such firms are usually the late adopters of the innovation cycle. They may not make the potentially large returns that accrue to first movers or early innovators, but neither do they face potentially large losses. And, given the economic, business and learning context they are operating in, this may be an appropriate strategy, especially if they can also tap into knowledge spillovers from other actors, with respect to their specific needs, resources and business objectives. While most tourism businesses are seeking to make a profit, many are not seeking rapid growth. In fact the lifestyle dimension of some smaller tourist firms means that they are seeking to maximize a range of social and economic goals that may be incompatible with some aspects of commercial innovation. And more prosaically, entrepreneurs in many small firms may be constrained (in terms of knowledge or capital), and they are passive innovators by default rather than as elective lifestyle choices. In contrast, governments, which are seeking to promote economic and employment growth strategies, and larger firms, particularly transnationals, are likely to be much more active in innovation, in the face of the intensification of competition, even if that innovation is sometimes imitative and often incremental rather than disruptive.

Arguably, the perspective that innovation is 'essential' has developed out of the discourse of competitiveness that dominates much policy and industry thinking (Cheshire and Malecki 2004; Bristow 2005). Several reasons can be given for this dominance. First, it is resonant with existing business discourse as well as providing an exciting image of business and territorial activity. Second, it suggests that policy makers as well as firms can actually strongly influence their own futures, and that innovations can bring results. Third, it is business and political interests rather than the intrinsic merits of ideas that shape innovation policy making. However, academic and other institutional interests are also significant, particularly the ways in which academic knowledge is also produced, framed, disseminated and received in relation to certain 'economic' knowledges. This last point is significant because academic research and knowledge transfer is an integral component of the soft infrastructure of innovation and place competitiveness (Hall 2007).

There is relatively little overt analysis of the policy role that academic creativity plays in regional economic development. Nor, just as significantly, as to *how* the credibility of such research is mobilized. For example, Gibson and Klocker (2004: 424) noted that research on the supposed creative city is being undertaken within a creative industry and is inherently a part of the discourse that it is trying to understand: 'Such research is now complicit within its own subject – a pursuit of creative information production.'

The above comments do not mean we discard either the importance of innovation for tourism or tourism for innovation systems. Rather we are seeking to highlight the need for caution and that innovation needs to be understood from a strategic perspective, whether that of a firm or a place. Innovation is not a goal in its own right, it is a means to an end. In fact, in some situations innovation is clearly required. We have already noted the tension between 'innovation or die' versus 'innovation and die', but innovation also has wider social ramifications. For example, innovation can have a positive role in sustainable tourism development. Technical innovation in terms of developing substitutes for scarce products may help to overcome the fact that natural capital cannot always be reproduced. In a similar vein social innovation and institutional redesign may help to overcome a crisis where the social capital is foundering, or to produce a redistribution of welfare (see Box 9.1).

Innovation is not about markets and unfettered competition, although of course most innovation occurs in markets, of varying contestability, and competition is a driver of, or driven by, innovation. But private capital is incapable of ensuring its own reproduction, and it is widely recognized that the workings of unhampered market forces will erode the basis of economic growth (Lundvall *et al.* 2002: 228). The key to economic growth, and innovation, lies in the specific institutions of capitalist economies, and proto-capitalist economies. That is why tourism innovation must be understood in terms of the variegations of capitalist societies and markets (Shaw and Williams 2004: chapter 2).

Box 9.1 Social innovation: an extreme makeover?

Societies advance through innovation every bit as much as economies do. But we still treat social innovation in a much more amateurish way than innovation in science or business. It remains roughly at the point where science was more than a century ago, when invention and innovation were left to the enthusiasm and energy of determined individuals. Although more policy ideas are now piloted than in the past, there are very few institutions devoted to social innovation, no widely accepted methods for doing it, no serious academic works analysing it and no widely used metrics for measuring it. Worse, there are strong disincentives to innovate in both the public and voluntary sectors. It is well-known that the penalties for failed innovations are often high while the rewards for successful ones are slim.

Over the past 40 years, a huge investment has gone into new ideas in IT, and has given us everything from iPods and Google to smart missiles and 3G mobiles. Just imagine if a similar investment had been made in innovations in homelessness, older people's care or zero-carbon housing, and with a similarly rigorous commitment to supporting ideas that work. It is not far-fetched to believe that an enormous amount of unnecessary human suffering could have been averted.

Source: Mulgan (2006).

Note: Geoff Mulgan is director of the Young Foundation. *Social Silicon Valleys: A Manifesto for Social Innovation* is available from the Young Foundation at www.youngfoundation.org.

Innovation is about adapting to or shaping change. Most innovation has a limited range or impacts, while the most holistic and radical – what Abernathy and Clark (1988) term architectural innovation – can reshape the larger board on which the intriguing but deadly earnest game of innovation is played out. In this sense, the biggest challenges to tourism innovation are likely to come not only from within the sector but also beyond it. Even a body as conservative as the OECD recognizes the uncertainties surrounding contemporary economic change of which tourism constitutes an important element:

> Two of the main engines that drive globalisation – liberalisation and progress in transport – may run out of steam. Further liberalisation is increasingly difficult to achieve because the issues to be addressed are more controversial and more actors are involved in the decision-making process.
> Further expansion of transport – notably the two fastest increasing components of the transport sector (road and air transport) often appear to be largely unsustainable. Moreover, other factors such as geopolitics or security, environmental concerns such as climate change, or demographic change could slow or undermine the process in different ways.
>
> (OECD 2007: 55)

Innovation is likely to become more rather than less important in the face of such potentially radical shifts in political economy (see Box 9.2).

Box 9.2 A prize to save the Earth?

In February 2007 Sir Richard Branson offered a US$25m (£12.8m) prize for scientists who find a way to help save the planet from the effects of climate change. Flanked by the former US vice-president Al Gore, the head of Virgin called for scientists to come up with a way to extract greenhouse gases from the atmosphere. Describing the prize as the largest ever offered, Branson compared it to the competition to devise a method of accurately estimating longitude. He denied that being the head of an airline prevented him from being concerned about climate change:

> Let's confront the airline question. I have an airline. I can afford to ground that airline today. My family have got businesses in mobile phones and other businesses, but if we do ground that airline today, British Airways will just take up the space. So what we are doing is making sure we acquire the most carbon dioxide-friendly planes. We're making sure that 100% of profits we make from our transportation businesses are put back into things like the prize we've offered today.
>
> (Cited in Sturcke 2007)

In commenting on the launch of the prize, Tony Jupiter, the Friends of the Earth's director, warned against wasting time waiting for new innovations:

> Technology has an important role to play in tackling climate change, and Sir Richard's initiative may encourage innovators to develop a wonder technology which takes carbon dioxide out of the atmosphere. But many of the ways of tackling climate change, such as energy efficiency and renewables, already exist, and it is essential that these are implemented as soon as possible. We cannot afford to wait for futuristic solutions which may never materialise. Sir Richard must also look at his business activities and the contribution they make to climate change. The world will find it very difficult to tackle climate change if air travel continues to expand and space tourism is developed.
>
> (Cited in Sturcke 2007)

This book has made a first step in understanding the relationship between innovation and tourism. Like many things in tourism it has emphasized that innovation in the field cannot be understood just by examining the tourism industry or the tourist. Rather it has highlighted that tourism's relationship with innovation needs to be contextualized with national, regional, spatial and sectoral innovation systems. Central to such innovation systems are the knowledge spillovers from universities and researchers as well as, of course, tourism firms. Tourism researchers, as much as tourism businesses and policy makers, neglect innovation at their peril.

References

Aaker, D.A. (2004) 'Leveraging the corporate brand,' *California Management Review*, 46(3): 6–18.

Abernathy, W.J. and Clark, K.B. (1988) 'Innovation: mapping the winds of creative destruction', in Tushman, M.L. and Moore, W.L. (eds), *Readings in the Management of Innovation*, 2nd edn, Cambridge, MA: Ballinger, pp. 55–78.

Adams, R., Tranfield, D. and Denyer, D. (2006) *Innovation Types: Configurations of Attributes as a Basis for Innovation Classification*, London: Advanced Institute of Management Research, Working Paper 46.

Agarwal, R. and Audretsch, D.B. (2001) 'Does size matter? The impact of the life cycle and technology on firm survival', *Journal of Industrial Economics*, 49: 21–43.

Aghion, P. (2007) 'Do we need less government for innovation-based growth?', presented at Festival of Economics, 30 May–2 June, Trento, Italy.

Aitken, C. and Hall, C.M. (2000) 'Migrant and foreign skills and their relevance to the tourism industry', *Tourism Geographies: An International Journal of Place, Space and the Environment*, 2(3): 66–86.

Aldrich, H.E. and Clift, J.E. (2003) 'The pervasive effects of family on entrepreneurship: toward a family embeddedness perspective', *Journal of Business Venturing*, 18: 573–96.

Amabile, T.M. (1998) 'How to kill creativity', *Harvard Business Review* September–October: 77–87.

Amin, A. (1999) 'An institutionalist perspective on regional economic development', *International Journal of Urban and Regional Research*, 23(2): 365–78.

Amin, A. (2002) 'Spatialities of globalization', *Environment and Planning A*, 34: 385–99.

Amin, A. and Thrift, N. (1995) 'European regions: from markets and plans to socio-economic and powers of association', *Economy and Society*, 24(1): 41–66.

Amit, R. and Zott, C. (2001) 'Value creation in e-business', *Strategic Management Journal*, 22(6–7): 493–520.

Andersen, B. (1998) *The Complexity of Technology Dynamics: Mapping Stylised Facts in Post Schumpeterian Approaches with Evidence from Patenting in Chemicals 1890–1990*, Manchester: University of Manchester, Centre for Research on Innovation and Competition, Working Paper 7.

Anderson, P., Cjayman, B., Holbrook, A., Lipsett, M., McCarthy, J. *et al.* (2006) *The Changing Conduct and Management of Science and Technology – CPROST*, a report to the Council of Science and Technology Advisors, Vancouver: Centre for Policy Research on Science and Technology, Simon Fraser University.

Anderson, R., Cohn, T., Day, C., Howlett, M. and Murray, C. (1998) 'Introduction: innovation systems in a global context', in Anderson, R., Cohn, T., Day, C., Howlett, M. and Murray, C. (eds), *Innovation Systems in a Global Context: The North American Experience*, Montreal and Kingston: McGill-Queens University Press, pp. 3–20.

Ansell, C.K. (2000) 'The networked polity: regional development in Western Europe', *Governance*, 13(2): 279–91.

Archibugi, D. and Michie, J. (1995) 'Technology and innovation: an introduction', *Cambridge Journal of Economics*, 19: 1–4.

Archibugi, D. and Michie, J. (1997) 'Technological globalization and national systems of innovation: an introduction', in Archibugi, D. and Michie, J. (eds), *Technology, Globalisation and Economic Performance*, Cambridge: Cambridge University Press, pp. 1–23.

Arrow, K.J. (1962) 'Economic welfare and the allocation of resources for invention', in Nelson. R.R. (ed.), *The Rate and Direction of Inventive Activity: Economic and Social Factors, vol. 13*, Princeton, NJ: NBER Special Conference Series, Princeton University Press, pp. 609–25.

Asheim, B.T. (2002) 'Temporary organisations and spatial embeddedness of learning and knowledge creation', *Geografiska Annaler: Series B Human Geography*, 84: 111–24.

Asheim, B.T. and Coenen, L. (2004) 'The role of regional innovation systems in a globalising economy: comparing knowledge bases and institutional frameworks of Nordic clusters', paper to be presented at the DRUID Summer Conference 2004 on Industrial Dynamics, Innovation and Development, Elsinore, Denmark, 14–16 June, Theme F: networks, clusters and other inter-firm relations as vehicles for knowledge building and transfer.

Asheim, B.T. and Coenen, L. (2006) 'Contextualising regional innovation systems in a globalising learning economy: on knowledge bases and institutional frameworks', *Journal of Technology Transfer*, 31: 163–73.

Asheim, B.T. and Isaksen, A. (2002) 'Regional innovation systems: the integration of local "sticky" and global "ubiquitous" knowledge', *Journal of Technology Transfer*, 27: 77–86.

Ateljevic, I. and Doorne, S. (2000) 'Staying within the fence: lifestyle entrepreneurship in tourism', *Journal of Sustainable Tourism*, 8(5): 378–92.

Ateljevic, I. and Doorne, S. (2003) 'Culture, economy and tourism commodities: social relations of production and consumption', *Tourist Studies*, 3(2): 123–41.

Ateljevic, I. and Doorne, S. (2004) 'Diseconomies of scale: a study of development constraints in small tourism firms in central New Zealand', *Tourism and Hospitality Research*, 5(1): 5–24.

Audretsch, D. (1995a) *Innovation and Industry Evolution*, Cambridge, MA: MIT Press.

Audretsch, D. (1995b) 'Innovation, growth, and survival', *International Journal of Industrial Organization*, 13: 441–57.

Australian Government (2003) *Tourism White Paper: A Medium to Long Term Strategy for Tourism*, Canberra: Commonwealth of Australia.

Australian Government (2004) *Tourism White Paper Implementation Plan: Achieving Platinum Australia. Implementation Plan 2004*, Canberra: Commonwealth of Australia.

Australian Government (2007) *New Elements of the R&D Tax Concession: An Evaluation*, Canberra: Commonwealth of Australia.

Autio, E., Sapienza, H.J. and Almeida, J.G. (2000) 'Effects of age at entry, knowledge intensity, and imitability on international growth', *Academy of Management Journal*, 43(5): 909–24.

Awad, E. and Ghaziri, H. (2004) *Knowledge Management*, Saddle River, NJ: Pearson Education.

Aydalot, P. and Keeble, D. (eds) (1988) *High Technology Industry and Innovative Environments: The European Experience*, London: Routledge.

Aynsley, B. (2006) 'City visions: the quest is on to create the perfect city, but how much say do we have in this?', *The Listener*, 27 May: 14–20.

Baker, M. and Li, B. (1996) 'A little of what you fancy does you good? Does IT make a positive contribution to the hospitality industry?', paper presented to the HITA conference, Edinburgh, 17–20 May.

Barro, R. and Sala-I-Martin, X. (2003) *Economic Growth*, 2nd edn, Boston: MIT Press.

Bartlett, C.A. and Ghoshal, S. (1989) *Managing Across Borders: The Transnational Solution*, Boston: Harvard University Press.

Bathelt, H., Malmberg, A. and Maskell, P. (2004) 'Clusters and knowledge: local buzz, global pipelines and the process of knowledge creation', *Progress in Human Geography*, 28(1): 31–56.

Baumol, W. (2002) *The Free Market Innovation Machine: Analyzing the Growth Miracle of Capitalism*, Princeton, NJ: Princeton University Press.

Baumol, W.J. (2003) 'Innovations and growth: two common misapprehensions', *Journal of Policy Modelling*, 25: 435–44.

Baumol, W., Panzar, J. and Willig, R. (1982) *Contestable Markets and the Theory of Industrial Structure*, New York: Harcourt Brace Jovanovich.

Bawden, A. (2007) 'Two leaders united in city pride', *Guardian*, Society, 13 July.

Bayraktaroglu, S. and Kutanis, R.O. (2003) 'Transforming hotels into learning organisations: a new strategy for going global', *Tourism Management*, 24: 149–54.

BBC (2005) 'Singapore approves casino plan', BBC News International, 18 April, http://news.bbc.co.uk/2/hi/asia-pacific/4457091.stm (accessed 5 October 2007).

BBC (2006a) 'Vegas Sands wins Singapore casino', BBC News International, 26 May, http://news.bbc.co.uk/2/hi/business/5019488.stm (accessed 5 October 2007).

BBC (2006b) 'Second Singapore casino approved', BBC News International, 8 December, http://news.bbc.co.uk/2/hi/business/6161177.stm (accessed 5 October 2007).

Beardsworth, A. and Bryman, A. (1999) 'Late modernity and the dynamics of quasification: the case of the themed restaurant', *Sociological Review*, 47(2): 228–57.

Bitner, M.J. (1992) 'Servicescapes: the impacts of physical surroundings on customers and employees', *Journal of Marketing*, 56: 57–71.

Blackler, F. (2002) 'Knowledge, knowledge work and organizations', in Choo, C.W. and Bontis, N. (eds), *The Strategic Management of Intellectual Capital and Organizational Knowledge*, New York: Oxford University Press, pp. 47–62.

Blake, A., Sinclair, M.T. and Soria, J.A.C. (2006) 'Tourism productivity: evidence from the UK', *Annals of Tourism Research*, 33(4): 1099–120.

Boschma, R.A. (2004) 'Competitiveness of regions from an evolutionary perspective', *Regional Studies*, 38(9): 1001–14.

Boschma, R.A. (2005) 'Rethinking regional innovation policy: the making and breaking of regional history', in Fuchs, G. and Shapira, P. (eds), *Rethinking Regional Innovation and Change: Path Dependency or Regional Breakthrough?*, Dordrecht: Springer, pp. 249–71.

Bowen, J. and Ford, R.C. (2002) 'Managing service organizations: does having a thing make a difference?', *Journal of Management*, 28(3): 447–69.

Bray, R. and Raitz, V. (2001) *Flight to the Sun: The Story of the Holiday Revolution*, London: Continuum.

Brenner, N. (1998) 'Global cities, glocal states: global city formation and state territorial restructuring in contemporary Europe', *Review of International Political Economy*, 5(1): 1–37.

Breznitz, D. (2006) 'Innovation and the state: development strategies for high technology industries in a world of fragmented production: Israel, Ireland, and Taiwan', *Enterprise & Society*, 7(4): 675–84.

Breznitz, D. (2007) *Innovation and the State: Political Choice and Strategies for Growth in Israel, Taiwan, and Ireland*, New Haven: Yale University Press.

Bristow, G. (2005) 'Everyone's a "winner": problematising the discourse of regional competitiveness', *Journal of Economic Geography*, 5: 285–304.

Brooks, S. (1993) *Public Policy in Canada*, Toronto: McClelland and Stewart.

Brown, D.E. and Lawler, E.E. (2002) 'The empowerment of service workers: what, why, how and when', in Henry, J. and Mayle, D, (eds), *Managing Innovation and Change*, London: Sage, pp. 243–57.

Brown, J.S. and Duguid, P. (1991) 'Organizational learning and communities-of-practice: towards a unified view of working, learning and innovation', *Organizational Science*, 2(1): 40–57.

Brown, J.S. and Duguid, P. (1998) 'Organizing knowledge', *California Management Review*, 40(3): 90–111.

Brynjolfsson, E. (1993) 'The productivity paradox of information technology: review and assessment', *Communications of the ACM*, 36(12): 67–77.

Buhalis, D. (2004) 'eAirlines: strategic and tactical use of ICTs in the airline industry', *Information & Management*, 41: 805–25.

Buhalis, D. (2006) 'The impact of information technology on tourism competition', in Papatheodorou, A. (ed.), *Corporate Rivalry and Market Power: Competition Issues in the Tourism Industry*, London: I.B. Tauris, pp. 143–71.

Buhalis, D. and Ujma, D. (2006) 'Intermediaries: travel agencies and tour operators', in Buhalis, D. and Costa, C. (eds), *Tourism Business Frontiers: Consumers, Products and Industry*, Oxford: Elsevier, pp. 172–80.

Bunnell, T.G. and Coe, N.M. (2001) 'Spaces and scales of innovation', *Progress in Human Geography*, 25(4): 569–89.

Burdon, N. (2007) '$188m Carisbrook stadium plan unveiled', *Southland Times*, 23 February.

Burgelman, R.A. and Sayles, L.R. (1986) *Inside Corporate Innovation. Strategy, Structure and Managerial Skills*, London: Free Press.

Butler, R.W. (1980) 'The concept of the tourism area cycle of evolution: implications for management of resources', *Canadian Geographer*, 24(1): 5–12.

Butler, R. and Russel, R. (2005) 'The role of individuals in the development and popularisation of tourist destinations', paper presented at Beijing conference of the International Academy for the Study of Tourism, July 2005.

Cainelli, G., Evangelista, R. and Savon, M. (2005) 'Innovation and economic performance in services: a firm-level analysis', *Cambridge Journal of Economics*, 30: 435–58.

Camagni, R. (ed.) (1991) *Innovation Networks: Spatial Perspectives*, London: Belhaven.

Canadian Tourism Commission (2006) *2007–2011 Strategic Plan: Moving Forward With Vision*, Ottawa: Canadian Tourism Commission, Industry Canada.

Carayannis, E.G. and Gonzalez, E. (2003) 'Creativity and innovation = competitiveness? When, how and why', in Shavinina, L.V. (ed.), *The International Handbook on Innovation*, Oxford: Elsevier, pp. 587–605.

Caves, R.E. (1998) 'Industrial organization and new findings on the turnover and mobility of firms', *Journal of Economic Literature*, 36(4): 1947–82.

Cefis, E. and Marsili, O. (2005) 'A matter of life and death: innovation and firm survival', *Industrial and Corporate Change*, 14(6): 1167–92.

Cefis, E. and Marsili, O. (2006) 'Survivor: the role of innovation in firms' survival', *Research Policy*, 35: 626–41.

Chaminade, C. and Edquist, C. (2006) 'From theory to practice: the use of the systems of innovation approach in innovation policy', in Hage, J. and Meeus, M. (eds), *Innovation, Science and Institutional Change: A Research Handbook*, Oxford: Oxford University Press, pp. 141–62.

Chan, A., Go, F.M. and Pine, R. (1998) 'Service innovation in Hong Kong: attitudes and practice', *The Service Industries Journal*, 18(2): 112–24.

Chang, Y.-H. and Chen, M.-H. (2004) 'Comparing approaches to systems of innovation: the knowledge perspective', *Technology in Society*, 26: 17–37.

Chell, E. (2001) *Entrepreneurship: Globalization, Innovation and Development*, London: Thomson Learning.

Chell, E., Haworth, J. and Brearley, S. (1991) *The Entrepreneurial Personality: Concepts, Cases and Categories*, London: Routledge.

Cheshire, P.C. and Gordon, I.R. (1998) 'Territorial competition: some lessons for policy', *Annals of Regional Science*, 32: 321–46.

Cheshire, P.C. and Malecki, E.J. (2004) 'Growth, development and innovation: a look backward and forward', *Papers in Regional Science*, 83: 249–67.

Choonwoo, L., Kyungmook, L. and Pennings, J.M. (2001) 'Internal capabilities, external networks and performance: a study on technology-based ventures', *Strategic Management Journal*, 22: 615–40.

Chouinard, H.H. (2005) 'Auctions with and without the right of first refusal and National Park Service concession contracts', *American Journal of Agricultural Economics*, 87(4): 1083–8.

Chrisman, J.J., Chua, J.H. and Steier, L.P. (2003) 'An introduction to theories of family business', *Journal of Business Venturing*, 18: 441–8.

Christensen, C.M. and Overdorf, M. (2001) 'Meeting the challenge of disruptive change', in *Harvard Business Review on Innovation*, Boston: Harvard Business School Press, pp. 103–30.

Christensen, C.M., Suarez, F.F. and Utterback, J.M. (1998) 'Strategies for survival in fast changing industries', *Management Science*, 44: S207–20.

Clark, H. (2002) *Growing an Innovative New Zealand*, Wellington: Office of the Prime Minister.

Clark, H. (2007) *Rugby Ball Venue to Showcase NZ, Press Release*, Wellington: Office of the Prime Minister.

Clark, J.R.A. (2005) 'The "New Associationalism" in agriculture: agro-food diversification and multifunctional production logics', *Journal of Economic Geography*, 5(4): 475–98.

Claver-Cortés, E., Molina-Azorín, J.F. and Pereira-Moliner, J. (2006) 'Strategic groups in the hospitality industry: intergroup and intragroup performance differences in Alicante, Spain', *Tourism Management*, 27: 1101–16.

CMM (2005) *Charting Our International Future: A Competitive Metropolitan Region, Economic Development Plan*, Montreal: CMM.

Coakes, E., Willis, D. and Clarke, S. (2002) *Knowledge Management in the Sociotechnical World*, London: Springer Verlag.

Coles, T. (2006) 'Enigma variations? The TALC, marketing models and the descendants of the product life cycle', in Butler, R.W. (ed.), *The Tourism Area Life Cycle, Vol. 2, Conceptual and Theoretical Issues*, Clevedon: Channel View Publications, pp. 49–66.

Coles, T. and Hall, C.M. (2008) *International Business and Tourism: Global Issues, Contemporary Interactions*, London: Routledge.

Commonwealth of Australia (2001) *Backing Australia's Ability: An Innovation Action Plan for the Future*, Canberra: Commonwealth of Australia.

Commonwealth of Australia (2002) *Australian Government Innovation Report 2001–02*, Canberra: Commonwealth of Australia.

Commonwealth of Australia (2003) *Australian Government Innovation Report 2002–03*, Canberra: Commonwealth of Australia.

Commonwealth of Australia (2004) *Australian Government Innovation Report 2003 04*, Canberra: Commonwealth of Australia.

Commonwealth of Australia (2005) *Australian Government Innovation Report 2004–05*, Canberra: Commonwealth of Australia.

Commonwealth of Australia (2006) *Australian Government Innovation Report 2005–06*, Canberra: Commonwealth of Australia.

Cooke, P. (1992) 'Regional innovation systems: competitive regulation in the new Europe', *Geoforum*, 23: 365–82.

Cooke, P. (2001) 'Regional innovation systems, clusters, and the knowledge economy', *Industrial and Corporate Change*, 10(4): 945 71.

Cooke, P. (2002) *Knowledge Economies: Clusters, Learning and Cooperative Advantage*, London: Routledge.

Cooke, P., Gomez Uranga, M. and Etxebarria, G. (1997) 'Regional systems of innovation: institutional and organisational dimensions', *Research Policy*, 26: 475–91.

Cooper, C. (2006) 'Knowledge management and tourism', *Annals of Tourism Research*, 33(1): 47–64.

Cooper, R.G. (1990) 'Stage-gate system: a new tool for managing new products', *Business Horizons*, May–June: 44–54.

Corbett, T. (2001) *The Making of American Resorts: Saratoga Springs, Ballson Spa, and Lake George*, New Brunswick: Rutgers University Press.

Coviello, N., Winklhofer, H. and Hamilton, K. (2006) 'Marketing practices and performance of small service firms: an examination in the tourism accommodation sector', *Journal of Service Research*, 9(1): 38–58.

Crevoisier, O. (2004) 'The innovative milieus approach: towards a territorialized understanding of the economy', *Economic Geography*, 80(4): 367–79.

Crouch, G.I. and Ritchie, J.R.B. (1999) 'Tourism, competitiveness, and social prosperity', *Journal of Business Research*, 44: 137–52.

CSTA (2005) *LINKS – Linkages in the National Knowledge System*, Ottawa: Industry Canada.

David, J., Graboski, S. and Kasavana, M. (1996) 'The productivity paradox of hotel-industry technology', *Cornell Hotel and Restaurant Administration Quarterly*, 37(2): 64–70.

David, P.A. and Foray, D. (2002) 'An introduction to the economy of the knowledge society', *International Social Science Journal*, 171: 9–24.

Davidsson, P. and Wiklund, J. (2001) 'Levels of analysis in entrepreneurship research: current research practice and suggestions for the future', *Entrepreneurship Theory and Practice*, 25(4): 81–99.

Deas, I. and Giordano, B. (2001) 'Conceptualising and measuring urban competitiveness in major English cities: an exploratory approach', *Environment and Planning A*, 33: 1411–29.

Department of Education, Science and Training (2005) *Joint Ministerial Announcement on Backing Australia's Ability Programme*, Canberra: Department of Education, Science and Training.

Department of Trade and Industry (2003) *Innovation Report: Competing in the Global Economy: The Innovation Challenge*, London: Department of Trade and Industry.

Djankov, S. and Hoekman, B. (2000) 'Foreign investment and productivity growth in Czech enterprises', *World Bank Economic Review*, 14: 49–64.

Doblin Inc. (2007) Innovation Landscape176, http://www.doblin,com/ (accessed 1 July 2007).

Doel, M.A. and Hubbard, P.J. (2002) 'Taking world cities literally: marketing the city in a global space of flows', *City*, 6: 351–68.

Downs, A. (1967) *Inside Bureacracy*, Boston: Little, Brown.

Dredge, D. and Jenkins, J. (eds) (2007) *Tourism Planning and Policy*, Brisbane: Wiley.

Drejer, I. (2004) 'Identifying innovation in surveys of services: a Schumpeterian perspective', *Research Policy*, 33: 551–62.

Drennan, M.P. (2002) *The Information Economy and American Cities*, Baltimore: John Hopkins University Press.

Drucker, P.F. (1992) 'The new productivity challenge', *Harvard Business Review*, 696: 69–79.

Duranton, G. and Puga, D. (2000) 'Diversity and specialisation in cities: why, where and when does it matter?', *Urban Studies*, 37: 533–55.

Earl, P.E. (1986) *Lifestyle Economics: Consumer Behavior in a Turbulent World*, Brighton: Wheatsheaf.

Ebner, A. (2007) 'Public policy, governance and innovation: entrepreneurial states in East Asian economic development', *International Journal of Technology and Globalisation*, 3(1): 103–24.

ECON Analysis (2006) *Innovation in Services: Typology, Case Studies and Policy Implications*, commissioned by the Norwegian Ministry of Industry and Trade, ECIN-Report no. 2006–025, Project no. 44720, AHA/LAG/pil, TVA, 28 February 2006, Oslo: Ministry of Industry and Trade.

Edquist, C. (ed.) (1997) *Systems of Innovation: Technology, Institutions and Organizations*, London: Pinter.

Edquist, C. (2001) 'The systems of innovation approach and innovation policy: an account of the state of the art', lead paper presented at the DRUID Conference, Aalborg, 12–15 June 2001, under Theme F: 'National systems of innovation, institutions and public policies', Aalborg: DRUID.

Edquist, C. (2006) *Industrial Policy from a Systems Innovation Perspective*, CIRCLE, Centre for Innovation, Research and Competence in the Learning Economy.

Edquist, C. and Johnson, B. (1997) 'Institutions and organizations in systems of innovation', in Edquist, C. (ed.), *Systems of Innovation: Technology, Institutions and Organizations*, London: Pinter, pp. 41–63.

Egle, V. (2006) *The Role of State in Promoting Innovation in Small Countries – Some Examples from Baltic Countries*, presented at IRC Annual Conference, Tartu, Estonia, 18 September.

Esping-Andersen, G. (1990) *The Three Worlds of Welfare Capitalism*, Cambridge: Polity Press.

Evans, G. (2003) 'Hard branding the cultural city – from Prado to Prada', *International Journal of Urban and Regional Research*, 27(2): 417–40.

Findlay, R. (1978) 'Relative backwardness, direct foreign investment and the transfer of technology. A simple dynamic model', *Quarterly Journal of Economics*, 62: 1–16.

Fischer, M.M. (2001) 'Innovation, knowledge creation and systems of innovation', *Annals of Regional Science*, 35: 199–216.

Florida, R. (2002) *The Rise of the Creative Class: And How it's Transforming Work, Leisure, Community, and Everyday Life*, New York: Basic Books.

Freeman, C. (1968) 'Science and economy at the national level', in OECD, *Problems of Science Policy*, Paris: OECD, pp. 58–65.

Freeman, C. (1987) *Technology Policy and Economic Performance: Lesson from Japan*, London: Frances Pinter.

Freeman, C. (1995) 'The "national system of innovation" in historical perspective', *Cambridge Journal of Economics*, 19(1): 5–24.

Freeman, J., Carroll, G.R. and Hannan, M.T. (1983) 'The liability of newness: age dependence in organizational death rates', *American Sociological Review*, 48: 692–710.

Frenken, K. (2000) 'A complexity approach to innovation networks. The case of the aircraft industry (1909–1997)', *Research Policy*, 29: 257–72.

Frenken, K., Van Oort, F.G , Verburg, T. and Boschma, R.A. (2005) 'Variety and regional economic growth in the Netherlands', *Papers in Evolutionary Economic Geography* #05.02, Utrecht: University of Utrecht.

Fuchs, G. and Shapira, P. (eds) (2005) *Rethinking Regional Innovation and Change. Path Dependency or Regional Breakthrough?*, Dordrecht: Springer.

Galbraith, J.K. (1969) *The New Industrial State*, Harmondsworth: Pelican.

Garvin, D. (1993) 'Building a learning organization', *Harvard Business Review*, 71(4): 78–91.

Gershuny, J. (2000) *Changing Times: Work and Leisure in Postindustrial Society*, New York: Oxford University Press.

Gertler, M.S. (2001) 'Best practice: geography, learning and in the institutional limits to strong convergence', *Journal of Economic Geography*, 1: 5–26.

Gertler, M.S. (2003) 'Tacit knowledge and the economic geography of context, or the undefinable tacitness of being (there)', *Journal of Economic Geography*, 3: 75–99.

Gibbons, M., Limoges C., Nowotny, H., Schwartzman, S., Scott, P. *et al.* (1994) *The New Production of Knowledge*, London: Sage.

Gibson, C. and Klocker, N. (2004) 'Academic publishing as "creative" industry, and recent discourse of "creative economies": some critical reflections', *Area*, 36(4): 423–34.

Glaeser E.L. (2000) 'The new economics of urban and regional growth', in Clark, G.L., Feldman, M.P. and Gertler, M.S. (eds), *The Oxford Handbook of Economic Geography*, Oxford: Oxford University Press, pp. 83–98.

Goodman, A. (2000) 'Implementing sustainability in service operations at Scandic hotels', *Interfaces*, 30(3): 202–14.

Görg, H. and D. Greenaway (2004) 'Much ado about nothing? Do domestic firms really benefit from foreign direct investment?' *World Bank Research Observer*, 19(2): 171–97.

Government Information Office (2002) *Challenge 2008: The Six-year National Development Plan*, Taipei: Government Information Office Republic of China, http://www.gio.gov.tw/taiwan-website/4-oa/20020521/2002052101.html (accessed 5 October 2007).

Government of Canada (2002) *Achieving Excellence: Investing in People, Knowledge and Opportunity, Canada's Innovation Strategy*, Ottawa: Government of Canada.

Government of Canada (2007) *Canada's New Government: Mobilizing Science and Technology to Canada's Advantage*, Ottawa: Government of Canada.

Grabher, G. (2001) 'Ecologies of creativity: the village, the group, and the heterarchic organisation of the British advertising industry', *Environment and Planning A*, 33: 351–74.

Graham, B. and Vowles, T.M. (2006) 'Carriers within carriers: a strategic response to low-cost airline competition', *Transport Reviews*, 26(1): 105–26.

Gratzer, M., Werthner, H. and Winiwarter, W. (2004) 'Electronic business in tourism', *International Journal of Electronic Business*, 2(5): 450–9.

Grönroos, C. (1994) 'From scientific management to service management: a management perspective for the age of service competition', *International Journal of Service Industry Management*, 5(1): 5–20.

Guerrier, Y. and Adib, A. (2003) 'Work at leisure and leisure at work: a study of the emotional labour of tour reps', *Human Relations*, 56(11): 1399–517.

Hall, C.M. (2005) *Tourism: Rethinking the Social Science of Mobility*, Harlow: Prentice Hall.

Hall, C.M. (2006) 'Space–time accessibility and the TALC: the role of geographies of spatial interaction and mobility in contributing to an improved understanding of tourism', in Butler, R.W. (ed.), *The Tourism Area Life Cycle, Vol. 2, Conceptual and Theoretical Issues*, Clevedon: Channel View Publications, pp. 83–100.

Hall, C.M. (2007) 'Tourism and regional competitiveness', in Tribe, J. (ed.), *Tourism Research: New Directions, Challenges and Applications*, Oxford: Elsevier, pp. 217–30.

Hall, C.M. (2008a) *Tourism Planning*, 2nd edn, Harlow: Prentice Hall.

Hall, C.M. (2008b) 'Regulating the international trade in tourism services', in Coles, T. and Hall, C.M. (eds), *International Business and Tourism: Global Issues, Contemporary Interactions*, London: Routledge, in press.

Hall, C.M. and Coles, T. (2008) 'Tourism and international business – tourism as international business', in Coles, T. and Hall, C.M. (eds), *International Business and Tourism: Global Issues, Contemporary Interactions*, London: Routledge, in press.

Hall, C.M. and Jenkins, J.M. (1995) *Tourism and Public Policy*, London: Routledge.

Hall, C.M. and Mitchell, R.M. (2008) *Wine Marketing*, Oxford: Butterworth-Heinemann.

Hall, C.M. and Page, S. (1999) *The Geography of Tourism and Recreation: Environment, Place and Space*, London: Routledge.

Hall, C.M. and Rusher, K. (2004) 'Risky lifestyles? Entrepreneurial characteristics of the New Zealand bed and breakfast sector', in Thomas, R. (ed.), *Small Firms in Tourism: International Perspectives*, Oxford: Elsevier, pp. 83–97.

Hall, C.M., Williams, A.M. and Lew, A.A. (2004) 'Tourism: conceptualisations, institutions and issues', in Lew, A.A., Hall, C.M. and Williams, A.M. (eds), *A Companion to Tourism*, Oxford: Blackwell, pp. 3–22.

Hansen, M.T., Nohria, N. and Tierney, T. (1999) 'What's your strategy for managing knowledge?' *Harvard Business Review*, March–April: 106–16.

Harrah's Entertainment (2007) *Form 10-K, Harrah's Entertainment Inc – HET, Filed: March 01, 2007 (period: December 31, 2006). Annual Report Which Provides a Comprehensive Overview of the Company for the Past Year*, Washington, DC: Securities and Exchange Commission.

Harrison, B. (1994) *Lean and Mean: Why Large Corporations Will Continue to Dominate the Global Economy*, New York: Guilford Press.

Harrison, J.T. (2003) 'Strategic analysis for the hospitality industry', *Cornell Hotel and Restaurant Administration Quarterly*, 44(1): 139–52.

Harvard Business Essentials (2003) *Managing Creativity and Innovation*, Boston: Harvard Business School Press.

Harvey, D. (1989) 'From managerialism to entrepreneurialism: the transformation in urban governance in late capitalism', *Geografiska Annaler*, 71B: 3–17.

Hatton, M.J. (1999) 'A living culture, Tamaki Maori Village', in Hatton, M.J. (ed.), *Community-based Tourism in the Asia-Pacific*, published as part of APEC, Forum Tourism Working Group Project, Toronto: School of Media Studies, Humber College, http://www.community-tourism.org/ (accessed 20 March 2007).

Henard, D.H. and Szymanski, D.M. (2001) 'Why some new products are more successful than others', *Journal of Marketing Research*, 38(3): 362–75.

Henry, N. and Pinch, S. (2000) 'Spatialising knowledge: placing the knowledge community of Motor Sport Valley', *Geoforum*, 31: 191–208.

Heskett, J.L., Jones, T.O., Loveman, G.W., Sasser, W.E. Jr. and Schlesinger, L.A. (1994) 'Putting the service profit chain to work', *Harvard Business Review*, March–April: 164–74.

Heskett, J., Sasser, E. and Schlesinger, L. (2003) *The Value Profit Chain: Treat Employees Like Customers and Customers Like Employees*, New York: Free Press.

Hitchcock, M. (2000) 'Ethnicity and tourism entrepreneurship in Java and Bali', *Current Issues in Tourism*, 3(3): 204–25.

Hitters, E. and Richards, G. (2002) 'The creation and management of cultural clusters', *Creativity and Innovation Management*, 11(4): 234–47.

Hjalager, A.-M. (1996) 'Tourism and the environment: the innovation connection', *Journal of Sustainable Tourism*, 4(4): 201–18.

Hjalager, A.-M. (1997) 'Innovation patterns in sustainable tourism: an analytical typology', *Tourism Management*, 18(1): 35–41.

Hjalager, A.-M. (2002) 'Repairing innovation defectiveness in tourism', *Tourism Management*, 23: 465–74.

Holbrook, J.A.D. and Hughes, L.P. (1999) *Characteristics of Innovation in the Service Sector in British Columbia*, CPROST Report 99–03, Vancouver: Centre for Policy Research on Science and Technology, Simon Fraser University.

Holbrook, J.A. and Wolfe, D.A. (eds) (2000) *Knowledge, Clusters and Regional Innovation: Economic Development in Canada*, Montreal and Kingston. McGill-Queen's University Press for the School of Policy Studies, Queen's University.

Hollingsworth, J.R. (2000) 'Doing institutional analysis: implications for the study of innovations', *Review of International Political Economy*, 7(4): 595–644.

Howells, J.R. (2003) *Innovations, Consumption and Knowledge: Services and Encapsulation*, Manchester: Centre for Research on Innovation and Competition, Discussion Paper 62.

Howells, J. and Roberts, J. (2000) 'From innovation systems to knowledge systems', *Prometheus*, 18: 17–31.

Hudson, R. (1999) 'The learning economy, the learning firm and the learning region: a sympathetic critique', *European Urban and Regional Studies*, 6(1): 59–72

Hudson, R. (2001) *Producing Places*, New York: Guilford Press.

Huybers, T. and Bennett, J. (2003) 'Inter-firm cooperation at nature-based tourism destinations', *Journal of Socio-Economics*, 32: 571–87.

Hymer, S.H. (1960) *The International Operations of National Firms: A Study of Direct Foreign Investment*, Cambridge, MA: MIT Press (thesis 1960; published 1976).

Industry Canada (2003) *Review of Federal Government and Agency Programs Related to Tourism 2003*, Ottawa: Industry Canada.

Industry Canada (2007) *Industry Canada 2007–2008 Estimates Report on Plans and Priorities*, Ottawa: Industry Canada.

Ioannides, D. and Petersen, T. (2003) 'Tourism non-entrepreneurship in peripheral destinations: a case study of small and medium enterprises on Bornholm, Denmark', *Tourism Geographies*, 5(4): 408–35.

Isaksen, A. and Hauge, E. (2002) *Regional Clusters in Europe*, Observatory of European SMEs Report 2002 No. 3, Luxembourg: European Communities.

Jacob, M. and Groizard, J.L. (2004) 'Technology transfer and multinationals: the case of tourism investments in two developing economies', unpublished manuscript, University of the Balearic Islands.

Jacob, M., Tintoré, J., Guiló, E.A., Bravo, A. and Mulet, J. (2003) 'Innovation in the tourism sector: results from a pilot study in the Balearic Islands', *Tourism Economics*, 9(3): 279–95.

Jacob, M., Tintoré, J., Simonet, R. and Aguiló, E. (2004) *Pautas de innovación en el sector turístico balear*, Series: Colección Estudios no. 25. Fundación Cotec para la Innovación Tecnológica, Madrid.

Janson, K. (2006) 'National tourism structures – Who's got it right?' *Caterer and Housekeeper*, 11 April.

Jessop, B. (1998) 'The narrative of enterprise and the enterprise of narrative: place marketing and the entrepreneurial city', in Hall, T. and Hubbard, P. (ed.), *The Entrepreneurial City*, Chichester: Wiley, pp. 77–99.

Jogaratnam, G. and Tse, E.C.-Y. (2004) 'The entrepreneurial approach to hotel operation: evidence from the Asia-Pacific hotel industry', *Cornell Hotel and Restaurant Administration Quarterly*, 45(3): 248–59.

Jones, T. (2002) *Innovating at the Edge: How Organizations Evolve and Embed Innovation Capability*, Oxford: Butterworth-Heinemann.

Judd, D.R. (2003) 'Building the tourist city: editor's introduction', in Judd, D.R. (ed.), *The Infrastructure of Play: Building the Tourist City*, Armonk, NY: M.E. Sharpe, pp. 3–16.

Kamakura, W.A., Mittal, V., de Rosa, F. and Mazzon, J. (2002) 'Assessing the service-profit chain,' *Marketing Science*, 21(3): 284–317.

Kanter, R.M. (1983) *The Change Masters*, London: Unwin.

Kassinis, G.I. and Soterlou, A.C. (2003) 'Greening the service profit chain: the impact of environmental management practices', *Productions and Operations Management*, 12(3): 386–403.

Keller, P. (2006) 'Innovation in tourism policy', in OECD (ed.), *Innovation and Growth in Tourism*, Paris: OECD, pp. 16–40.

Kelley, M.R. and Helper, S. (1999) 'Firm size and capabilities, regional agglomeration, and the adoption of new technology', *Economics of Innovation and New Technology*, 8: 79–103.

Keltner, B., Finegold, D., Mason, G. and Wagner, K. (1999) 'Market segmentation strategies and service sector productivity', *California Management Review*, 41(Summer): 84–102.

Kets de Vries, M.F.R. (1977) 'The entrepreneurial personality: a person at the cross-roads', *Journal of Management Studies*, February: 34–57.

Kim, W.C. and Mauborgne, R. (1999) 'Strategy, value innovation and the knowledge economy', *MIT Sloan Management Review*, Spring: 41–54.

Kim, W.C. and Mauborgne, R. (2004) 'Value innovation: the strategic logic of high growth', *Harvard Business Review*, 82(7–8): 172–80.

Kindleberger, C.P. (1969) *American Business Abroad*, New Haven: Yale University Press.

Kingston, J. (2004) *Conducting Feasibility Studies for Knowledge Based Systems*, Joseph Bell Centre for Forensic Statistics and Legal Reasoning, Report Series No. 32.

Klein, S. and Loebbecke, C. (2003) 'Emerging pricing strategies on the web: lessons from the airline industry', *Electronic Markets*, 13(1): 46–58.

Komninos, N. (2002) *Intelligent Cities: Innovation, Knowledge Systems and Digital Spaces*, London: Spon Press.

Kooiman, J. (ed.) (1993) *Modern Governance: New Goverment–Society Interactions*, London: Sage.

Kooiman, J. (2003) *Governing as Governance*, London: Sage.

Kotilainen, H. (2005) *Best Practices in Innovation Policies*, Technology Review 177/2005. Helsinki: Tekes.

Kotler, P. and Armstrong, G. (1997) *Marketing: An Introduction*, 4th edn, Englewood Cliffs, NJ: Prentice Hall.

Kotler, P., Haider, D.H. and Rein, I. (1993) *Marketing Places: Attracting Investment, Industry, and Tourism to Cities, States, and Nations*, New York: Free Press.

Koutoulas, D. (2006) 'The market influence of tour operators on the hospitality industry', in Papatheodorou, A. (ed.), *Corporate Rivalry and Market Power: Competition Issues in the Tourism Industry*, London: I.B. Tauris, pp. 94–123.

Kozak, M. (2004) *Destination Benchmarking: Concepts, Practices and Operations*, Wallingford: CABI Publishing.

Lagendijk, A. and Oinas, P. (eds) (2005) *Proximity, Distance and Diversity: Issues in Economic Interaction and Local Development*, Aldershot: Ashgate.

Lam, A. (2000) 'Tacit knowledge, organizational learning and societal institutions: an integrated framework', *Organization Studies*, 21: 487–513.

Larédo, P. and Mustar, P. (eds) (2001) *Research and Innovation Policies in the New Global Economy: An International Comparative Analysis*, Cheltenham: Elgar.

Larsen, K. (2004) 'Modes and nodes of innovation: conditions and systems of innovation in tourism and the food sector in the region of Dalarna in Sweden', paper presented at CESIS Conference: Innovation and Entrepreneurship, Stockholm, 18–20 November.

Law, C. (2002) *Urban Tourism: The Visitor Economy and the Growth of Large Cities*, 2nd edn, London: Continuum.

Laws, E. (1997) *Managing Packaged Tourism: Relationships, Responsibilities, and Service Quality in the Inclusive Holiday Industry*, London: International Thomson Business Press.

Lazonick, W. (1991) *Business Organization and the Myth of the Market Economy*, New York: Cambridge University Press.

Lee, J. (2006) 'Free trade agreement, the role of the state, and the survival of small and medium-sized business', APEC SME Innovation Briefing No. 3, December.

Lei, Z. (2006) 'The theoretical pillars of industrial organization in tourism', in Papatheodorou, A. (ed.), *Corporate Rivalry and Market Power: Competition Issues in the Tourism Industry*, London: I.B. Tauris, pp. 20–34.

Leitner, H. and Sheppard, E. (2002) 'Economic uncertainty, interurban competition and the efficacy of entrepreneurialism', in Hall, T. and Hubbard, P. (eds), *The Entrepreneurial City: Geographies of Politics, Regimes and Representation*, Chichester: Wiley, pp. 285–307.

Levinthal, D.A. (1998) 'The slow pace of rapid technological change: gradualism and punctuation in technological change', *Industrial and Corporate Change*, 7: 217–47.

Lew, A.A. and Wong, A. (2002) 'Tourism and the Chinese diaspora', in Hall, C.M. and Williams, A.M. (eds), *Tourism and Migration: New Relationships between Production and Consumption*, Dordrecht: Kluwer Academic Publishers, pp. 205–20.

List, F. (1856) *National System of Political Economy*, translated by G.A. Matile and H. Richelot, Philadelphia: J.B. Lippincott & Co.

Longhi, C. and Keeble, D. (2000) 'High technology clusters and evolutionary trends in the 1990s', in Keeble, D. and Wilkinson, F. (eds), *High Technology Clusters, Networking and Collective Learning in Europe*, Aldershot: Ashgate, pp. 21–56.

Lovering, J. (1999) 'Theory led by policy: the inadequacies of the "New Regionalism" (illustrated from the case of Wales)', *International Journal of Urban and Regional Research*, 23: 379–96.

Lundvall, B.-Å. (ed.) (1992) *National Systems of Innovation: Towards a Theory of Innovation and Interactive Learning*, London: Pinter.

Lundvall, B.-Å. and Borrás, S. (1997) *The Globalising Learning Economy: Implications for Innovation Policy*, report based on contributions from seven projects under the TSER programme DG XII, Commission of the European Union, December, Luxembourg: European Communities.

Lundvall, B.-Å. and Johnson, B. (1994) 'The learning economy', *Journal of Industry Studies*, 1: 23–42.

Lundvall, B.-Å., Johnson, B., Andersen, E.S. and Dalum, B. (2002) 'National systems of production, innovation and competence building', *Research Policy*, 31: 213–31.

Löfgren, O. (1999) *On Holiday: A History of Vacationing*, Berkeley: University of California Press.

Ma, J.X., Buhalis, D. and Song, H. (2003) 'ICTs and internet adoption in China's tourism industry', *International Journal of Information Management*, 23: 451–67.

McClelland, D.C. (1985) *Human Motivation*, Glenview, IL: Scott, Foreman.

McDowell, L. (1997) 'A tale of two cities? Embedded organisations and embodied workers in the City of London', in Lee, R. and Wills, J. (eds), *Geographies of Economies*, London: Arnold, pp. 118–29.

Macfarlane, I. (2007) *Tax Concession Changes Boost Australian R&D*, media release the Hon. Ian MacFarlane MP, Ministers and Parliamentary Secretary, Industry, Tourism and Resources, 11 July, Canberra.

McKercher, B. (1999) 'A chaos approach to tourism', *Tourism Management*, 20: 425–34.

Maillat, D. (1995) 'Territorial dynamic, innovative milieus and regional development', *Entrepreneurship and Regional Development*, 7: 157–65.

Majone, G. (1996) *Regulating Europe*, London: Routledge.

Malecki, E.J. (2002) 'Hard and soft networks for urban competitiveness', *Urban Studies*, 39: 929–45.

Malecki, E.J. (2004) 'Jockeying for position: what it means and why it matters to regional development policy when places compete', *Regional Studies*, 38(9): 1101–20.

Malerba, F. (2001) *Sectoral Systems of Innovation and Production: Concepts, Analytical Framework and Empirical Evidence*, presented at conference 'The Future of Innovation Studies', Eindhoven University of Technology, the Netherlands, 20–3 September 2001, Eindhoven: Eindhoven Centre for Innovation Studies.

Malerba, F. (2002) 'Sectoral systems of innovation and production', *Research Policy*, 31: 247–64.

Malerba, F. (2005a) 'Sectoral systems of innovation: basic concepts', in Malerba, F. (ed.), *Sectoral Systems of Innovation: Concepts, Issues and Analyses of Six Major Sectors in Europe*, Cambridge: Cambridge University Press, pp. 9–41.

Malerba, F. (ed.) (2005b) *Sectoral Systems of Innovation: Concepts, Issues and Analyses of Six Major Sectors in Europe*, Cambridge: Cambridge University Press.

Malerba, F. and Orsenigo, L. (1996) 'The dynamics and evolution of industries', *Industrial and Corporate Change*, 5(1): 51–87.

Malerba, F. and Orsenigo, L. (1997) 'Technological regimes and sectoral patterns of innovation activities', *Industrial and Corporate Change*, 6(1): 83–118.

Malerba, F. and Orsenigo, L. (2000) 'Knowledge, innovative activities and industrial evolution', *Industrial and Corporate Change*, 9(2): 289–314.

Mallard, T. (2006a) *Economic Transformation – The Kiwi Way – Minister of Economic Development Media Statement*, 7 November, Wellington: Ministry of Economic Development.

Mallard, T. (2006b) *Seeking New Zealand's Future Prosperity*, Cabinet Paper, Wellington: Ministry of Economic Development.

Manyika, J. (2006) 'The coming imperative for the world's knowledge economy', *Financial Times*, 16 May 2006.

Maori Innovation Summit (2007) *Speakers*, http://www.mis.maori.nz/speakers.htm (accessed 15 March 2007).

Marinova, D. and Phillimore, J. (2003) 'Models of innovation', in Shavinina, L.V. (ed.), *The International Handbook on Innovation*, Oxford: Elsevier, pp. 44–53.

Marshack, K.J. (1994) 'Copreneurs and dual-career couples: are they different?', *Entrepreneurship: Theory and Practice*, 19(1): 49–70.

Martinez-Fernandez, M.C., Soosay, C., Krishna, V.V., Toner, P., Turpin, T. *et al.* (2005) *Knowledge-intensive Service Activities (KISA) in Innovation of the Tourism Industry in Australia*, Sydney: AEGIS, University of Western Sydney.

Maskell, P. and Malmberg, A. (1999) 'Localised learning and industrial competitiveness', *Cambridge Journal of Economics*, 23: 167–85.

Matthing, J., Sandén, B. and Edvardsson, B. (2004) 'New service development: learning from and with customers', *International Journal of Service Industry Management*, 15(5): 479–98.

MCC (2007) *Our Creative City: Manchester's Cultural Strategy*, Manchester: MCC.

Medina, C.C., Lavado, A.C. and Cabrera, R.V. (2005) 'Characteristics of innovative companies: a case study of sectors', *Creativity and Innovation Management*, 14(3): 272–87.

Mercer, D. (1979) 'Victoria's land conservation council and the alpine region', *Australian Geographical Studies*, 17(1): 107–30.

Metcalfe, J.S. (2001) 'Consumption, preferences, and the evolutionary agenda', *Journal of Evolutionary Economics*, 11: 37–58.

Metcalfe, J.S. (2005) 'Innovation, competition and enterprise: foundations for economic evolution in learning economies', Manchester: University of Manchester, Centre for Innovation and Competition, Discussion Paper 71.

Michael, E. (2006) *Micro-clusters and Networks: The Growth of Tourism*, Oxford: Elsevier.

Millar, C., Choi, C. and Chu, R. (2005) 'The state in science, technology and innovation districts: conceptual models for China', *Technology Analysis & Strategic Management*, 17(3): 367–73.

Ministry of Economic Development (2005) *The Growth and Innovation Framework Sector Taskforces: Progress with Implementation – 2005 Report*, Wellington: Ministry of Economic Development.

Ministry of Economic Development (2007) *SMEs in New Zealand: Structure and Dynamics*, Wellington: Ministry of Economic Development.

Ministry of Tourism (2007) *Draft New Zealand Tourism Strategy 2015*, Wellington: Ministry of Tourism.

Ministry of Trade and Industry (2003) *Plan From Idea to Value: The Government's Plan for a Comprehensive Innovation Policy*, Oslo: Ministry of Trade and Industry.

Ministry of Trade and Industry (2007) 'Travel industry, Oslo', http://www.regjeringen.no/en/dep/nhd/selected-topics/travel-industry/Travel-Industry.html?id=449229 (accessed 1 August 2007).

Mitchell, D. and Coles, C. (2003) 'The ultimate competitive advantage of continuing business model innovation', *Journal of Business Strategy*, 24(5): 15–21.

Mitev, N.N. (1999) 'Electronic markets in transport: comparing the globalization of air and rail computerized reservation systems', *Electronic Markets*, 9(4): 215–25.

Morales-Moreno, I. (2004) 'Postsovereign governance in a globalizing and fragmenting world: the case of Mexico', *Review of Policy Research*, 21(1): 107–17.

Morgan, G. (2001) 'Transnational communities and business systems', *Global Networks*, 1(2): 113–30.

Morrison, A., Rimmington, M. and Williams, C. (1999) *Entrepreneurship in the Hospitality, Tourism and Leisure Industries*, Oxford: Butterworth-Heinemann.

Mulgan, G. (2006) 'Extreme makeover: from health to housing, social innovation is the key to making public services smarter and more efficient. It's time to take it more seriously', *Guardian*, 26 April.

Nauwelaers, C. and Reid, A. (1995) *Innovative Regions? A Comparative Review of Methods of Evaluating Regional Innovation Potential*, European Innovation Monitoring System (EIMS) Publication No. 21, Luxembourg: European Commission, Directorate General XIII.

Nelson, R.R. (ed.) (1993) *National Innovation Systems: A Comparative Analysis*, New York: Oxford University Press.

Nelson, R.R. and Rosenberg, N. (1993) 'Technical innovation and national systems', in Nelson, R.R. (ed.), *National Innovation Systems: A Comparative Analysis*, New York: Oxford University Press, pp. 3–21.

Ng, J.J.M. and Li, K.X. (2003) 'Implications of ICT for knowledge management in globalization', *Information Management & Computer Security*, 11(4): 167–74.

Nielsen, K., Jessop, B. and Hausner, J. (1995) 'Institutional change in post-socialism', in Hausner, I., Jessop, B. and Nielsen, K. (eds), *Strategic Choice and Path Dependency in Post Socialism: Institutional Dynamics in the Transformation Process*, Aldershot: Edward Elgar, pp. 3–44.

Nonaka, H. and Takeuchi, I. (1995) *The Knowledge Creating Company: How Japanese Companies Create the Dynamics of Innovation*, New York: Oxford University Press.

Nordlinger, E. (1981) *On the Autonomy of the Democratic State*, Cambridge, MA: Harvard University Press.

Normann, R. (1984) *Service Management: Strategy and Leadership in Service Businesses*, New York: Wiley.

Nowotny, H., Gibbons, M. and Scott, P. (2001) *Rethinking Science: Knowledge and the Public*, Cambridge: Polity Press.

Nussbaum, B. (2005) 'Virgin mainstreams space tourism', *Businessweek*, 23 October http://www.businessweek.com/innovate/NussbaumOnDesign/archives/2005/10/virgin_airways.html (accessed 5 October 2007).

O'Connell, J.F. (2006) 'Corporate rivalry and competition issues in the airline industry', in Papatheodorou, A. (ed.), *Corporate Rivalry and Market Power: Competition Issues in the Tourism Industry*, London: I.B. Tauris, pp. 54–75.

O'Connor, P., Buhalis, D. and Frew, A.J. (2001) 'The transformation of tourism distribution channels through information technology', in Buhalis, D. and Laws, E. (eds), *Tourism Distribution Channels: Practices, Issues and Transformations*, London: Continuum, pp. 332–50.

OECD (1997) *Managing National Systems of Innovation*, Paris: Committee for Science and Technology Policy, OECD.

OECD (2000) *A New Economy? The Role of Innovation and Information Technology in Recent OECD Economic Growth*, Paris: OECD.

OECD (2003) *Proceedings of the OECD Conference on Innovation and Growth in Tourism, Lugano, Switzerland 18–19 September 2003*, Paris: OECD.

OECD (2007) *Globalisation and Regional Economies*, Paris: OECD.

Oinas, P. and Malecki, E.J. (1999) 'Spatial innovation systems', in Malecki, E.J. and Oinas, P. (eds), *Making Connections: Technological Learning and Regional Economic Change*, Aldershot: Ashgate, pp. 7–33.

Oinas, P. and Malecki, E.J. (2002) 'The evolution of technologies in time and space: from national and regional to spatial innovation systems', *International Regional Science Review*, 25(1): 102–31.

One News (2006) 'Business boosts Dunedin revival', One News, Television New Zealand, 27 September, http://tvnz.co.nz/view/page/411419/837111 (accessed 25 December 2006).

Orfila-Sintes, F., Crespí-Cladera, R. and Nez-Ros, E.M. (2005) 'Innovation activity in the hotel industry: evidence from Balearic Islands', *Tourism Management*, 26: 851–65.

Osterwalder, A., Pigneur, Y. and Tucci, C.L. (2005) 'Clarifying business models: origins, present, and future of the concept', *Communications of the Association for Information Systems*, 15(May): 1–38.

OSVC (2007a) 'New heart of the region will pump', http://www.ourstadium.co.nz/newheart.html (accessed 1 July 2007).

OSVC (2007b) 'Our stadium – bring it on' (home page), http://www.ourstadium.co.nz/index.html (accessed 1 July 2007).

Otago Daily Times (2007) '82% back stadium in poll', *Otago Daily Times*, 24 February.

Ottawa Business Journal (2007) 'Discussions: flight from Ottawa to Silicon Valley', *Discussion Page, initiated 01:59 pm January 31 2007*, http://discussion.ottawabusinessjournal.com/article.php?sid=539 (accessed 1 August 2007).

Ottawa International Airport Authority (2007) 'Yes, tou can fly there from Ottawa' (sponsored article), *Ottawa Business Journal*, 5 April, http://www.ottawabusinessjournal.com/288592332410371.php (accessed 1 August 2007).

Page, C. (2006) '$180m stadium to replace Carisbrook', *New Zealand Herald*, 10 August, http://subs.nzherald.co.nz/location/story.cfm?l_id=141&objectid=10395411 (accessed 5 October 2007).

Page, S. and Hall. C.M. (2003) *Managing Urban Tourism Destinations*, Harlow: Prentice Hall.

Papatheodorou, A. (2006) 'Corporate rivalry, market power and competition issues in tourism: an introduction', in Papatheodorou, A. (ed.), *Corporate Rivalry and Market Power: Competition Issues in the Tourism Industry*, London: I.B. Tauris, pp. 1–18.

Parasuraman, A. and Grewal, D. (2000) 'The impact of technology on the quality-value-loyalty chain: a research agenda', *Journal of the Academy of Marketing Science*, 28(1): 168–74.

Parasuraman, A., Zeithaml, V.A. and Berry, L.L. (1985) 'A conceptual model of service quality and its implications for future research', *Journal of Marketing*, 49(4): 41–50.

Pavitt, K. (1984) 'Sectoral patterns of technical change: towards a taxonomy and a theory', *Research Policy*, 13: 343–73.

Peck, J. (2005) 'Struggling with the creative class', *International Journal of Urban and Regional Research*, 29(4): 740–70.

Peck, J. and Tickell, A. (2002) 'Neoliberalizing space', *Antipode*, 34: 380–403.

Pedler, M., Burgoyne, J.G. and Boydell, T. (1991) *The Learning Company: A Strategy for Sustainable Development*, London: McGraw Hill.

Peredo, A.M., Anderson, R.B., Galbraith, C.S., Honig, B. and Dana, L.P. (2004) 'Towards a theory of indigenous entrepreneurship', *International Journal of Entrepreneurship and Small Business*, 1(1–2): 1–20.

Peters, B.G. (1996) *The Future of Governing*, Lawrence: University Press of Kansas.

Peters, B.G. (1998) 'Globalization, institutions and governance', Jean Monnet Chair Paper RSC No. 98/51, Florence: European University Institute.

Peters, B.G. and Pierre, J. (2001) 'Developments in intergovernmental relations: towards multi-level governance', *Policy and Politics*, 29(2): 131–5.

Petit, P. (1995) 'Employment and technological change', in Stoneman, P. (ed.), *Handbook of the Economics of Innovation and Technological Change*, Oxford: Blackwell, pp. 366–408.

Pfeffer, J (2002) 'Competitive advantage through people', in Henry, J. and Mayle, D. (eds), *Managing Innovation and Change*, London: Sage, pp. 61–73.

Phan, P.H. (2004). 'Entrepreneurship theory: possibilities and future directions', *Journal of Business Venturing*, 19: 617–20.

Pil, F.K. and Holweg, M. (2006) 'Evolving from value chain to value grid', *MIT Sloan Management Review*, 47(4): 72–80.

Pine II, B.J. and Gilmore, J.H. (1999) *The Experience Economy: Work is Theatre and Every Business a Stage: Goods and Services Are No Longer Enough*, Boston: Harvard Business School Press.

Piore, M. and Sabel, C. (1984), *The Second Industrial Divide*, New York: Basic Books.

Polanyi, M. (1958) *Personal Knowledge*, London: Routledge and Kegan Paul.

Polanyi, M. (1966) *The Tacit Dimension*, London: Routledge and Kegan Paul.

Poon, A. (1993) *Tourism, Technology, and Competitive Strategies*, Wallingford: CAB International Books.

Porter, M. (1990) *The Competitive Advantage of Nations*, London: Macmillan.

Porter, M.E. (2000a) 'Location, competition, and economic development: local clusters in a global economy', *Economic Development Quarterly*, 14(1): 15–34.

Porter, M.E. (2000b) 'Locations, clusters and company strategy', in Clark, G., Feldman, M. and Gertler, M. (ed.), *The Oxford Handbook of Economic Geography*, Oxford: Oxford University Press, pp. 253–74.

Porter, M. (2001) 'Strategy and the internet', *Harvard Business Review*, 103D(March): 63–78.

Powell, T.C. (1995) 'Total quality management as competitive advantage: a review and empirical study', *Strategic Management Journal*, 16(1): 15–37.

Prahalad, C.K. and Ramaswarmy, V. (2003a) 'Co-creating unique value with customers', *Strategy & Leadership*, 32(3): 4–9.

Prahalad, C.K. and Ramaswarmy, V. (2003b) 'The new frontier of experience innovation', *MIT Sloan Management Review*, 44(4). 12–18.

Prahalad, C.K. and Ramaswarmy, V. (2004) *The Future of Competition: Co-creating Unique Value With Customers*, Boston: Harvard Business School Publishing.

Pratten, J.D. (2003) 'The importance of waiting staff in restaurant service', *British Food Journal*, 105(11): 826–34.

Preissl, B. (2000) 'Service innovation: what makes it different? Empirical evidence from Germany', in Metcalfe, J.S. and Miles, I. (eds), *Innovation Systems in the Service Economy: Measurements and Case Study Analysis*, Dordrecht: Kluwer, pp. 125–48.

Pyka, A. and Küppers, G. (eds) (2002) *Innovation Networks: Theory and Practice*, Cheltenham: Edward Elgar.

Pyo, S. (2005) 'Knowledge map for tourist destinations – needs and implications', *Tourism Management*, 26: 583–94.

Pyo, S., Uysal, M. and Chang, H. (2002) 'Knowledge discovery database for tourist destinations', *Journal of Travel Research*, 40: 396–403,

Quemener, T. (2007) 'Boeing unveils lighter, "greener" airliner of future', *The Age*, 10 July.

Quigley, J.M. (1998) 'Urban diversity and economic growth', *Journal of Economic Perspectives*, 12: 127–38.

Quinn, J.B., Baruch, J.J. and Zein, K.A. (2002) 'Intellect, innovation and growth', in Henry, J. and Mayle, D. (eds), *Managing Innovation and Change*, London: Sage, pp. 5–22.

Ramirez, R. (1999) 'Value co-production: intellectual origins and implications for practice and research', *Strategic Management Journal*, 20(1): 49–65.

Reardon, J. and Vida, I. (1998) 'Measuring retail productivity: monetary vs. physical input measures', *International Review of Retail, Distribution and Consumer Research*, 8(4): 399–413.

Rhodes, R.A.W. (1994) 'The hollowing out of the state', *Political Quarterly*, 65(2): 138–51.

Rhodes, R.A.W. (1996) 'The new governance: governing without government', *Political Studies*, 44: 652–67.

Rhodes, R.A.W. (1997) *Understanding Governance: Policy Networks, Governance, Reflexivity and Accountability*, Milton Keynes: Open University Press.

Riley, M., Ladkin, A. and Szivas, E. (2002) *Tourism Employment: Analysis and Planning*, Clevedon: Channel View Publications.

Ritter, T. and Walter, A. (2003) 'Relationship-specific antecedents of customer involvement in new product development', *International Journal of Technology Management*, 26(5–6): 482–501.

Rogers, E. (2003) *Diffusion of Innovations*, 5th edn, New York: The Free Press.

Roper, S. and Crone. M. (2003) 'Knowledge complimentarity and coordination in the local supply chain: some empirical evidence', *British Journal of Management*, 14(4): 339–55.

Rosa, P. and Scott, M. (1999) 'Entrepreneurial diversification, business-cluster formation and growth', *Environment and Planning C: Government and Policy*, 17(5): 527–48.

Rothwell, R. (1983) 'Innovation and firm size: the case of dynamic complementarity', *Journal of General Management*, 8(6): 5–25.

Rubin, R.M. and Joy, J.N. (2005) 'Where are the airlines headed? Implications of airline industry structure and change for consumers', *Journal of Consumer Affairs*, 39(1): 215–28.

Santarelli, E. (1998) 'Start-up size and post-entry performance: the case of tourism services in Italy', *Applied Economics*, 30(2): 157–63.

Saxenian A. (1994) *Regional Advantage: Culture and Competition in Silicon Valley and Route 128*, Aldershot: Ashgate.

Schaper, M. and Volery, T. (2004) *Entrepreneurship and Small Business: A Pacific Rim Perspective*, Singapore: Wiley.

Scheidegger, E. (2006) 'Can the state promote innovation in tourism? Should it?', in OECD (ed.), *Innovation and Growth in Tourism*, Paris: OECD, pp. 11–16.

Schmookler, J. (1966) *Invention and Economic Growth*, Cambridge, MA: Harvard University Press.

Schneider, B. and Bowen, D.E. (1995) *Winning the Service Game*, Boston: Harvard Business School Press.

Schumpeter, J. (1934) *The Theory of Economic Development*, Cambridge, MA: Harvard University Press.

Schumpeter, J.A. (1942) *Capitalism, Socialism and Democracy*, New York: Harper & Row.

Scottish Executive (2006a) *Scottish Tourism: The Next Decade – A Tourism Framework for Change*, Edinburgh: Scottish Executive.

Scottish Executive (2006b) *Summary of Comments: Tourism Framework for Change*, Edinburgh: Scottish Executive Tourism Unit.

Selby, M. (2004) 'Consuming the city: conceptualizing and researching urban tourist knowledge', *Tourism Management* 6(2): 186–207.

Senge, P. (1990) *The Fifth Discipline: The Art and Practice of the Learning Organization*, New York: Currency Doubleday.

Shaw, G. and Williams, A.M. (1998) 'Entrepreneurship and tourism development', in

Ioannides, D. and Debbage, K.G. (eds), *The Economic Geography of the Tourist Industry*, London: Routledge, pp. 235–55.

Shaw, G. and Williams, A.M. (2002) *Critical Issues in Tourism: A Geographical Perspective*, 2nd edn, Oxford: Blackwell.

Shaw, G. and Williams, A.M. (2004) *Tourism and Tourism Spaces*, London: Sage.

Shipton, H., Fay, D., West, M., Patterson, M. and Birdi, K. (2005) 'Managing people to promote innovation', *Creativity and Innovation Management*, 14(2): 118–28.

Sigala, M. (2002) 'The impact of multimedia on employment patterns in small and medium hospitality and tourism enterprises (SMHTEs) in the UK', *Information Technology and Tourism*, 4(3–4): 175–89.

Sigala, M. (2003) 'The information and communication technologies productivity impacts on the UK hotel sector', *International Journal of Operations and Production Management*, 23(10): 1224–45.

Sigala, M. and Mylonikis, J. (2005) 'Developing a data envelopment analysis model for measuring and isolating the impact of contextual factors on hotel productivity', *International Journal of Business Performance Management*, 7(2): 174–90.

Sigala, M., Airey, D., Jones, P. and Lockwood, A. (2004) 'ICT paradox lost? A stepwise DEA methodology to evaluate technology investments in tourism setting', *Journal of Travel Research*, 43: 180–92.

Siguaw, J.A., Enz, C.A. and Namasivayam, K. (2000) 'Adoption of information technology in U.S. hotels: strategically driven objectives', *Journal of Travel Research*, 39: 192–200.

Simeon, R. (1976) 'Studying public policy', *Canadian Journal of Political Science*, 9(4): 558–80.

Simmie, J. (2004) 'Innovation and clustering in the globalised international economy', *Urban Studies*, 41(5 6): 1095 112.

Sinclair, M.T. and Stabler, M. (1997) *The Economics of Tourism*, London: Routledge.

Sirilli, G. and Evangelista, R. (1998) 'Technological innovation in services and manufacturing: results form Italian survey', *Research Policy*, 27(9): 881 99.

Skordoulis, R.T. (2005) 'TGI Friday's UK: a case of innovation', *Corporate Reputation Review*, 8(1): 73–9.

Smith, D. (2006) 'France fights back against New World wine rivals', *The Observer*, 22 October.

Smith, R. and Liu, C. (2002) 'Mike and Doug Tamaki: Tamaki Tours Ltd', in Cameron, A. and Massey, C. (eds), *Entrepreneurs at Work: Successful New Zealand Business Ventures*, Auckland: Pearson Education, pp. 24–33.

Sorensen, J.B. and Stuart, T.E. (2000) 'Aging, obsolescence, and organizational innovation', *Administrative Science Quarterly*, 45: 81–112.

Ståhle, P. (ed.) (2007) *Five Steps for Finland's Future*, Technology Review 202/2007, Helsinki: Tekes.

Stamper, C.L. and van Dyne, L. (2003) 'Organizational citizenship: a comparison between part time and full time service employees', *Cornell Hotel and Restaurant Administration Quarterly*, Feburary: 33–42.

Starbuck, W.H. (1992) 'Learning by knowledge-intensive firms', *Journal of Management Studies*, 29(6): 713–40.

Statistics New Zealand (2006) *Business Operations Survey*, Wellington: Statistics New Zealand.

Statistics New Zealand (2007) *Innovation in New Zealand 2005*, Wellington: Statistics New Zealand.

STCRC (2005) *STCRC Promotional Flier*, Gold Coast: CRC for Sustainable Tourism Pty Ltd, http://www.crctourism.com.au/Documents/general/2005%20STCRC %20profile_v2.pdf (accessed 1 August 2005).

Sternberg, R. and Arndt, O. (2001) 'The firm or the region: what determines the innovation behaviour of European firms', *Economic Geography*, 77(4): 364–82.

Sternberg, R.J., Pretz, J.E. and Kaufman, J.C. (2003) 'Types of innovation', in Shavinina, L.V. (ed.), *The International Handbook on Innovation*, Oxford: Elsevier, pp. 158–69.

Sturcke, J. (2007) 'Virgin boss offers $25m reward to save Earth', *Guardian*, 9 February.

Sundbo, J. (1994) 'Modulization of service production and a thesis of convergence between service and manufacturing organisations', *Scandinavian Journal of Management*, 10(3), 245–66.

Sundbo, J. (1998) *The Theory of Innovation: Entrepreneurs, Technology and Strategy*, Cheltenham: Edward Elgar.

Sutton, J. (1995) 'The size distribution of business. Part I: a benchmark case', *The Economics of Industry Group Discussion Paper Series E1/9*, London: London School of Economics.

Swarbrooke, J. (2002) *The Development and Management of Visitor Attractions*, 2nd edn, Oxford: Butterworth-Heinemann.

Tamaki Heritage Experiences (2007) *The Story*, http://www.maoriculture.co.nz/ Maori%20Village/The%20Story. (accessed 15 March 2007).

Tan, W.L. and Fock, S.T. (2001) 'Coping with growth transitions: the case of Chinese family businesses in Singapore', *Family Business Review*, 14: 123–39.

Te Puni Kōkiri (2001) *He Mātāi Tāpoi Māori: A Study of Barriers, Impediments and Opportunities for Māori in Tourism*, Wellington: Te Puni Kōkiri.

Teece, D.J. (2000) *Managing Intellectual Capital*, Oxford: Oxford University Press.

Tekes (2007) *Seizing the White Space: Innovative Service Concepts in the United States. Peer Insight*, Technology Review 205/2007, Helsinki: Tekes.

Terry, D.J., Hogg, M.A. and White, K.M. (1999) 'The theory of planned behaviour: self-identity, social identity, and group norms', *British Journal of Social Psychology*, 38: 225–44.

Tether, B. (1999) *Small Firms in Employment Creation in Business and Europe, a Question of Expectations*, Manchester: University of Manchester, Centre for Innovation and Competition, Briefing Paper 2.

Tether, B. (2004) *Do Services Innovate Differently?*, Manchester: University of Manchester, Centre for Innovation and Competition, Discussion Paper 66.

Tether, B.S. and Metcalfe, J.S. (2005) 'Services and systems of innovation', in Malerba, F. (ed.), *Sectoral Systems of Innovation: Concepts, Issues and Analyses of Six Major Sectors in Europe*, Cambridge: Cambridge University Press, pp. 287–323.

Tether, B., Miles, I., Blind, K., Hipp, C., Liso, N. de *et al.* (2002) *Innovation in the Service Sector*, Manchester: University of Manchester, Centre for Research on Innovation and Competition, Working Paper 11.

Te Velde, R. (2004) 'Schumpeter's theory of economic development revisited', in Uljin, J. and Brown, T.E. (eds), *Innovation, Entrepreneurship and Culture, a Matter of Interaction between Technology, Progress and Economic Growth*, Cheltenham: Edward Elgar, pp. 103–29.

Thomas, R. (ed.) (1998) *The Management of Small Tourism and Hospitality Firms*, London: Cassell.

Thomas, R. (ed.) (2004) *Small Firms in Tourism: International Perspectives*, Oxford: Elsevier.

Tidd, J., Bessant, J. and Pavitt, K. (2002) 'Learning through alliances', in Henry, J. and Mayle, D. (eds), *Managing Innovation and Change*, London: Sage, pp. 167–88.

Timmons, J.A. and Spinelli, S. (2007) *New Venture Creation: Entrepreneurship for the 21st Century*, International 7th edn, Singapore: McGraw Hill.

Tödtling, F. and Kaufmann, A. (1998) 'Innovation systems in regions of Europe – a comparative perspective', paper presented to the 38th Congress of the European Regional Science Association, 28 August–1 September, Vienna.

Tödtling, F. and Wanzenböck, H. (2003) 'Regional differences in structural characteristics of start-ups', *Entrepreneurship & Regional Development*, 15(4): 351–70.

Tourism New Zealand (2007) *Maori Creativity*, http://www.newzealand.com/travel/en/media/ (accessed 15 March 2007).

Tourism Strategy Group (2001) *New Zealand Tourism Strategy 2010*, Wellington: Tourism Strategy Group.

Tracey, P. and Clark, G.L. (2003) 'Alliances, networks and competitive strategy: rethinking clusters of innovation', *Growth and Change*, 34(1): 1–16.

Tushman, M.L. and O'Reilly, C.A. (1996) 'Ambidextorous organizations: managing evolutionary and revolutionary change', *California Management Review*, 38(4): 8–30.

Tushman, M. and Scanlan, T. (1981) 'Boundary spanning individuals: their role in information transfer and their antecendants', *Academy of Management Journal*, 24(2): 289–305.

Ulijn, J. and Brown, T.E. (2004) 'Innovation, entrepreneurship and culture, a matter of interaction between technology, progress and economic growth? An introduction', in Ulijn, J. and Brown, T.E. (eds), *Innovation, Entrepreneurship and Culture, a Matter of Interaction between Technology, Progress and Economic Growth*, Cheltenham: Edward Elgar, pp. 1–38.

Uriely, N. (2001) '"Travelling workers" and "working tourists": variations across the interaction between work and tourism', *International Journal of Tourism Research*, 3: 1–8.

Urry, J. (1990) *The Tourist Gaze: Leisure and Travel in Contemporary Societies*, London: Sage Publications.

Utterback, J.M. (1994) *Mastering the Dynamics of Innovation*, Boston: Harvard Business School Press.

Van der Aa, W. and Elfring, J. (2002) 'Realizing innovation in services', *Scandinavian Journal of Management*, 18: 155–71.

Vandermerwe, S. (1993) *From Tin Soldiers to Russian Dolls: Creating Added Value through Services*, London: Butterworth-Heinemann.

Von Hippel, E., Thomke, S. and Sonnack, M. (2001) 'Creating breakthroughs at 3M', in *Harvard Business Review on Innovation*, Boston: Harvard Business School Press, pp. 31–54.

Walsh, K. (2002) 'Service-delivery strategies: three approaches to consulting for hospitality', *Cornell Hotel and Restaurant Administration Quarterly*, December: 37–48.

Weaver, A. (2005) 'Interactive service work and performative metaphors: the case of the cruise industry', *Tourist Studies*, 5(1): 5–27.

Weber, M. (1994) 'The nation state and economic policy (inaugural lecture)', in Lassman, P. and Speirs, R. (ed.), *Weber: Political Writings*, Cambridge: Cambridge University Press, pp. 1–28.

Weiermair, K. (2006) 'Product improvement or innovation: what is the key to success in tourism', in OECD, *Innovation and Growth in Tourism*, Paris: OECD, pp. 53–69.

Welsh Assembly Government (2006) *Achieving Our Potential 2006–2013: Tourism Strategy for Wales Mid-term Review*, Cardiff: Welsh Assembly Government.

Wenger, E. (1998) *Communities of Practice: Learning, Meaning, and Identity*, Cambridge: Cambridge University Press.

Wenger, E. (2000) 'Communities of practice and social learning systems', *Organizations*, 7(2): 225–46.

Werthner, H. and Klein, S. (1999) 'ICT and the changing landscape of global tourism distribution', *Electronic Markets*, 9(4): 256–62.

Wiig, K.M. (1993) *Knowledge Management Foundations: Thinking About Thinking – How People and Organizations Create, Represent, and Use Knowledge*, Arlington, TX: Schema Press.

Williams, A.M. (2005) 'Tourism, migration and human capital: knowledge and skills at the intersection of flows', paper presented at the 2005 Conference of the International Academy for the Study of Tourism, Beijing, July 2005.

Williams, A.M. (2006) 'Lost in translation? International migration, learning and knowledge', *Progress in Human Geography*, 30(5): 588–607.

Williams, A.M. (2007) 'Listen to me, learn with me: international migration and knowledge', *British Journal of Industrial Relations*, 45(2): 361–82.

Williams, A.M. and Balaz, V. (2000) *Tourism in Transition: Economic Change in Central Europe*, London: I.B. Tauris.

Williams, A.M. and Shaw, G. (1992) 'Tourism research: a perspective', *American Behavioral Scientist*, 36(2): 133–43.

Williams, A.M., Shaw, G. and Greenwood, J. (1989) 'From tourist to tourism entrepreneur, from consumption to production: evidence from Cornwall, England', *Environment and Planning A*, 21: 1639–53.

Williamson, O.E. (1975) *Markets and Hierachies*, New York: Free Press.

WIPO (2006) *About Geographical Indications*, http://www.wipo.int/about-ip/en/about_geographical_ind.html#P16_1100 (accessed 5 October 2007).

Witz, A., Warhurst, C. and Nickson, D. (2003) 'The labour of aesthetics and the aesthetics of organization', *Organization: The Critical Journal of Organization, Theory and Society*, 10(1): 33–54.

Woolthuis, K.R., Lankhuizen, M. and Gilsing, V. (2005) 'A system failure framework for innovation policy design', *Technovation*, 25(6): 609–19.

Yim, D.S. and Nath, P. (2005) 'National innovation systems in the Asian context', *Science Technology and Society*, 10(1): 1–10.

Yuan, Y.-L., Gretzel, U. and Fesenmaier, D.R. (2006) 'The role of information technology use in American convention and visitor bureaus', *Tourism Management*, 27: 326–41.

XCOR Aerospace (2007) *Boston Harbor Angels Invests in XCOR Aerospace Investment Fuels Expansion Into New Markets*, press release, 7 June, Mojave: XCOR Aerospace.

Zahra, S.A. (2003) 'International expansion of U.S. manufacturing family businesses: the effect of ownership and Involvement', *Journal of Business Venturing*, 18: 495–512.

Zapalska, A.M. and Brozik, D. (2004) 'Economic transition: a case study for Polish tourism and hospitality businesses', *Journal of East–West Business*, 10(2): 65–92.

Index